Call Center Technology Demystified

The No-Nonsense Guide to Bridging Customer Contact Technology, Operations and Strategy

Lori Bocklund and Dave Bengtson

What Others Are Saying about this Book

"This book clarifies the key elements you need to understand your business drivers and your current call center operation, as well as the steps to plan for the coming contact center evolution. Chapters are arranged in a logical manner that's to the point. This is one book you will have a hard time putting down; it will remain a treasured reference."
Mike Horn, Senior Consulting Call Center Specialist, Wachovia Corporation

"An instantly credible reference guide… it strikes a comfortable balance between high-level business strategy and technical granularity. Used with proper care, this book can bridge the ever-widening gap between operations and IT. The authors have taken the phrase 'no-nonsense' to a new level, producing an engaging read that's brimming with valuable information and refreshingly devoid of fluff."
Matthew Flemming, Director, Hospitality Systems, Foxwoods Resort Casino

"One of the greatest challenges for a call center director is ensuring that his or her management staff has a full grasp of how the technology in a call center environment functions. This book will enable my staff to be forward-thinking individuals who will make better use of technology… It's a must-read for anyone who is looking for ways to educate staff on current and future call center technology."
Jill LaVigne, Customer Contact Center Director, Xcel Energy

"A refreshing approach that puts technology in its rightful place, as the supporter and enabler of a well-thought-out business strategy. A must-read for decision-makers – it provides a comprehensive picture of contact center dynamics, bridging the divide between business and technology."
Christopher J. Whiteley, Channel Integration and Strategy Manager,
ABN AMRO N.A.

"Educational, insightful and well-written. This book is a business tool that creates a universal reference point for call center technology. It should be mandatory reading for call center managers and the business partners on whom they depend. It's easy to read and gives actionable ideas that can be immediately utilized on a strategic or tactical level to investigate, purchase and implement technology solutions for your contact centers."
Thomas J. Reilly, Director, Customer Service, NetBank/RBMG

"Finally a book about the newest call center technology that is really understandable and easy to read!"
Günter Greff, Publisher, Call Center Profi, Germany

"There are few resources available that capture the 'total' of call center technology... this book does it. It helps the reader understand the complete picture of call center technologies by explaining the applications as well as the underlying concepts, principles and value to the call center."
Fredia Barry, President, Call Center Industry Advisory Council (CIAC)

"With today's call center and telecom technology changing so fast, we need a tool that can help us develop our overall strategy for today and tomorrow. This book is that tool! It successfully presents highly sophisticated technologies in an easy-to-read manual that's helpful to everyone associated with call centers – from the CEO down."
Butch Mercier, Director, Telecommunications, Navigant International

"A long-needed book that should be required reading for everyone who plans, manages or supports call centers. Buy it, read it and keep it next to your desk for frequent reference. Highly recommended."
Ian Angus, President, Angus TeleManagement Group

"This book comes to grips with the challenges all call centers are facing today. Providing 'world-class' customer support while driving profitability and growth will differentiate the winners from the losers. *Call Center Technology Demystified* delivers clear alternatives and straightforward answers to a very complex subject. It contains the foundation of knowledge needed in all areas of a customer-focused, call center-driven company to deliver testimonial quality service to customers."
Julie S. Mantis, VP, Sales Support Management, EarthLink, Inc.

"Lori Bocklund and Dave Bengston have compiled an excellent guide for contact center professionals to effectively network their centers for optimal efficiency. It provides specific details on the day-to-day operational issues, backs up the information with a technology road map for successful integration – all while keeping the needs of the customer in mind. It's well-written and easy to read."
Milly Probst, Customer Contact Center Manager, Riggs Bank

"Dang... this is good stuff! Nuts and bolts. Solid. Informative. What a treat to read – straightforward material without a clever marketing twist or 'whiz-bang' hype to distract you from really learning. If you want a handle on where we've been as an industry, where we are and where we are going, this is it. If you need ready research to build, modify or strategize your contact center operation, this is it. This goes on the recommended reading list!"
Mary Beth Ingram, Founder, Phone Pro

Published by:
Call Center Press
A Division of ICMI, Inc.
Post Office Box 6177
Annapolis, Maryland 21401 USA

Call Center Technology Demystified

The No-Nonsense Guide to Bridging Customer Contact Technology, Operations and Strategy

Lori Bocklund and Dave Bengtson

Call Center Press
A Division of ICMI, Inc.

Acknowledgements

Of course a book like this doesn't get written without a lot of support and assistance from some special people. We have many to thank.

First and foremost are our colleagues at Vanguard Communications. They contributed to this book throughout the review cycles. In addition, their collaboration with us on client projects always makes us better consultants, and therefore, better authors. Our thanks go out to Madeleine Ashe, Elaine Cascio, Areg Gharakhanian, David Powis, Gail Sprague, Maren Symonds and Linda Van Doren, all of whom provided ideas, edits and insights that made this a better book. It's a privilege to work with this talented group.

A special thanks to Don Van Doren, our president, who encouraged us and supported us throughout this effort, in addition to reading every last word and helping us find our way through a few messy sections. Thanks for your guidance.

We also want to thank the people who teach us – our clients and our students. We can't list them, but you know who you are. Every client project presents an opportunity for us to apply what we know, while also giving us the chance to expand our knowledge. No consultant is successful without fantastic clients who present interesting problems to solve, challenge us to think critically and creatively, and teach us a few things from their own experiences. Our students who come to class to learn about call center technologies also teach us about call center technologies. Each story they share and every question they ask is an opportunity for us to learn. The content of this book is enriched by the real-life experiences we've had with our clients and students. Thanks to those of you who have been a part of that experience.

Our appreciation also goes out to our partners at Incoming Calls Management Institute and Call Center Press. Brad Cleveland, Susan Hash and Ellen Herndon, in particular, had a hand in the review, edit and production of the book. Thanks also to the support team that includes Linda Harden, Debbie Harne, Ted Hopton, Cara Visconti and the rest of the ICMI team.

And finally, we thank our spouses – Mike Mulligan and Sheila Bengtson. They share critical and cherished characteristics to be married to a couple of crazy consultants/writers: patience, understanding, respect, support and a fantastic sense of humor. And somehow they know just when to tell us to turn off the darn computer and have dinner, and when to let us run with the thoughts and ideas that need to get out of our heads and onto the paper. We love you and we thank you from the bottom of our hearts.

Foreword

When Lori and Dave asked us to write the foreword for *Call Center Technology Demystified*, we enthusiastically agreed. It is the right book, at the right time, with the right message. The call center is changing rapidly, with an explosion of new capabilities, new responsibilities, and perhaps most importantly, new recognition by senior management of the center's growing importance.

This book works for three reasons. First, it successfully reaches both those who direct and manage call centers (users) and the technologists (IT and telecom). As the authors point out, technology is an enabler of new functionality, not an end in itself. Therefore, implementation is most successful when technical staff and users work together. The book emphasizes the interconnection between the technology and the business issues in a way that will help each group better understand the other's viewpoint. Then, technology, strategy and operations align. The book truly lives up to its subtitle.

Second, it is well-done and easy to read. The charts and graphs alone are a gold mine. The sidebars provide additional insights. The writing is clear, the recommendations are sound and the book's organization provides a logical, integrated progression through key topics. It will also be a powerful reference work long after the initial read.

Third, the book has staying power. Yes, technology progresses by the minute. Sure, products will evolve and the supplier landscape will continue to change. But this book provides a framework, underlying principles and guidance about thinking through the issues that will continue to be the basis for sound analysis and decision-making for many years.

So, it's our privilege to congratulate Lori and Dave on a job well done – and to commend you, the reader, on securing a resource that can positively impact your customers, your organization and your career.

Brad Cleveland
President and CEO
Incoming Calls Management Institute (ICMI)
Annapolis, Maryland

Don Van Doren
President
Vanguard Communications Corp.
Morris Plains, New Jersey

In memory of my dad.

Lori

For Sheila, you will always be my lovely bride.

Dave

Table of Contents

Call Center Technology Demystified

*The No-Nonsense Guide
to Bridging Customer Contact Technology,
Operations and Strategy*

Lori Bocklund and Dave Bengtson

Introduction: Before You Get Started

As consultants who work in call centers (or contact centers) and lead seminars on call center technology, we're often asked, "Is there a book on call center technologies that will help me to understand this stuff better?" This book is for everyone who has ever asked that question. Specifically, it is written for:

• **Call center directors and managers** who want to apply technology more effectively, and who want to have more productive conversations with technology staff and vendors.

• **Technologists,** including information systems, telecommunications and business analyst staff who are just getting into call center work, as well as experienced professionals who would like to brush up on the latest trends.

• **Business managers,** including marketing, sales, service and finance professionals looking to execute business strategies in call center environments.

There are three themes that make *Call Center Technology Demystified: The Nononsense Guide to Bridging Customer Contact Technology, Operations and Strategy* unique:

1. **It "demystifies" call center technology:** Call center technology veterans (your colleagues or vendors) have their own language. They may be great at making hardware and software work, but their focus (or forte) may not be educating you on these technologies. So it is sometimes difficult to make sense of what you have or what you're getting, or know its full potential and pitfalls. In this book, we cut through the call center technology acronyms and jargon, and offer clear, concise explanations. We begin with foundations and fundamentals, and build on those with advanced capabilities and multimedia.

2. **It takes a "no-nonsense" approach:** There are a myriad of alternatives for applying technology – and every option has inherent strengths and weaknesses. Technologists are usually very passionate about their approaches and, similarly, vendors are understandably enthusiastic about their products and services. We'll help you take a step back to analyze the pros and cons of your options.

3. **It helps to "bridge" technology, operations and strategy gaps:** One of the true needs in our industry is to create a better understanding and working relation-

ship between business people and technology people. This book can help to bridge that gap and promote effective communication and collaboration. When presenting technological capabilities, we also let you know about the operations, processes and organizational impacts. It's important for everyone to understand those impacts as well as the interests of your business or technology counterparts.

This book was developed to serve as a handbook on call center technologies. It will be most successful if it's not read once and put on a shelf – but rather serves as a desk reference (one that we hope has flagged or dog-eared pages and notes in the margins!). Don't just read it on your commute; take it with you to meetings.

We provide you with key information about the variety of call center technologies you'll encounter. To dig further, conduct online research, attend courses and conferences, and read the trade publications. Meet with vendors, but drive the conversations based on what you learn in this book so that you can really benefit from these discussions. Also, be sure to talk extensively with colleagues and peers inside and outside of your own organization, and apply what you learn in your environment.

Objectives

This book will enable you to:

• **Understand key technology infrastructure options and issues.** The core infrastructure of call center technology is changing as call routing, resource management and reporting functions move to server-based solutions, and Internet Protocol (IP) enters the picture. As you work with contact center technologies, it's critical to understand infrastructure options and tradeoffs, as well as where they fit and in which directions they're heading.

• **Understand essential and advanced technologies for the call center.** There are a wide range of capabilities in today's call center for routing, reporting and management, media and information management. Understanding the basics and how to build on them helps to make this complex world a bit more manageable.

• **Identify capabilities and applications that make sense in your environment.** Reading trade publications and listening to vendors may lead you to think you need to do everything tomorrow (or yesterday!). We want to help you get past the hype and focus on how to decide what makes sense for your particular environment and unique business vision, functions, size, customer base, competition, tolerance for risk and support capabilities.

• **Build a vision of a "world-class," integrated solutions.** Everyone wants to know who's the best and what their call center looks like. How do we make ourselves a "world-class" or "best-in-class" center? Building a vision within the context of a strategy and developing a plan to get there are keys to success in using call center technologies.

• **Plan for deployment of call center solutions.** It's not just theory; it's practice. Planning how to do this stuff right – identifying needs, defining requirements, selecting solutions and implementing systems – ultimately makes the understanding practical.

We also want to point out some things this book cannot do for you. It is not intended to be a crystal ball, although we do discuss where things are headed so you can make sound decisions today that will serve you well tomorrow. It is not intended to be a guide on how to operate a call center – that is already covered well in many industry publications.* We'll highlight the implications and ripple-effects of the technologies on operations and organizations so that you can assess the potential impact and make adjustments to use the technology more effectively.

This book won't define your business goals, but we will show you how technology enables you to achieve your objectives, while highlighting the impacts it has on your organization. Also, the book is not a "how-to" guide to setting up a call center, although the information here should certainly help a new center with technology planning and deployment.**

Finally, it's important to note that there are usually no black-and-white solutions to planning for and using call center technologies. The answer to your question: "What should I do?" is often, "It depends." It would be nice if we could tell you with certainty what to do, when to do it and absolutely how to do it right,

---

* For a book on call center management, see *Call Center Management on Fast Forward: Succeeding in Today's Dynamic Inbound Environment* by Brad Cleveland and Julia Mayben, available through ICMI at www.incoming.com.
** A good source for setting up a center is Prosci's "Call Center Planning and Design Toolkit." Visit www.call-center.net.

given this or that set of variables. But, there are too many dependencies for that and, as we'll point out repeatedly, every center is different in its business goals and needs, technology infrastructure, the pain points it's trying to address, and in the operations and processes that leverage the technology.

In the end, these realities make this book even more important. We'll provide you with guidance to help you sort through your issues and options, and make decisions. We'll "arm you for the discussion" so that your conversations about these technologies – internally and with vendors, service providers and other partners – will be more efficient, accurate and fruitful.

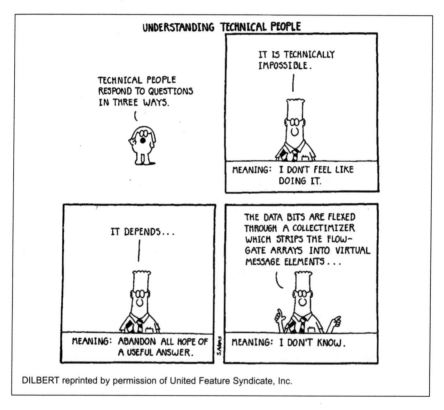

DILBERT reprinted by permission of United Feature Syndicate, Inc.

A Caveat about Vendors

It would be nice to avoid mentioning specific vendors in this book. They're changing constantly – the result of new names, new lines of business, and mergers and acquisitions. But vendor examples can provide additional context and understanding. When we mention specific vendors, we're not saying they're the best or the only provider of a particular capability – we only offer the example to help you better understand the technology and its realities in the marketplace.

If you would like vendor lists for the various technology areas, visit the Web. There are many online sources for buyers' guides and other lists. For instance, we keep an updated vendor list on the Vanguard Communications Web site (www.vanguard.net). The list was created for attendees of our courses, it can be useful to anyone who is in the technology-selection process. There is also a list of resources that will point you to additional online research, conferences, publications and more.

A Word About Our Experience and Views

We work for Vanguard Communications Corp., an independent consulting firm with more than 20 years' experience in the industry. We have worked with call centers and call center technologies for a long time (more than 27 years' experience between us) as consultants and as vendors. We're also drawing from the skills and insights of the rest of our Vanguard team.

We're using our combined experience to give you the straight scoop on technology, based on numerous and varied company and project experiences. In our consulting work, we see good and bad applications of technology every day, with a variety of approaches and vendor solutions. We have worked with large call centers, and very small ones, long-established centers and start-ups. We draw from our extensive exposure to various types of operations to put the technology and its realities in perspective. And a key fact that differentiates Vanguard is that we are independent: We don't partner with or promote any specific vendor.

Those Darn Americans Can't Spell!

We're Americans. We teach, speak and consult on projects around the world, but the reality is, we write about what we know best – the U.S. market. So when we offer input on technology costs, it's in U.S. dollars for the U.S. market. When we give examples, most often, they are based on U.S. companies. When we discuss vendors, it's based on the U.S. market. And worst of all, we spell "center" wrong to a large portion of the English-speaking world (we know, it's "centre"!). Our apologies to those of you in call centers outside of the United States.

But there is good news: Call centers around the world have a lot in common. They tackle the same challenges and, in many cases, work with the same technologies from the same global suppliers. Call center capabilities are advancing rapidly in many parts of the world, and different languages, accents and spelling notwithstanding, this has truly become a global community.

Terminology

The following conventions apply to terms used throughout this book:

• We use the term "agent" throughout the book to refer to the person handling contacts in the center. You may call them Customer Service Representatives (CSRs), Telephone Service Representatives (TSRs), Sales Reps, Customer Advocates or any number of other titles.

• We use "call center" and "contact center" somewhat interchangeably. We'll use contact center more as we get into the later chapters and multimedia issues. And we use "multimedia" to describe handling Web contacts, email, fax, mail or other contacts along with voice.

• We use the term "voice switch" or "switch" to describe the system that manages and connects voice communications. You may refer to it as your PBX, PABX, ACD, phone system or communications server.

• We use lots of acronyms – no surprise there! We provide a thorough acronym list and glossary on pages 328 and 333, respectively, that should help you work your way through any call center technology conversation or paragraph.

A Roadmap of the Book

Figure 1 illustrates the overall call center technology environment. You'll see this picture at the beginning of each chapter with specific areas highlighted corresponding to the technologies discussed in that chapter.

Figure 1: The Call Center Technology Environment

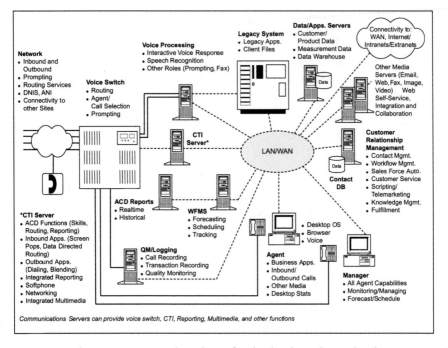

Communications Servers can provide voice switch, CTI, Reporting, Multimedia, and other functions

Figure 2 depicts a conceptual roadmap for this book. It shows the chapters, topics and relationships. In Part One, we build the foundation with strategy and infrastructure, and look at the questions they present. In Part Two, we cover the fundamental technologies used for routing, reporting and managing voice calls. In Part Three, we expand to the data side of the equation and look at Computer Telephony Integration (CTI), and business applications and architectures, including Customer Relationship Management (CRM) technologies. Part Four then moves into self-service options and multimedia environments. Finally, in Part Five, we present issues and considerations for implementing call center technologies and take a brief look into the future.

Figure 2: A Roadmap of *Call Center Technology Demystified*

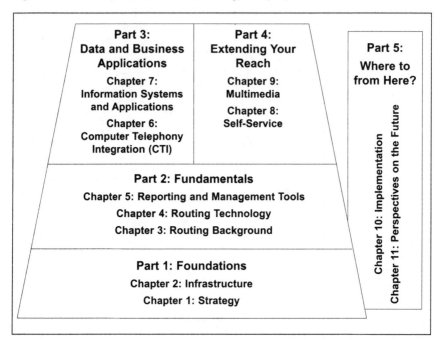

Here's a summary of the topics covered by each chapter, and how the chapters are arranged within the five main sections of the book:

Part One: Foundations

Chapter 1: Strategic Context for Your Call Center Technology. This chapter emphasizes the need for congruence among three elements: business strategy, call center strategy and technology strategy. Technology serves as an enabler for your strategy. We give you a framework for thinking about the appropriate strategy for your business and its impact on call center technology planning.

Chapter 2: Infrastructure Changes Force Big Architectural Decisions. Here, we define big changes in application infrastructure and network infrastructure. We talk about PBX, ACD, hybrid, CTI and communications server architectures and where the application "smarts" reside. Also, network infrastructures and the transition from circuit-switched to packet-switched technologies like Asynchronous Transfer Mode (ATM) and Internet Protocol (IP) are described.

Part Two: Fundamentals

Chapter 3: Principles and Enablers for Routing and Queuing. Without background knowledge of the principles of routing theory, the tools for queuing and routing cannot be fully understood. We provide that insight, along with a description of some of the key enablers for call routing, such as network information and prompting.

Chapter 4: Call Center Matchmaking: Routing Callers to the Right Resource. This chapter defines different levels of sophistication – and complexity – in routing, from basic ACD queuing to conditional routing, skills-based routing and data-directed routing. Single-site and multisite routing are addressed. The various technology elements where this routing can reside are tied into the infrastructure discussion.

Chapter 5: Tools for Measuring, Managing and Optimizing Your Center. We address the gamut of reporting and management tools: ACD reports, wallboards, workforce management systems, logging and quality monitoring systems, as well as simulation tools. And we put it all in the context of developing your reporting strategy.

Part Three: Data and Business Applications

Chapter 6: CTI: Screen Pops and So Much More. We define the many things you can do with CTI and the architectures that support it. We walk through a call flow to emphasize how it works. As the book progresses into these more advanced technologies, we spend more time on the challenges and keys to success.

Chapter 7: Information and Applications Bring CRM Strategies to Life. This chapter first lays the groundwork for business applications by discussing some fundamental things about information systems architectures in the call center and the transition to Web-enabled and Web-architected approaches. Then we address the monster concept of "CRM" and its ties to business strategy, as well as the technology tools that can enable it.

Part Four: Extending Your Reach

Chapter 8: Building IVR and Web-Based Self-Service. This chapter reviews Interactive Voice Response (IVR) and Web-based options within the context of an overall self-service strategy. We also take a look at speech recognition and other advanced capabilities that are beginning to change the landscape for self-service – and we look at moving beyond phone-based self-service to using the Web.

Chapter 9: Multimedia: Transitioning from Call Center to Contact Center. The nonvoice contacts are introduced with a focus on Web-enabling contact methods, such as email, text-chat, Web calls and collaboration tools. We highlight the best-in-class strategy of weaving the Web into a contact center and show you how to tackle it. It all comes together with a discussion of universal queues and the architectures for, and implications of, managing all media cohesively.

Part Five: Where to from Here?

Chapter 10: Making It Happen: Implementation Considerations. Here, we provide a framework for implementing call center technologies, including building a strategy, planning and implementing. We also address challenges concerning the vendor marketplace, and provide advice on making sourcing decisions.

Chapter 11: Perspectives on the Future. In this final chapter we take a brief look into the crystal ball, but with a practical perspective. We give you some direction as you tackle the big decisions about what to do and when to do it.

Part 1: Foundations

Anyone seeking to understand and apply call center technology today needs a solid foundation on which to build. Your foundation must be built on strategies for the business, contact center and technology. Once you have that in place, core architectural decisions can be made to create a direction for your call center technology environment.

Chapter 1: Strategic Context for Your Call Center Technology

Chapter 2: Infrastructure Changes Force Big Architectural Decisions

Chapter 1:

Strategic Context for Your Call Center Technology

Key Points Discussed in this Chapter:

Business Strategy Is the Foundation

Aligning Business, Call Center and Technology Strategies

The Role of Technology in Strategy: Automation Vs. Transformation

Tying Technology Planning to Call Center Strategy

Call center technology planning, investment and implementation should be undertaken within the context of your company's overall business strategy and goals. This seems obvious and yet we continually come across technology projects that don't link to business strategy, let alone call center strategy. *It's so easy for this to happen.* Given the fascination with new and exciting technology, and management pressure to do something now, even the best intentions can be derailed.

The pressure and changes introduced to our industry by Customer Relationship Management (CRM) concepts and multiple-media channels – especially the Web – make strategic planning more important than ever. When technology investments are not placed in context, you run the risk of operating far below your potential – and even at cross-purposes with your company's mission.

Business Strategy Is the Foundation

Strategy helps you to develop a blueprint for the future. It provides the framework for near-term and long-term decisions. Call centers are guided by three levels of strategy: 1) business strategy, 2) call center strategy, and 3) technology strategy. The key elements of each strategy, and the relationships between them, are depicted in Figure 1-1 (on page 6).

The guiding vision for a particular organization is defined by senior management in the *business strategy*. Its fundamental purpose is to identify attractive business opportunities through which the organization can build and sustain competitive advantage. The business strategy defines the organization's target customers, the products and services to be offered, the means through which those products and services will be assembled and delivered, and the revenues and costs associated with delivery. It is the foundation upon which *every other aspect* of the business is built.

Is business strategy relevant to call centers? Absolutely! Your call center is a vital link to one of your company's most important strategic assets – your customers.

Figure 1-1: Strategic Relationships

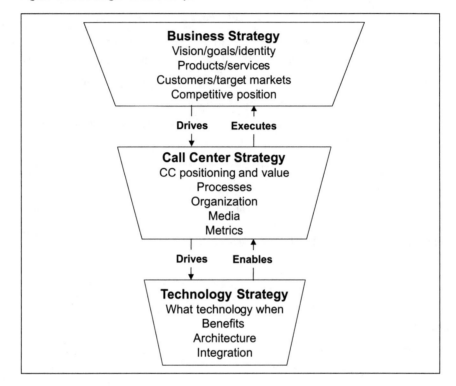

In our consulting practice, we're seeing more and more call center projects driven from the top down. In these cases, the executives understand the influence of the call center on customer acquisition, retention, satisfaction and growth. They know that call center excellence translates into increased profitability. For example:

• Decreasing the customer defection rate by 5 percent translates into profitability increases of 25 percent to 100 percent, depending on the industry (*The Loyalty Effect*, Frederick Reichheld).

• When customers leave a company, 75 percent of the time it has nothing to do with the product (*Fortune* Magazine).

• The No. 1 reason for customer defection is poor service (*Business Week*).

• Numerous studies have determined that it is significantly more expensive to acquire new customers than retain existing ones (three times, 10 times or more!).

Clearly, call centers can directly affect these factors and other measures of business success.

A better understanding of business strategy also helps you to drive projects from the bottom up. Connecting with the issues that senior management cares about and communicating the value of your work in their terms will help them to appreciate the call center role and how it supports the business goals. While you create visibility for your center, you also gain insights into business directions. That insight can be used to further enhance your strategic positioning.

© 2000 Ted Goff

"We need to cut down on productivity, quality and customer service to save money."

Alternative Strategy Models

There are numerous books on business strategy available. Harvard Professor Michael Porter is author of *Competitive Strategy, Competitive Advantage* and *On Competition*. He introduces models for competitive advantage (differentiation, cost leadership and focus). He also writes about the "five forces" model for assessing the external environment, and the "value chain" for systematically analyzing a company's discrete business functions for sources of competitive advantage. He notes that companies can choose not to seek competitive advantage in a specific business function, but instead focus on operational effectiveness.

Michael Treacy and Fred Wiersema, authors of *The Discipline of Market Leaders*, identify three strategies companies can use to become leaders in a particular industry:

- **Operational excellence** calls for a focus on relentless cost reduction, convenience and quality.
- **Product leadership** companies provide the best product possible, and constantly push the existing product boundaries.
- **Customer intimacy** builds strategic advantage around in-depth knowledge of target markets and customer needs.

Companies excel by choosing the strategy that is consistent with their resources and market opportunities and focusing on it. Keep in mind, you can't be all things to all people. Tradeoffs will help you to define and execute successful business strategy.

Aligning Business, Call Center and Technology Strategies

The *call center strategy* defines the processes, organizational structure, operations blueprint and metrics that help the business to achieve its strategic objectives. The associated *technology strategy* helps to translate the call center strategy into reality.

So how do you align the three strategies? Let's look at an example of three companies in the same industry that are pursuing three different business strategies. Company A wants to be the absolute *low-cost leader*; Company B chooses to compete by offering the *best products*; and Company C is staking out its competitive ground by having the *best sales and service organization*. Although they're in the same industry, they are pursuing different approaches to the market, and hence, attract different buyers. Table 1-1 summarizes the differences in business strategies, call center strategies and call center technology strategies for Companies A, B and C.

In the examples, all three approaches work well – even though they are radically different. The key is that, within each company, the three strategies are consistent and well-conceived to support, enable and drive each other. None of these companies tries to "do it all." Each picks and chooses what makes sense within its strategic framework.

Table 1-1: Strategic Positioning

	Company A	Company B	Company C
Unique position	Low-cost leader	Best products	Best sales and service
Sources of competitive advantage	• Manufacturing • Linkages to suppliers • Financial management • Automation • Call center	• Research and development • Engineering • Hiring practices • Indirect sales and distribution (dealers)	• Sales force • Service force • Customer knowledge • Call center
Corporate culture	Discipline: • Interdepartmental coordination • Tight financial control	Innovation: • Product leadership • Value designers and engineers	Customers first: • Provide choice and control of contacts • Know them intimately • Grow relationships
Values of target customers	Are cost-conscious – decide on price	Want innovative products with the most advanced features and best performance (and willing to pay for it)	Want companies that are "easy to do business with" and want to be treated special
Call center makes a strategic contribution?	Yes – deliver decent service while containing costs	No – investments are focused on product development	Yes – call center on the front line of providing best sales and service
Call center positioning	Valued asset: • Inbound and outbound sales • Customer service • Linked to other parts of business for process efficiency	Necessity: • Gather information to support product development • Dealer support as needed • Outsourcer for basic dealer or product information	Service differentiator: • Sales and service teams support customers and field • Tightly tied to other parts of business for customer knowledge and support
Call center focus and examples of execution	Efficiency: • Streamlined processes • Metrics focused on cost per contact, resource utilization, handle time	Best practices: • Manage to best practices • Balanced metrics across productivity, cost, resource utilization	Service and sales: • Customer-focused processes • Customer-focused metrics (service level, customer value, quality)

continued on next page

	Company A	Company B	Company C
Unique position	Low-cost leader	Best products	Best sales and and service
Technology used	• Single switch, universal agents • Web (call avoidance) • IVR (call avoidance) • Predictive dialer for outbound contact efficiency • Reporting linked to financial management • Workforce management scheduling and adherence • CTI screen pops • Integration to manufacturing	• Capture and categorize information gleaned from call center contacts and deliver to product development teams • Basic routing • Basic reporting • Basic forecasting • Outsourcers handle majority of call center technology • Minimize customization and integration	• Comprehensive CTI-enabled CRM • CTI data-directed routing • Skills-based routing • Knowledge base • Business applications with scripts, call flows, work flows • Self-service for 24x7 customer access • Integration to marketing and field sales and service

The Role of Technology in Strategy

The examples illustrate the role of technology in creating or supporting strategic value. It's important to understand, though, that off-the-shelf call center technology by itself usually isn't a source of sustainable competitive advantage because it is available to anybody.

Does this mean that companies should build custom system solutions? Not usually. Rather, it's important to use these systems in unique ways that further the company's strategic goals. When call center technology is uniquely configured, surrounded by unique processes and linked to other information systems and management practices, it can be a source of competitive advantage. Technology is an enabler. It is not generally a standalone answer to a problem, but it can be a powerful factor when aligned with the overall business strategy and call center strategy.

There is another key issue to consider when developing a technology implementation strategy. Technology can play two roles: it can automate or transform. With automation, the business outcome and the fundamental nature of the work stays the same, but it is achieved better, faster or cheaper. With transformation, the technology changes the actual nature of the work. Automation changes *how* things get done, while transformation changes the nature of *what* gets done. Table 1-2 illustrates the differences.

Table 1-2: Technology Automation Vs. Transformation

Technology	Automation	Transformation
Routing	Virtual operations to add efficiency through larger agent groups	Skill segmentation and virtual operations to get caller to best person to handle call
Reporting	Basic tools to manage efficiency, meet targets (service level, handle time, occupancy)	Advanced tools to create customer-focused reports, business intelligence (retention, revenue, business growth)
Quality monitoring and logging systems	Recordings for risk and loss management, continuous improvement	Evaluation for talent development, career pathing
Workforce management systems	Forecasting and scheduling for headcount minimization	Forecasting and scheduling for optimized accessibility across varying volumes (and media), planning for growth and new initiatives
Computer telephony integration	Pop screens, automate outbound dialing or other functions to save time	Use data-directed routing for customer segmentation, integrated reporting to analyze relationships
Business applications and databases (CRM, knowledge base, etc.)	Use contact-logging, knowledge base, and transactional tools to streamline interactions	Create an enterprise view of the customer relationships and personalize interactions
Self-service technologies and integration	Force or encourage customers to self-serve to drive down costs (contact avoidance)	Offer customer choices, 24x7 access, and assisted service that is readily accessible and integrated with the call center
IP telephony	Lower capital and operation costs by simplifying to one network	Enable media-rich collaboration using Web calls and co-browsing

Transformational technology implementations offer powerful benefits. However, executing a transformational project is significantly more difficult than automating. With automation, you keep existing processes and operating principles. With transformation, the underlying call center processes, management practices and operating assumptions need to change. Process reengineering and organizational development work has to be done before, or in parallel with, the technology implementation.

Transformational projects affect power and influence, reporting relationships, organizational structures, senior management visibility, pay plans, agent recruitment and retention programs, and cross-functional teams (call center operations, telecom, IS/IT, marketing, sales and human resources). As you plan for transformational technologies, understand that the organizational and process implications are likely greater than the technology challenges.

Tying Technology Planning to Call Center Strategy

Figure 1-2 shows the progression of call center technology arrayed against the positioning, or strategic value, of the call center. We use this tool with companies to help them develop call center technology strategies – it triggers discussions about the match (or mismatch) of business needs and the technology to enable it.

Figure 1-2: Call Center Technology's Strategic Value

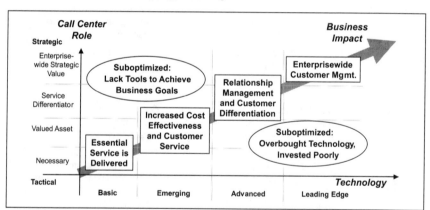

The vertical axis defines where a call center is positioned within the organization: Is it a strategic imperative or a tactical necessity? What is its role in developing and managing relationships with customers? The horizontal axis identifies the technology tools required, from basic to leading edge. While there aren't rigid boundaries here, Table 1-3 provides a framework for technology evolution within these categories.

Table 1-3: Technology Progression Framework

Basic	Emerging	Advanced	Leading edge
• Basic routing • Basic reporting • Basic systems • Basic forecasting	• Advanced routing and reporting • Self-service (IVR, Web) • Workforce management • Quality monitoring • CTI screen pops • Contact management • Knowledge management • Multisite virtual center	• CTI routing and reporting • CRM workflows, scripts • Web integration (email, calls, text-chat, collaboration) • Personalized self-service	• Integrated multimedia queue • Cross-channel contact tracking • Data analysis (analytics) for customer-focused reporting and personalization

The diagonal line (Figure 1-2) shows the intersection of the call center positioning with the technology tools to enable it, and the business outcome that results. Companies can be anywhere along the diagonal line, depending on the role that the call center plays in their overall business strategy. A call center that has a more significant (strategic) role in the business needs more powerful technology tools and would gravitate toward the upper right of the diagonal line. A center whose role is to deliver essential services would likely be found toward the lower left of the diagonal, and would have a hard time justifying advanced technologies.

However, the call center positioning and technology investment don't always match. When centers are above or below the diagonal line, their technology investment is suboptimized. Call centers below the diagonal line have overinvested – the technology tools exceed their business vision – resulting in highly under-utilized technologies. Those above the diagonal line are underinvested in call center technology – the call center is strategic, but the technology deployed doesn't enable them to achieve their business goals. The goal is to be along the diagonal, where the role of the call center is supported by the right amount of technology investment.

Execution Is the Really Hard Part

Developing call center and technology strategies can be exciting and fun. But once you define your strategies, it's time to execute on your intent. As you increase the strategic positioning of your call center, and associated technological complexity, there is an increasing premium on some critical skills:

- **Organization and operations:** change management, organizational development, business process reengineering, cross-functional team management and general project management skills.
- **Human resources:** training, skill development, recruiting and screening, career paths and job design, and compensation management
- **Technology management:** technical project management, systems architecting, systems integration, operations, administration and support, and specialized support staff development.

The bottom line: In your enthusiasm about strategy and technology, don't forget the huge implications for people and processes, and include them in your planning.

Build a Strategy for Success

Part of building a strategy is understanding where you are today and defining where you need to be tomorrow. It starts with identifying the call center's role in the organization and the technologies required to enable the center to succeed in that role. With the current and target position defined and an understanding of what technology can do, you can start considering how to get from one place to the other. Our aim is to help you in that quest!

Points to Remember

- Business strategy, call center strategy and the call center technology strategy must align. You should care what your executives are thinking about business strategy, because it will define the call center position within the company and the technology you need to support your strategic goals.
- Technology itself is generally not a source of competitive advantage because it is freely available to all competitors. How you use it is a competitive advantage.

• A call center technology strategy will help you make technology prioritization decisions that will enable you to meet your business goals.

• Linking to business strategy can raise your visibility and educate senior management.

Actions to Take

• Understand your company's business strategy. Build a contact center strategy if you don't already have one and define your technology strategy within that context. Chapter 10 provides a framework for developing a technology strategy.

Chapter 2:

Infrastructure Changes Force Big Architectural Decisions

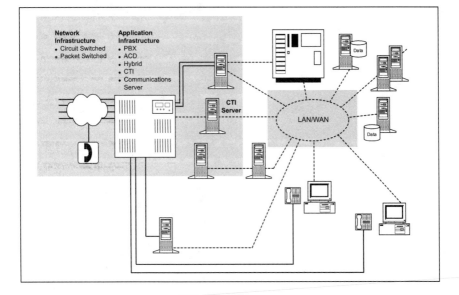

Key Points Discussed in this Chapter:

A Brief History of Voice and Data Systems Infrastructures

Application Infrastructure Options
PBXs, Standalone ACDs, Hybrids, CTI, Communications Servers and others

Network Infrastructure Options
Circuit-Switching, Digital Communications, Signaling Methods, Packet-Switching and Data Networks

Packetizing Voice
Internet Protocol
VoIP Requirements, Considerations and Standards

Now that we've set the overall stage of call center and technology strategy, it's time to dig into two fundamental call center technology questions:

- What are the options for my application infrastructure?
- What are the options for my network infrastructure?

Application and network infrastructures are foundational technologies with wide-ranging ripple effects. Because other call center technologies depend on these infrastructures, your choice of infrastructure can limit or expand future options. Some options can also lock you into a long-term relationship with a vendor. Additionally, infrastructure choices have other organizational ramifications, like the depth and breadth of IT support skills required and the relationships between departments.

The term *application infrastructure* means the core technology of the voice switch (or the phone system) that routes and manages calls.* The voice switch is the device that connects callers to agents. Application logic is used to route and queue calls to agents; the theory and technology behind it is discussed in detail in Chapters 3 and 4. As you'll see, there are many options for this infrastructure. Because of the variety of choices, making decisions about which products and vendors fit best can be a bit confusing.

We use the term *network infrastructure* to denote the underlying technology that physically transports the caller-agent conversations. Until the past few years, there has been only one choice for voice networking: circuit-switching. This is the technology used for telephones for more than 100 years.

With the advent of high-bandwidth, ubiquitous data networks, a second alternative has emerged: packet-switching. With this option, all types of communications traffic – data, voice and even video – can be carried on the same network. Packet-switching of voice includes technologies like the much-hyped Voice over Internet Protocol (often referred to as "Voice over IP" or VoIP).

We'll interweave some history on how these two infrastructures evolved and how they are continuing to evolve. These markets are changing very rapidly.

---

* The focus of this discussion is on call center functionality. There is also a set of functions for basic call management (such as dial plan, call coverage, least-cost routing) often referred to as PBX functionality.

Because of the constant stream of innovations hitting the marketplace (literally on a daily basis), use the content of this chapter as a guideline for framing infrastructure discussions. Keep up-to-date by attending trade shows, reading call center technology magazines and reviewing industry analyst reports.

The options for both application and network infrastructure are many. And eventually, you'll have to answer the question: "What do I do?" The answer: "It depends." (You'll hear this more than once in this book!) Businesses and their call centers are like snowflakes – each is unique (we'll also remind you of this!). However, we do provide you with the advantages and disadvantages of the alternatives. Much will depend on the risk profile of your organization and the aggressiveness of your company's attitude toward deploying new technologies.

A Brief History

Four key developments have spurred the evolution of application and network infrastructure: PCs, data networking technology, client/server computing and the explosion of the Internet.

Since the birth of telephony in the late 1800s, voice has been the center of the communications universe. Very specialized voice equipment, optimized to manage voice connections, was manufactured by a variety of companies. These voice switches came as an all-in-one package. Vendors provided all hardware and software, right down to the telephones. In the call center world, these switches are called PBXs and ACDs (we'll describe them more further on). Once a vendor choice was made, only that vendor could supply you with technology. If you wanted someone else's hardware or software, all of the previous vendor's technology had to be replaced. The only salvageable investment was building wiring.

This proprietary approach was paralleled in the world of data processing. Until the late 1970s, the mainframe and minicomputer reigned supreme, and these systems came as packages consisting of hardware, operating systems, application software, networking equipment and terminals. If you wanted to change vendors, then all of your previous investments were scrapped.

So until the 1970s, the worlds of voice and data were closed and highly proprietary.

Figure 2-1: Voice and Data Technology Evolution

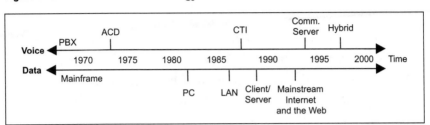

The PC Is First on the Scene

The development of the PC in the late '70s and early '80s started to change this situation in the data world. With PCs, you could make separate hardware, operating system and application software decisions. These different components began to interoperate and this unbundling spawned a proliferation of vendor options for both hardware and software. De facto standards emerged and solidified – and when standards solidify, interoperability reigns, buyers have choices and prices drop.

Enter the LAN

Standalone personal computers were great for personal productivity (word processing) and decision support (spreadsheet, database applications), but users wanted to share information and resources. This need led to the development of the Local Area Network (LAN) with networking technologies like Ethernet and Token Ring. In the LAN's first iteration, users were limited to sharing files and printers.

Next Comes Client/Server Computing

Even as PCs and LANs became widespread, the majority of business applications (e.g., order entry, manufacturing, financial systems) still resided on very expensive and inflexible minicomputers and mainframes. The desire to migrate from the costly mainframe/minicomputer world drove the development of client/server computing in the late '80s and early '90s. With client/server computing, business applications shifted to servers that allowed users to access applications over the network with PCs. Data and applications also remained on the mainframe or minicomputer, and could be accessed by the server for data retrieval and updating. The server managed the heavy computational and query functions, while the

Graphical User Interface (GUI) on the PC served as an easy-to-use navigational tool.

This scenario offered compelling economic advantages. Because de facto standards and industry standards existed, the situation allowed hundreds of hardware and software firms to participate in the industry. Pick your hardware (client, server, networking equipment); pick your software (operating system, database engine, and business application). It was all about choice, standards, economics and not being locked into proprietary vendor arrangements.

Then Comes the Internet

The last big trend that accelerated the change in thinking about infrastructure was the explosive growth of the Internet and the Web. The use of email exploded, along with Web self-service capabilities, and the potential for chat, Web calls and Web collaboration. All of a sudden, claims on agent resources were being stretched with nontelephone customer requests. Data communications traffic volume skyrocketed, overtaking voice traffic volume.

Voice Technology – Late to the Party

While the scenario of choice was well-accepted – even expected – in the data world, voice technology moved slower. Why? In the United States, voice communications was regulated and basically operated as a monopoly in equipment until the late 1960s and a monopoly in network services until the early 1980s. Even with deregulation, the culture was slow to change. But users and technologists began to ask the question: "Why can't I have the benefits of open systems in the voice world?"

First came Computer Telephony Integration (CTI). Early CTI developers thought that, because companies had invested significant sums of money in both voice infrastructure and data infrastructure, they would want to leverage that existing investment. Voice equipment, with typical depreciation cycles of five to 10 years, could not be simply tossed and replaced. So CTI vendors drew from the best of both worlds – existing voice functionality and existing data functionality – and created additional value by making them work together, creating new applications. CTI vendors used standard server-based application platforms that integrated with proprietary PBXs and ACDs.

The next school of vendors took it a step further. They believed people should have even more choices of voice hardware, operating system, database engine and voice application software. Startups emerged promoting this PC/data-networking/ software-centric approach for voice. Infrastructure providers that seek to achieve this vision are generally referred to as Communications Server companies.

This evolution leaves us with three vendor groupings in the voice world today:

• The _PBX_ and _ACD_ vendors who, although their history is rooted in proprietary platforms, are (somewhat slowly) migrating their architectures.

• The _CTI_ providers who were the first to push for intelligence outside of proprietary switching platforms.

• The _Communications Server_ vendors who dared to say telephony applications could run on a standard PC server.

Each of these application infrastructure options can be implemented with either a circuit- or packet-switched (IP) network infrastructure.

Application Infrastructure Options

The good news is that all of these historical influences have spurred rapid innovation among vendors. Traditional PBX and ACD vendors are working very hard to open up their systems, and the newer kids on the block are becoming more reliable, scalable and manageable. Five application infrastructure options are presented: PBX, ACD, Hybrid, CTI and Communications Server. The first two are more traditional, while the latter three are becoming more mainstream as the closed proprietary approach fades. So, let's dig in and take a look at these options.

Private Branch Exchange

The PBX, or Private Branch Exchange, is the core voice switch for most medium and large organizations. People in your organization probably just call it the "phone system." The PBX serves all departments and functions in an organization in addition to call center personnel.

A PBX is a specialized computer for managing phone connections. It has a Central Processing Unit (CPU, which is basically the core computer), memory, storage devices (disk, tape, flash ROM), an operating system and application software. Other components include cabinets and circuit cards (also referred to as circuit boards or blades) that provide connections to telephones as well as to network service providers for local and long-distance service. The underlying transport mechanism is Time Division Multiplexing (TDM) – more on that later in this chapter.

For the call center, PBX providers have specialized software (generally referred to as "ACD software") that they turn on to provide core call center functionality. This software runs on a processing complex right on the PBX itself. In each of the application infrastructure options, we point out where the core call center functions reside. These functions include queuing, routing, agent work state management and monitoring, and other capabilities that are discussed in detail in Chapters 3 and 4.

Figure 2-2: PBX Application Infrastructure

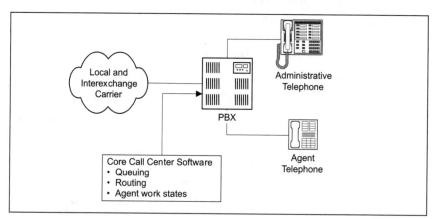

Call Center Technology Demystified ■

Table 2-1: Advantages and Disadvantages of PBX Application Infrastructure

Advantages of a PBX	Disadvantages of a PBX
• One system serves the entire organization • Highly scalable – serves thousands of users • Very high reliability – 99.999%* (a few minutes of downtime per year) • Good administration and maintenance tools • Good distribution and support networks • Suites of products and services; relationships with other call center technology vendors • Robust call treatment capabilities (announcements, music in queue) built in • Proven technology	• Proprietary: hardware and software from a single manufacturer • Expensive because of proprietary nature • Call center Research and Development (R&D) dollars compete with other projects • Original development optimized for voice channel; less elegant architecture for multimedia • Original development for circuit-switched network; less elegant architecture for packet-based voice communications

Likely Sales Messages from a PBX Vendor

"We've been around for a long time. We're stable, proven and we're here for the long haul. This is a no-risk decision for you. Is the PBX changing? Yes, but it's an evolutionary change as opposed to a revolutionary one. Because we bundle our hardware and software, we are the most reliable piece of equipment in your entire technology base. Further, we service everything end to end – if you have a problem, you make one phone call (there is no finger-pointing between vendors with us). Our solution, which includes call center and administrative applications like advanced call coverage and voice-messaging applications running on our hardware, has been improved upon for years; it is time-tested and is used by tens of thousands of companies."

The top three PBX vendors in the call center arena are Avaya, Nortel and Siemens. Other notable vendors include Ericsson, Fujitsu, Mitel, NEC and Toshiba.

Who are the likely buyers of this type of applications infrastructure? They tend to be organizations in which the telecom departments have greater influence over call center technology buying decisions.

---

* 99.999% reliability is often referred to as the "five nines" of reliability.

Standalone ACD

An automatic call distributor (ACD) is a specialized voice switch that is optimized for the call center. With this option, the business thinking is that the call center is such a specialized business function it needs a separate, dedicated application infrastructure.

A standalone ACD has its own dedicated cabinets, circuit packs, CPU, operating system, storage and memory. From a hardware perspective, it is very similar to a PBX.

With the ACD, non-call center functions are usually served by another voice switch. It is common to see a PBX installed side-by-side with the ACD. The ACD serves the call center while the PBX serves the rest of the business (non-call center users are sometimes referred to as administrative users). Users communicate between the two different systems using tie trunks. The ACD and PBX usually have their own dedicated sets of trunks to both long-distance and local network service providers.

Figure 2-3: ACD Application Infrastructure

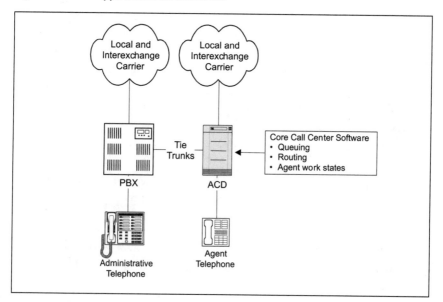

Table 2-2: Advantages and Disadvantages of ACD Application Infrastructure

Advantages of an ACD	Disadvantages of an ACD
• Highly scalable – serves hundreds or thousands of users • Highly reliable – comparable to PBX reliability • Advanced features and functions specific to call center needs • Suites of call center products and third-party application relationships • Marketing, sales and service staff are very call center literate and focused • 100% of R&D is focused on call center solutions • Very good call center application development toolkits	• Duplicate infrastructures to administer, maintain and manage • Costly because of dual investments for call center and administrative functions • Proprietary architecture • PBX call center functionality is very close to parity • Original development optimized for voice channel; less elegant architecture for multimedia • Original development for circuit-switched network; less elegant architecture for packet-based voice communications

Likely Sales Messages from a Standalone ACD Vendor

"These aren't just phone calls coming in – these are customer relationships, and meeting your sales, service and other business objectives is at stake. We understand that operating a call center poses a unique managerial challenge – and it's because of that uniqueness that you need a dedicated ACD. We've optimized our software to give you the routing and reporting functionality you need to be successful. We have a non-blocking switching matrix and, by keeping your administrative traffic separate from your mission-critical customer traffic, you'll never have blocked or uncompleted customer calls. Botched customer calls mean lost revenue and damaged business relationships. Use your PBX for what it was designed – general business users. Service your customers on our platform. You've invested tens of millions of dollars in building those relationships. Invest a bit more in our dedicated ACD, because it's not just a phone system; it's a platform for customer access and satisfaction."

Aspect and Rockwell are examples of standalone ACD vendors. The buyers of this type of solution are often the end-users – call center management.

The Hybrid

As customers began to demand more functionality and open architectures from their PBXs and ACDs, some vendors migrated some of the application intelligence off of the switching matrix and placed it on a standard server and operating system. We call this arrangement a Hybrid. Vendors have done this to meet their customer's demands and to stay competitive, as well as to take advantage of powerful, cost-effective server technology and new development tools to create additional functionality.

This Hybrid approach signals a more open technology attitude to the marketplace. As you'll see, it looks much like the CTI application infrastructure approach. However, these Hybrid arrangements work with only the PBX or ACD vendor's proprietary switching matrix and use a proprietary link between the PBX or ACD and the Hybrid server.

Figure 2-4: Hybrid Application Infrastructure

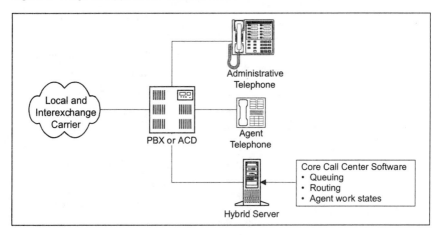

Table 2-3: Advantages and Disadvantages of Hybrid Application Infrastructure

Advantages of a Hybrid	Disadvantages of a Hybrid
• Increased functionality • Improved capacities • Runs on more open, standard server platform (standard operating system and database) • Improved system administration and reporting interfaces • Extends the useful life of switching matrix and telephones • Provides a path for multimedia queuing and routing	• Proprietary to vendor's switching matrix (uses a proprietary link between switch and server) • Many still require all hardware and software be purchased from same vendor • May require dual administration on both the PBX or ACD and the external server

Likely Sales Messages from a Vendor with a Hybrid Approach

"Our call center solution represents a gradual evolution to open systems. By migrating the core functions to an external server, we're able to support advanced functionality and feature capacities like very sophisticated skill groups, multimedia and very granular routing, while still providing you the 99.999 percent uptime you demand. It also serves as a path for multimedia integration. This is the lowest-risk, highest-reliability, best-supported path to open systems."

Examples of vendors in this space include traditional PBX and ACD vendors. The Hybrid is likely to be bought by telecom departments that are in transition in their thinking and position, or companies trying to leverage their existing investments while moving into newer architectures.

Computer Telephony Integration

Computer Telephony Integration (CTI) bridges the world of traditional telephony with the newer world of client/server computing. CTI applications infrastructure can augment or replace the existing switch (PBX or ACD) application infrastructure.

Some CTI applications *augment* the switch's functionality, because a PBX or ACD can't do some things on its own without additional external computer-based software. These capabilities leverage the data side of the equation to a great degree. Examples are screen pops, softphones, data-directed routing, predictive dialing, integrated multisource reporting and multimedia integration (email, fax, chat, Web calls). These applications increase functionality.

Other CTI applications *replace* the core ACD or PBX call center functionality (internal to the voice switch) with software and hardware that resides outside the voice switch. Functions such as routing, agent work states, skills management and reporting move from being controlled by the voice switch to an external server-based software environment. This doesn't dramatically increase functionality, but rather changes where the functionality resides and executes.

This approach to migrating the functionality off of the PBX or ACD is some-times (disparagingly) referred to as "dumbing down the switch." CTI vendors that are proponents of this replacement approach also provide augmentation applications.

The Difference Between CTI and a Hybrid

The architecture of CTI looks a lot like the Hybrid option described on page 28. And physically, implementations of these solutions can all look the same on the surface. But the reality is there is tremendous variation in the amount of application "smarts" moved off the switch onto the server and the variety of switches supported. In our definition, CTI software supports a variety of PBXs and ACDs, while Hybrid software only supports a PBX or ACD from the same vendor (no true interoperability). The spectrum of intelligence levels is discussed in Chapter 6.

CTI software and hardware typically run on a Microsoft (NT/Windows 2000/XP) or Unix-based server. It is connected to the switch through a CTI link, which uses software on the switch and a LAN interface (generally Ethernet TCP/IP) from the switch to exchange monitoring and control messages between the switch and the CTI applications. CTI is discussed at length in Chapter 6.

Figure 2-5: CTI Application Infrastructure

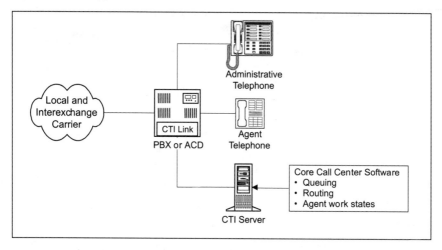

Table 2-4: Advantages and Disadvantages of CTI Application Infrastructure

Advantages of CTI	Disadvantages of CTI
• Re-use existing PBX/ACD hardware investment • Variety of PBX/ACD interoperability • Broad software technology support: Visual Basic, Java, C++, Active X • Extensive support of standards like TAPI, SQL, ODBC and TCP/IP • Toolkits and integrated development environments (IDE) • Highly customizable • Choice of preferred OS, RDBMS and hardware servers • Positions for suite of CTI applications (screen pops, softphone, etc.) • Path to multimedia queuing and routing (email, fax, Web calls)	• Scalability may be somewhat limited • Reliability issues may still require using ACD/PBX functionality as a backup • Significant customization and system integration efforts may be required • May require dual administration on both the PBX or ACD and the CTI server • Potential lock-in to a proprietary software application suite • Support may be difficult due to multiple vendors and customization • Quality of the application is highly dependent on the voice-switch CTI link capabilities • Call treatment may require an IVR port for every call queued

Likely Sales Messages from a CTI Vendor

"Deploying your call center applications on our software platform gives you strategic choice. We don't care what your ACD or PBX telephony hardware environment is – we support our application on all the major ACDs and PBXs. In today's business world of mergers and acquisitions, we can integrate your call center operations very quickly by using the acquired company's telephony assets. We can normalize any PBX or ACD environment. Besides standardizing your environment today, we put you on the path to advanced applications like multimedia integration, data-directed and multisite routing, integrated reporting and outbound applications. Your previous vendors have locked you into their application infrastructures. Their expertise is hardware, ours is software. Software functionality is what makes the difference in meeting your business goals today."

Vendor examples for the top-tier CTI solutions are Alcatel (formerly Genesys Labs and IBM CallPath) and Cisco. The PBX and ACD vendors often have their own CTI platforms, as well. These CTI platforms differ from the Hybrid platforms in that they interface with multiple switch vendors.

Who is buying CTI-oriented architectures? Primarily, organizations where IT has greater influence on call center technology buying decisions, and where decision-makers value open platforms and vendor independence.

Communications Server

With the Communications Server option, the "phone system" runs on a standard PC server with standard operating systems, such as NT, Unix or Linux. It is very software-oriented. You may be able to choose certain components from your preferred vendors: operating system, database engine, hardware server and telephony cards. Or the vendor provides a set of "approved" or certified vendor options and specifications from which to choose.

This type of infrastructure provides highly integrated or bundled capabilities for basic voice-switch functions as well as optional suites of call center capabilities. Besides the core call center application functionality (agent states, routing, skills, etc.), this server-based infrastructure also has highly integrated voice-processing capabilities (interactive voice response and voicemail), reporting, multimedia queuing and desktop CTI applications. These providers label it an "all-in-one" solution – with their proprietary software, APIs and toolkits for complete customization. Because these companies were established in the 1990s, they were able to take advantage of the core technology available at that time: advanced object-oriented programming languages, off-the-shelf operating systems and database engines, standard server technology and standard telephony cards. Because Communications Server vendors source so many core components from other technology vendors, they can focus their efforts on developing their call center application software, management tools and customized Applications Programming Interfaces (APIs).

Because of the fear of downtime, Communications Servers used in mission-critical call center environments need to use industrial-strength server technology (redundant fans, redundant power supplies, RAID storage) and hot standby technologies like clustering. An interesting facet of the Communications Server, which is not necessarily an advantage or disadvantage ("it depends"), is that it is not always clear who should manage and maintain it. A Communications Server requires some IT support because the core architecture and associated maintenance and troubleshooting needs are outside of the comfort zone for most telecom shops. But it's a "phone system," so some think that the telecom group should manage it.

Figure 2-6: Communications Server Application Infrastructure

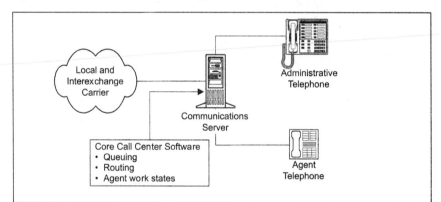

Table 2-5: Advantages and Disadvantages of a Communications Server

Advantages of a Communications Server	Disadvantages of a Communications Server
• Highly integrated ACD routing and reporting, IVR, CTI, voicemail and multimedia capabilities • Some choice of software components (operating systems, Web servers, database engine) • Options for hardware components (servers, telephony cards, telephones) • Toolkits for customization • Rich application functionality for small and medium-size centers • Good option for organization that prefers to do its own IT support	• Reliability and uptime is highly dependent on the server, operating system, application software and application development quality • Scalability can be limited • Relatively young market so call center applications and features are not mature in some cases • Support and maintenance may be difficult because of multiple components, suppliers • Customization costs can be high • Multisite capabilities somewhat limited

Likely Sales Messages from a Communications Server Vendor

"We represent the cutting edge of call center technology. We're extremely open and flexible. With our solution, you avoid having to stitch together a solution of ACD, IVR, reporting, multimedia and desktop CTI applications. We provide you with that functionality right out of the box. Although you do have to configure our solution, minimal integration is required. We've integrated all the application components from Day 1. And as hardware and software vendors improve their infrastructure components, we're able to take advantage of those improvements with you. You've been taken advantage of by your incumbent vendor – it's time to make the move to a truly open solution."

Communications Server vendor examples include Interactive Intelligence, Altigen, Cisco, Cosmocom and Telephony@Work. The first two vendors come from a heritage of circuit-switching, while the last three vendors come from a heritage of packet-switching (more to come on circuit- and packet-switching in the second half of this chapter). Most of the major PBX and ACD vendors offer Communications Servers as part of their product lines now, as well.

Communications Servers are most likely to be bought by companies with smaller centers and those in which IT is driving the decisions. Communications servers are also attractive to new centers and those who want a broad set of functionality quickly.

Other Options: Centrex, Key Systems and Application Service Providers

Three other options for the core applications infrastructure are Centrex, Key systems and Application Service Providers (ASPs).

• With *Centrex*, you essentially outsource your key call center voice-switching and applications infrastructure to your local telecom company (RBOC or PTT). You pay for the service on a monthly basis (no capital), and the telecom company manages the system changes, upgrades and maintenance. This may be a good option if you have small groups scattered around a metropolitan area. The phone companies have excellent backup power and equipment security, and they also offer 24-hour support. The downside to this approach is that the monthly service charges may become cost-prohibitive, and advanced functionality may be thin or nonexistent. Centrex-based solutions have been slower to evolve than premise-based solutions.

• *Key systems* present an option for small call centers. This option typically has limited call center functionality (simple routing, queuing and reporting), and usually supports around 50 total users (agents and administrative users). Like a PBX or an ACD, the call center functions reside right on the voice system. Third parties sometimes offer application packages for more advanced call center functions. This option is viable for a center with a dozen or so agents without significant growth or advanced functionality requirements.

• *ASPs* were a great hope during the dot-com boom of the late 1990s. With this option, the ASP hosts the telephony hardware and software in their facilities. ASPs source best-of-breed application software, integrate the components, house the infrastructure in a highly secure environment and furnish highly reliable power sources and communications circuits. With ASPs, a company outsources call center technology. This option is similar in concept to Centrex: You pay the ASP a monthly per-user fee and they manage the entire infrastructure for you. The ASP industry is not yet mature. If you pursue this option, due diligence is in order, especially around financial strength and long-term viability. (See Chapter 10 for more about ASPs.)

So there are many options for application infrastructure. Before you make an application infrastructure decision, or as you evolve your existing application infrastructure, consider the following questions:

• What are your driving business requirements, considering contact strategy, size and growth, media and financial goals?

• What technology infrastructure do you have today that you want to continue to leverage?

• What is your corporate and IT/telecom posture? Aggressive or cautious? Early adopter or follower?

• What resources do you have to implement, support and apply call center technologies?

The answers to these questions will put you on the proper application infrastructure path for your center.

Network Infrastructure Options

The application infrastructure decision addresses the question: Where do I place my core call center functionality? We now turn our focus to the question: What are my options for network connectivity?

Until just a few years ago, all voice traffic was carried over circuit-switched facilities. Then a new way of transporting voice emerged – packet-switching. Packet-switching is the underlying technology behind VoIP (Voice over Internet Protocol). Lots of wild vendor claims are being made about VoIP. In this section, we'll give you our view from the street and help you to sort myth from reality.

For some companies, VoIP is a hot topic *today*. For others, it is on the horizon and the posture is to "wait and see." We provide the basics for anyone here, as well as the depth needed for those who are ready to take the plunge. While we address this second infrastructure question, keep in mind that the application infrastructure and network infrastructure options can be used in any combination. Although the traditional call center approach is circuit-switched, you can use IP as your network infrastructure with any of the application infrastructure options.

Circuit-Switching

The Public-Switched Telephone Network (PSTN) was developed to support voice traffic. From the time of its invention to the present, voice traffic was carried using a technology called *circuit-switching*. With circuit-switching, an end-to-end temporarily dedicated connection path is set up from the time a call starts ringing at the called party's telephone until disconnect. No other caller has use of the transmission path for the duration of the call. Voice communication is a real-time form of communication – an utterance can't be delayed – and voice interactions tend to be fairly short (most telephone conversations last only a few minutes). Circuit-switching has been around for decades, it's highly reliable and it works extremely well.

Figure 2-7: Circuit-Switching: Temporary Dedicated Paths

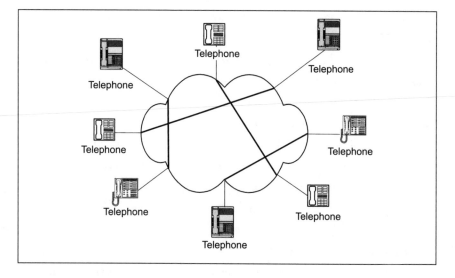

Digital Communications

Today, most voice calling is digital. Although human speech is analog, business telephones immediately convert the analog source to a digital format. The technique that puts analog voice input into a digital format is called Pulse-Code Modulation (PCM); the conversation is converted to a standard 64,000 bits per second digital stream. Through an additional technique called Time-Division Multiplexing (TDM), multiple conversations are placed on a common transmission circuit. Each discrete conversation is placed on the circuit into assigned "time slots" based on a very precise timing scheme. Time-Division Multiplexing is used in voice-switching of both network service providers (local and long distance) and premise equipment providers (PBX, ACD, Communications Server).

The transmission paths that run from a network service provider to your voice switch are known as "trunks" (alternatively, some people refer to these as "lines"). These trunks use either analog or digital transmission. For call center applications, the vast majority of trunks utilize a special digital circuit called a T1 or E1. In North America and Japan, a T1 circuit carries 24 simultaneous conversations over the same set of wires; in Europe, the E1 standard is 31 multiplexed conversations (a 32nd channel is used for timing and synchronization). Multiple T1s can be aggregated onto a single transmission facility. Large call centers often use a DS-3, which is 28 T1s.

In call center applications, digital transmission is a superior alternative to analog transmission for many reasons:

• **Sound quality:** Digital voice is very clear and much less susceptible to popping, hissing, crackling and background noises.

• **Cost effectiveness:** Time-Division Multiplexing allows the phone companies to get more information on a given set of wires and, therefore, keeps costs down.

• **Ease of maintenance:** Digital facilities are easy to maintain – they either work or they don't. Analog facilities' intermittent problems are more difficult to troubleshoot.

• **Equipment density:** Because of the density of conversations handled on a T1/E1, the connecting equipment takes up less room in a voice switch, potentially decreasing the footprint of the voice system in an equipment room.

• **Simpler wiring plan:** A T1/E1 runs over one set of wires. The analog equivalent would require 24 (T1) or 31(E1) wire runs to support the same traffic level.

• **Application sharing:** Dialed Number Identification Service (DNIS) digits are sent over digital circuits to identify the caller's purpose for calling. Different 800 numbers (for example, sales, service and billing) send different DNIS digits, and the information is then used for routing the call to the correct agent group. Literally hundreds of different 800 numbers can use the same T1, helping to contain costs.

Even with all the advantages of digital circuits, it's a good idea to use some regular analog facilities for disaster recovery planning (cable cuts, power failure, failure on the voice switch or network service provider equipment).

Signaling Methods

The T1 or E1 circuit is simply the format for multiplexing the conversation. In order to function, the digital circuit needs a method for setting up and taking down transmission paths. There are two methods for doing this: in-band and out-of-band. With in-band signaling, the signaling information is sent in the same channel as the voice call. With out-of-band signaling, all signaling and control information for all conversations travels in a separate, dedicated signaling channel. In-band signaling is used in features like the caller ID service you might receive in your home. This is why you generally need to wait one or two rings to receive caller ID – it is sent in between ringing signals on the same line that you answer and talk on. Most call centers avoid in-band signaling as it is slower and more limited. Out-of-band signaling is most common in call centers for its speed and feature set.

For call center applications, a very common method for out-of-band signaling is Integrated Services Digital Network (ISDN) Primary Rate Interface (PRI). In North America and Japan, 23 channels of a T1 are used for the voice conversations, while the 24th channel is used for signaling, control and caller-specific information. The 23 channels used for voice transmission paths are called "bearer" or B channels, while the 24th channel that carries the data for setup, teardown and caller information, is called the "data" or D channel. In Europe, 30 conversations are carried on the B channels, and one D channel carries the signaling information. It's possible (and highly dependent on your voice-switching equipment and network vendors) to aggregate the signaling for multiple ISDN PRI circuits onto a single D channel by a technique called non-facility associated signaling (NFAS).

This grouping may lower monthly telecommunications carrier charges for D channels.

Out-of-band digital signaling has a big advantage: more information, faster. For example, DNIS digits are sent to identify the call purpose; Automatic Number Identification (ANI) digits are sent to identify the caller or their geographic location. This information can be delivered faster using out-of-band ISDN PRI signaling. Circuit setup and teardown is also much faster with out-of-band signaling.

Packet-Switching

While voice conversations traditionally use circuit-switching, data communications – or computer-to-computer communications – use *packet-switching*. With packet-switching, information gets chopped into smaller pieces, a process called "packetizing." These smaller pieces of information are called frames, cells or, most often, packets.

Once packetized, the information is sent over a shared network. This brings up the question: why are voice and data communications technologies so different?

• **Data is "bursty":** The nature of data communications is "bursty," which means that data arrives in short and intensive spurts. Computers will sit idle for minutes, sometimes hours, before transmitting any information. Circuit-switching is simply a bad fit for data – when the two computing devices sit idle, the circuit is underutilized. Computers can share the network because of the burstiness – when one set of computers is sitting idle, another set of computers can use the transmission path in the network, resulting in better asset utilization.

• **Data needs exceptional error detection and correction:** Error correction is the other reason that packet-switching is more appropriate for data than circuit-switching. For voice traffic, a slight perturbation in the circuit that momentarily distorts the voice usually doesn't affect overall comprehension. But changing a single zero to a one in a data string could have significant impact. Therefore, data communication needs a mechanism for error detection and correction. When data is put it into packets, error-checking mechanisms are added. When the packet is received at the far end, an algorithm processes the packet and sees that the data is correct. If not, the packet can be resent or otherwise corrected. If a packet, frame or cell is damaged or missing, the receiving device sends the originating device a request to retransmit a specific packet instead of having to resend the entire transmission.

Figure 2-8: Packet-Switching: Permanent Shared Network

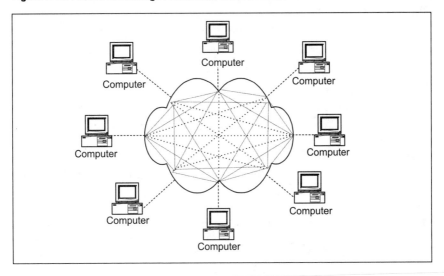

Data Networks

Data communications use two types of networking technologies: Local Area Networks (LANs) and Wide Area Networks (WANs). LAN technologies encompass all the technologies that are utilized inside of a building or a self-contained multibuilding campus. LAN technologies include things like data switches and transmission formats like Ethernet, Token Ring and Asynchronous Transfer Mode (ATM). WAN technologies include devices like routers and services from network service providers like Frame Relay, ATM (used in both LAN and WAN), X.25 and IP over SONET.

Each packet has a sender address, receiver address and sequence number in the packet header. Data-networking devices like data switches and routers interpret the addresses and forward each packet on a packet-by-packet basis. The route taken to the destination may be different for each packet, depending on congestion and route availability. The receiving device then reorders the packets. Compare this data scenario with the voice communications scenario: Each voice conversation has a dedicated path for the duration of the conversation and a transmission never gets out of order.

Two Different Worlds

Until the mid-1990s, network infrastructure was essentially duplicated. There were two parallel networks: one for voice and one for data. The following table summarizes the differences between the two worlds:

Table 2-6: Voice and Data Communications Characteristics

Characteristic	Voice	Data
Communication Source	Telephone	Computer
Switching Method	Circuit	Packet
Communication Session Time	Short	Long
Transmission	Temporary dedicated path per call	Permanent shared network for two or more computers
Wide Area Network Service	Circuit-based	ATM, Frame Relay, IP, X.25
Switching Device	Circuit-based voice switch (e.g., PBX, ACD, Communications Server)	Packet-based data switches and routers
Error Tolerance	Low	Zero
Delay Tolerance	Extremely low	Medium
Communication Sequencing	Always in order	Sometimes out of order
Communications Flow	Continuous	Bursty

Figure 2-9: Traditional Voice and Data Worlds

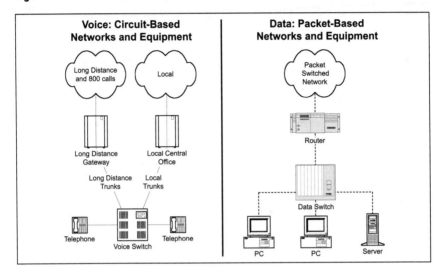

Packetizing Voice

Data traffic has grown at a much faster rate than voice traffic. For years, networking experts predicted that aggregate data traffic would eventually be larger than voice traffic. With the Internet becoming a mainstream business tool, it's estimated that, today, the volume of data transmissions is twice that of voice transmissions. Network engineers theorized that, if the smaller voice traffic volume could be put on a data network, the entire voice network could converge with the data network. All of the duplication of the voice world would be eliminated and significant savings would result from economies of scale and better asset utilization.

Internet Protocol Surpasses ATM

Quite a bit of research had already been done with a converged transmission technology called Asynchronous Transfer Mode (ATM). ATM was engineered to provide quality of service, or a method to give real-time packets (like voice and video) priority over data packets. The original converged protocol was ATM. It was, and is still, used as a backbone technology in the service provider market. But the ubiquity of IP deployment has put the momentum behind VoIP (even though IP can be, and is, used in conjunction with ATM).

Although ATM is a first-rate technology, the understanding of its use is not widespread. Knowledge of IP, on the other hand, is pervasive and builds on Ethernet technology, which is also widespread and extremely cost-effective.

The downside to VoIP is the underlying assumptions of the data network. The data protocols were set up for unreliable networks. Data networks most commonly use a protocol called TCP/IP (Transmission Control Protocol/Internet Protocol). Damaged packets are retransmitted, and because packets can travel a variety of routes, packets can arrive out of order – that's great for data, but it doesn't work for real-time applications like voice and video. To adjust for these issues, VoIP uses other protocols out of the TCP/IP suite:

• **User Datagram Protocol (UDP)** is a fast (low overhead), best-effort protocol. The network makes a best effort to deliver the packet and, if a packet arrives damaged, the VoIP application simply throws it out. Voice can tolerate the loss of a few damaged packets. It's a good fit for voice because speed is more important than reliability.

• **Real-Time Transport Protocol (RTP)** helps with the ordering of packets. It puts a time stamp on each voice packet. The VoIP application reads the time stamp on each packet coming in, and if the packet is out of order, it simply throws the packet away. If this happens only occasionally, the human cognitive sense fills in the blanks to make sense of the information. If it happens too frequently, the quality of the conversation degrades and a "clipping" symptom occurs in which pieces of the conversation are lopped off. Clipping sounds similar to a bad cell phone connection where the conversation gets garbled in a weak signal area.

Benefits to Using VoIP in a Call Center

The theoretical benefits to a converged network are many. In a perfect world, VoIP provides the following benefits to a call center:

• **Improves asset utilization.** Uses the data network asset base (data switches, router, WAN) further by carrying voice and data.

• **Decreases capital costs.** Eliminates the TDM-based switch infrastructure of a PBX or ACD, or the TDM-based circuit cards of a Communications Server.

• **Enables cost-effective multisite networking.** Links outsourcers or other call center locations for load balancing.

- **Enables call center telecommuting and remote agent groups.** Cost-effectively connects at-home agents and remote agent groups in branch offices.

- **Provides the foundation for a multimedia contact center.** Packet technology is used in the transport of email, chat and Web collaboration.

- **Reduces internal support costs.** Separate voice and data networking staffs are no longer needed because of the common network.

- **Eliminates PBX/ACD switch maintenance.** No PBX or ACD – no maintenance!

- **Eliminates PBX/ACD switch upgrades (pain and costs).** No PBX or ACD – no upgrades!

- **Simplifies the wiring plan.** Dedicated voice wiring is eliminated; only one wire is run for both voice and data.

- **Simplifies moves, adds and changes.** IP addresses are automatically established so it's plug-and-play.

- **Reclaims desktop space.** Eliminate the telephone and talk through the PC.

- **Lowers long-distance expenses.** Minimize voice circuits; carry voice traffic on the data network.

- **Cuts 800 expenses.** Customers call over the Internet.

Figure 2-10: Converged Voice and Data World

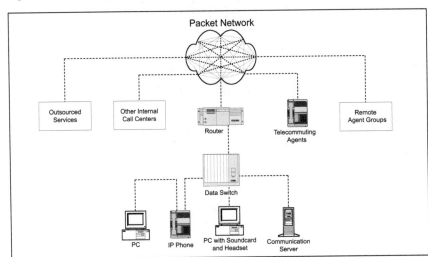

Sound and look compelling? Sound too good to be true? Read on...

Requirements for VoIP

Although the benefits of VoIP are theoretically real, there is a small matter of requirements to make the dream a reality...

You need a perfect (or near-perfect) data network. Literally. The network requirements for VoIP are brutal. A very secure, high-performance data network that works great for applications like email, Web browsing, printing and file management may perform no better than tin cans and string when it comes to VoIP. What's the deal? Data networking technologies were optimized for providing non-real-time communications with reliable delivery over unreliable networks. What about voice? Voice networks were engineered to provide real-time communications over reliable networks. That's right – voice requirements are basically the opposite of data requirements.

Here are the issues associated with a data network:

• **Latency.** Latency is the total end-to-end delay in a network. In the world of VoIP, delay kills. According to the International Telecommunications Union (ITU), the upper limit of latency for good voice quality is 150 milliseconds. Sources of delay in transmitting and receiving VoIP include the PSTN (circuit) to LAN (packet) conversion, end-user IP phones, PC sound card, packetizing algorithms, LAN, router, firewall, Virtual Private Network (VPN) encryption/decryption and the WAN.

Latency is a lower risk proposition in a LAN-only deployment because of higher bandwidth (switched 10 or 100 Mbps to each desktop) and internal control of the network. However, it presents much higher risk in a WAN deployment (for example, multisite networking, remote agent groups and telecommuters) because of lower bandwidth and because network control is ceded to a network service provider.

Figure 2-11: Sources of Delay in a VoIP Environment

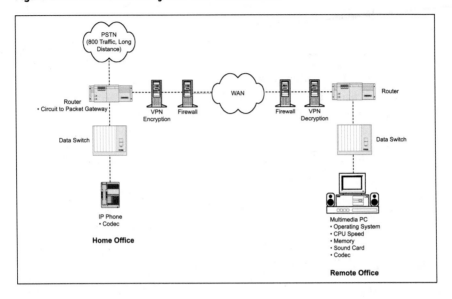

If the total endpoint-to-endpoint delay exceeds 150 milliseconds, callers start to talk over each other – parties in the conversation think the other person has stopped speaking and then both simultaneously start to speak. This is the same symptom experienced in a bad cell phone connection or an international satellite call. In addition, the latency items noted are for business-to-business across LAN/WAN. Latency can be further impacted by a low bandwidth connection.

  • **Variable delay (also known as "jitter").** A variation in packet delivery delay between two endpoints of more than 20ms causes clipping. Parts of words and syllables get dropped, and excess clipping can make a conversation unintelligible. VoIP vendors try to circumvent this problem by building "jitter buffers" into their products. Jitter buffers smooth the delivery of the voice packets to the handset or headset, minimizing conversation choppiness.

  • **Packet loss.** Packet loss in excess of 0.2 percent causes clipping. As noted, excessive clipping can make a conversation unintelligible.

  • **Echo.** Data networks providing only data applications do not have to account for echo cancellation. Unfortunately, VoIP does. The speaker usually hears the echo, but the listener does not. Echo-cancellation equipment and software can reside in an IP phone, IP softphone, IP-enabled PBX or a router.

Who Is Using VoIP?

VoIP is going through the product-adoption lifecycle. The way in which it is applied will expand over time as companies gain confidence in using it and begin to measure the true benefits. Here are some examples of where VoIP is making early inroads:

- New centers (no legacy equipment), especially ones with remote sites or telecommuters.
- High-tech companies that are early adopters of new technology applications.
- Traditional companies that are dabbling first with VoIP between sites on a private Wide Area Network.

Minimizing Risk, Maximizing Success

Scared yet? Seriously, we're not knocking VoIP – we think that it will eventually be the only way to go. In the near term, however, please cover all your bases. The implicit assumption when you plan to implement VoIP is that you are in possession of a network that meets all of the previously mentioned criteria. If you aren't, do one of two things: Stay with your existing TDM-based network or upgrade your LAN and WAN before proceeding.

Consider setting up a VoIP lab for testing different calling scenarios prior to production deployment. Network performance and analysis tools that measure delay, jitter and packet loss, as well as examine packet content are invaluable for VoIP deployments. LAN/WAN simulation tools are also extremely helpful in identifying potential problem areas. If your organization does not have the in-house skills or you prefer to outsource, get your network assessed by a network consulting firm or your VoIP vendor. The money spent doing this will prevent days of frustrating troubleshooting and embarrassment down the road. Be a hero, not a goat!

VoIP Organizational Ramifications

In many organizations, the various technology components in a VoIP environment are typically managed by different external and internal groups:

- Desktop support team (PCs, wiring, desktop applications)
- LAN support team (data switches, servers)
- WAN support team (routers/network design)
- Telecom team (voice switch, IVR, voice circuits)
- Security team (Firewalls and VPN)
- Data network service providers (data circuits)
- Voice network service providers (voice circuits)

Because of the diversity of people and groups involved, there is significant risk of finger-pointing. Here are some actions to minimize the challenges:

- Appoint a "VoIP Czar" with accountability and authority over all VoIP technology and support decisions.
- Document and communicate your VoIP operations, administration and maintenance plan. Provide plenty of detail for troubleshooters. Include internal and external escalation points.
- Build a VoIP lab with network diagnostic, simulation and modeling tools. Use it for testing network design options and new software and hardware releases.

VoIP Design Considerations

Danger, danger – geek speak ahead! Are you ready to implement VoIP? Want to dig into more on the design and standards? If so, you'll appreciate the rest of this chapter. If not, feel free to go straight to the "Points to Remember" on page 58.

Besides having your network in great shape, here are some other decisions that you have to make when implementing VoIP:

- **Application infrastructure.** Where will your core call center functionality reside? A PBX, ACD, Hybrid, CTI or a Communications Server? Although PBXs and ACDs were originally designed for the TDM network, all of the major vendors are racing to make their core products VoIP-compatible. Some of the Communications Server vendors have designed their systems with VoIP from the start.

• **Gateway.** The gateway is the device that converts a VoIP stream to a circuit-switched format (most likely with ISDN signaling). There are three basic options –

1. Integrated PBX, ACD or Communications Server-based "blade" or circuit card: Used in scenarios where the call center is leveraging PBX or ACD infrastructure. The voice switch provides the application intelligence and streams the packetized voice (this approach is often referred to as "IP-enabled).

Figure 2-12: Integrated PBX/ACD/Communications Server Gateway

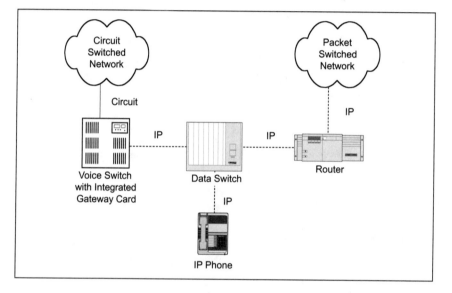

2. Standalone gateway: Connects the voice switch to the data network, usually to enable a multisite call center network. Intersite traffic is IP over the LAN/WAN, then converted to circuit-switched for the voice switch. The voice switch supplies the application intelligence while the gateway streams the packetized voice.

Figure 2-13: Standalone Gateway

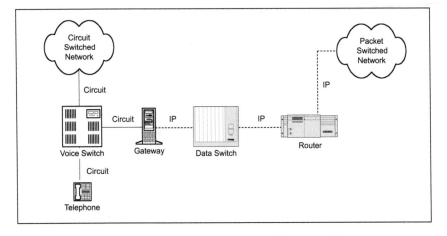

3. Router or data switch-based blade: Frequently used in environments where application infrastructure is server-based and the call center is leveraging the data infrastructure. The voice switch (usually a Communications Server) provides the application intelligence, while the router or data switch streams the packetized voice.

Implications of VoIP for Other Call Center Technology

VoIP doesn't just impact voice-switch architectures. It impacts other elements of the call center that interact with the voice switch or handle voice contacts: IVR, Quality Monitoring/logging and CTI. As we discuss each of these technologies in the book, we'll highlight the implications of VoIP for them. Here's the gist of it:

- IVR will handle packets instead of circuits. Applications won't change as a result of IP, but the architecture and the way an IVR listens to contacts, plays messages and plays responses will.
- Quality Monitoring (QM) and logging systems will need to record packet voice streams instead of circuit-switched calls.
- CTI will still monitor and control what's going on in the switch – but it will be an IP switch, not a TDM switch.

Figure 2-14: Integrated Router/Data Switch Gateway

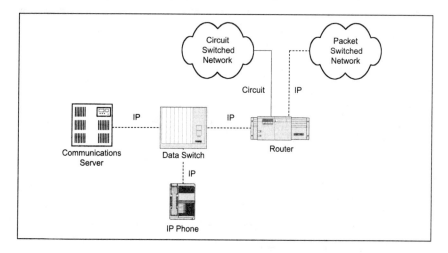

• **Codecs.** Codecs are the devices in an IP phone or softphone that take the analog voice input and convert it to packetized voice. Besides performing the analog-IP conversion, the codecs also perform compression. Compressed voice is highly desirable in a multisite remote group or remote agent scenarios. Because WAN bandwidth is expensive, the smaller and fewer the voice packets, the lower the chance of WAN congestion. However, you must trade voice sound quality for bandwidth consumption. The higher the compression, the worse the sound quality. Compression is generally not required in a LAN-only environment where bandwidth is more readily available (100 Mbps). Standards include (in order of lowest to highest compression):

G.711: 64 kbps – the same as PCM- and TDM-based voice. This provides the highest quality voice.

G.726: 16, 24, or 32 kbps – at the highest compression rate, it is four times more efficient than G.711.

G.729: 8 kbps voice – eight times more efficient than G.711.

G.723: 5.3 or 6.3 kbps voice – at the highest compression rate, it is 12 times more efficient than G.711.

• **IP phones.** Which would your agents prefer to work with – an IP-based telephone or a PC-based softphone? It's largely a matter of preference. The risk with the PC softphone is that if the PC crashes, the agent can't take calls at that position. Most vendors will allow you to mix and match. With the PC softphone option, make sure that the PC has a fast enough CPU, adequate memory, a full duplex, high-quality sound card and supported operating system. With the IP phone option, most vendors include an integrated two port (some vendors offer three ports) data switch. One port connects to the LAN, while the second port connects a PC to the IP phone.

Figure 2-15: IP Phones and Connectivity Options

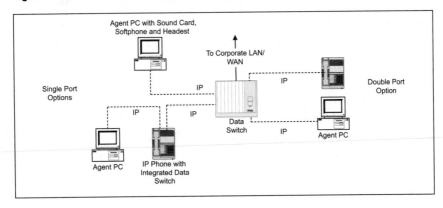

• **Endpoint power.** IP phones require power to function. There are two methods for supplying power: individual power supplies for each phone (make sure that you have an available outlet in each workstation area!) or inline power supplied from the data switch over the LAN cabling. The draft standard for Ethernet inline power is IEEE 802.3af. Ideally, mission-critical call centers use line-powered phones.

• **SNMP manageability.** Some vendors offer Simplified Network Management Protocol (SNMP) compliant VoIP management modules. SNMP tools can be very helpful in identifying problems, troubleshooting and generating performance reports on the VoIP applications.

Other Considerations for VoIP

Here are some other considerations to make your VoIP applications perform well:

• **Switched infrastructure.** Do not consider using VoIP unless you are running switched LAN segments to each desktop. The contention of shared hubs leads to poor performance.

• **Virtual LANs (VLANS).** VLAN technology groups endpoints in common user communities to contain network broadcasts, improving performance of network-based applications (defined in the IEEE 802.1Q standard). Because broadcast traffic propagates throughout the entire network, a network that is very "chatty" with service advertisements will impair VoIP performance if not segmented into VLANs. Preferably, the PCs get assigned to one VLAN, while VoIP phones get assigned to another VLAN. This segmentation shields the VoIP traffic from the data traffic, yielding higher performance.

The OSI Model

Anyone working in a TCP/IP environment, whether dealing with data or voice, needs to understand the International Standards Organization (ISO) Open Systems Interconnection (OSI) reference model. The model has seven layers that define the communications between systems and isolate the roles at each level. Some layers package information, detect errors and transport packets, while others provide value-added applications. Figure 2-16 shows the seven layers.

If you're coming from a voice background, and aren't familiar with this model, take time to learn more about it.

• **Single-port and double-port options.** IP hardphones are implemented in single-port or double-port configurations. With the single-port option, the IP phone uses its integrated data switch. The IP phone uses a single wire run to the Ethernet switch, and the Agent PC is connected to the IP phone. Both voice and data traffic share the single wire run and LAN segment to the Ethernet switch. With the double-port option, the IP phone and the PC each have a wire run to the Ethernet switch. The double-port option yields higher performance because the voice and data traffic have dedicated bandwidth. However, it doubles the Ethernet port and wire run requirements and increases network management complexity. VLANs are still used with both configurations. The single- and double-port options are shown in Figure 2-15 on page 53.

Figure 2-16: OSI Seven-Layer Model

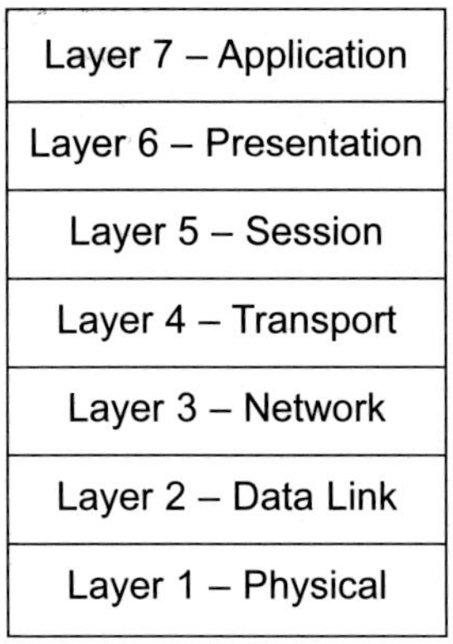

Layer 7 – Application
Layer 6 – Presentation
Layer 5 – Session
Layer 4 – Transport
Layer 3 – Network
Layer 2 – Data Link
Layer 1 – Physical

• **Quality of Service (QoS) and Class of Service (CoS).** Quality of Service refers to giving certain types of packets priority when there is congestion in the network. Class of Service is a methodology of tagging packets for special handling. Here are some options:

802.1p: This networking standard works at layer 2 in an Ethernet LAN environment. If there is congestion on an Ethernet switch port, this allows the VoIP traffic to pass before other application data.

DiffServ: This networking standard works at layer 3 in routed networks. If there is congestion putting packets on the WAN, this standard allows VoIP packets to be tagged with a unique identifier. Routers then use these tags to queue voice packets at a higher priority level than other nonreal-time applications. DiffServ only identifies packets for router prioritization. After the priority tagging, it is the router's queuing algorithms and speed at putting VoIP packets on the network that determines the application's effectiveness.

UDP port prioritization: Working at layer 4, this scheme allows layer 4

devices to prioritize specific UDP ports. The transmission of the actual packe-
tized-voice conversation is done with UDP packets. Layer 4 aware networking devices forward these packets at a higher priority, helping to ensure better
voice quality.

WAN services management: Router capabilities like RSVP (Resource
Reservation Protocol) and MPLS (Multiprotocol Label Switching) address
the real-time service requirements of VoIP applications for improved performance.

VoIP Standards

The standards for VoIP are in a state of flux. H.323 was the first, and Session
Initiation Protocol and Megaco H.248 have come on the scene in the past few
years. At this point, it's not clear what standard will dominate.

• **H.323.** Ratified by the International Telecommunications Union in 1996,
this was the first standard that addressed putting real-time communications (both
video and voice) on an unreliable packet network. H.323 is an umbrella standard
that has extensive references to other ITU standards. In an H.323-compliant application, there are four components:

1. **Terminal:** Addresses the endpoints that contain the codec for converting
   analog voice input to packetized voice.
2. **Gateway:** Converts the PSTN circuit-switched voice to packetized voice.
3. **Gatekeeper:** Provides network management (registration, admission and
   status functions) and call control functionality.
4. **Multipoint Control Unit (MCU):** Controls multiparty sessions (confer-
   encing and transfers).

H.323 specifies the above functions at a fairly high level and it makes no rec-
ommendation for where the functionality has to reside. The terminal can be an IP
phone or a multimedia PC with sound card. The remaining three components can
all be co-resident on a single device or disaggregated onto separate devices. For
purposes of a call center, any of the application infrastructure options can provide
gateway, gatekeeper and MCU functions.

The advantage to H.323 is that there is widespread vendor support and it has evolved through four versions. The downside is that underlying protocols are fairly complex, with lots of communications overhead.

• **Session Initiation Protocol (SIP).** SIP is a proposed standard of the Internet Engineering Task Force (IETF), and it is addressed in RFC 2543. SIP is a lighter weight (less overhead), less complex protocol than H.323, and it specifically addresses end-user mobility. It is text-based and readable; examples of SIP addresses are sip: lori@vanguard.net or tel: 973 605 8000. The big idea behind SIP is to make it very similar in concept to hypertext transfer protocol (HTTP), the protocol of the World Wide Web; by doing so, SIP potentially taps into the creativity of millions of Web developers. There are four components to SIP:

1. **User Agent:** Encompasses the IP endpoints.
2. **Proxy Server:** Receives end-user requests and forwards them onto the destination endpoints.
3. **Redirect Server:** Provides network management and call control functions.
4. **Registrar:** Redirects calls to the user's current location.

• **Megaco/H.248.** Megaco/H.248 is a standard proposed jointly by the IETF (RFC 3015) and the ITU (H.248). It is the descendant of the Media Gateway Control Protocol (RFC 2705), and it decomposes a monolithic voice switch into separate components. The benefit of this decomposition is scalability and multivendor interoperability and sourcing. Components of the proposed standard:

1. **Media Gateway:** Provides packet-to-circuit conversion; carries the actual voice conversation (similar in concept to an ISDN B channel). Very limited intelligence is resident on this device; it is a slave to the media gateway controller.
2. **Signaling Gateway:** Provides call setup and teardown capabilities.
3. **Media Gateway Controller:** The device that provides call control; it is the master over the media gateway. The media gateway controller is also known as a softswitch or a call agent.
4. **Media Gateway Control Protocol (MGCP):** The protocol used between the media gateway and the media gateway controller.

What to do about standards? If you're considering VoIP, ask potential vendors about compliance with the existing standard, H.323, as well as their development plans to support SIP and Megaco/H.248. The last thing you need is a supposedly "open" system that doesn't interoperate.

Points to Remember

• Application infrastructure provides core call center functionality, including agent work states, routing, prioritization, call treatment, call selection and agent selection. Application infrastructure options include the PBX, ACD, Hybrid, CTI and the Communications Server.

• Network infrastructure is the technology that physically transports agent/caller interactions. Network infrastructure for voice has traditionally been circuit-switching or TDM-based. Data has traditionally been packet-switched. New options have emerged for integrating voice with data onto a converged packet network, including VoIP.

• Application and network infrastructures are undergoing seismic shifts. Application infrastructure is increasingly open and standards-based. Network infrastructure will increasingly become packet-switching-based.

• There is no one answer for what is the best infrastructure option. Each company must carefully evaluate the options in the context of its strategy, business needs, existing environment, culture and directions.

Actions to Take

• Carefully weigh infrastructure options in the context of your call center strategy – consider where you are today and where you want to be in several years. Make informed decisions by assessing tradeoffs on reliability, quality, scalability, manageability, openness and support options.

Part 2: Fundamentals

The most fundamental call center processes involve routing calls and managing resources. Understanding the principles on which routing and management work and the available technology options is a start, and routing and reporting strategies will further set the stage. Then routing and management tools can be effectively applied to your environment.

Chapter 3: Principles and Enablers for Routing and Queuing

Chapter 4: Call Center Matchmaking: Routing Callers to the Right Resource

Chapter 5: Tools for Measuring, Managing and Optimizing Your Center

Chapter 3:

Principles and Enablers for Routing and Queuing

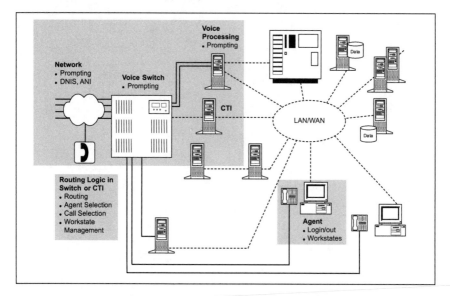

Key Points Discussed in this Chapter:

Random Call Arrival and Random Agent Availability

Erlang Calculations

Technology Implications of Random Call Arrival

Routing Principles: Matching Callers to Agents

Call-Routing Enablers

Identifying Caller and Call Purpose – Network Information and Prompting

Identifying Agents and Availability

Incoming Calls Management Institute (ICMI) defines call center management as: "The art of having the right number of properly skilled people and supporting resources in place at the right times to handle an accurately forecasted workload, at service level and with quality."

Let's take a look at the science behind this art before we launch into the key technologies to make your center a routing (or rousing) success.

Random Call Arrival and Random Agent Availability

Call centers must deal with routine randomness. Callers pick up the phone and contact your organization whenever they please (darn them!). Although calls can be forecasted with a fair amount of certainty over any interval (say, 15 or 30 minutes), it is very uncertain at any point *within* that interval how many callers will choose to contact you. Random call arrival is further complicated by randomness of agent availability: Agent interactions with your callers will have an element of variability (some short calls, some long calls), as well as a variety of longer and shorter wrap-up tasks (research, followup, data entry). Brad Cleveland, president of ICMI, sums up all this behavior nicely with the statement: "Calls bunch up."

This random phenomenon is the biggest problem for senior managers trying to understand call centers. They ask: Why are people sitting idle sometimes? Why do our callers have to wait in queue? Why do we have to play those delay messages to our callers? If I give you 20 percent more resources, the problem will get 20 percent better, right?

Erlang Calculations

Fortunately, this phenomenon has been researched and written about for decades. Much of the thinking around the concepts of random call arrival, staffing and service level was done in 1917 by a Danish telecommunications engineer named A.K. Erlang, and his work lives on in engineering tools called Erlang tables. Today, Erlang's model has been incorporated into computer programs that allow you to estimate staffing and trunking required, given the volume and duration of calls and service level desired.

Figure 3-1 shows a screenshot of ICMI's QueueView, one such Erlang tool. The inputs are shown at the top, and the outputs are shown in the rows. Each row in the table shows the resulting relationship between number of agents (column labeled "Agents") and the percentage component of Service Level (SL%). In addition, many other statistics associated with the number of agents are also produced.

To use the table, look down the SL% column (service level percentage) until you reach or exceed the percentage desired. That row specifies the number of agents needed to achieve that objective and the accompanying statistics.

In our example, the service level objective for answering the call is 90 percent in 30 seconds. In a 30-minute interval, 250 calls arrive, the average talk time is three minutes (180 seconds) and after-call work or wrap-up time is 30 seconds.

Figure 3-1: Erlang C: Relationship of Call Volume, Staffing, Queuing and Trunk Load

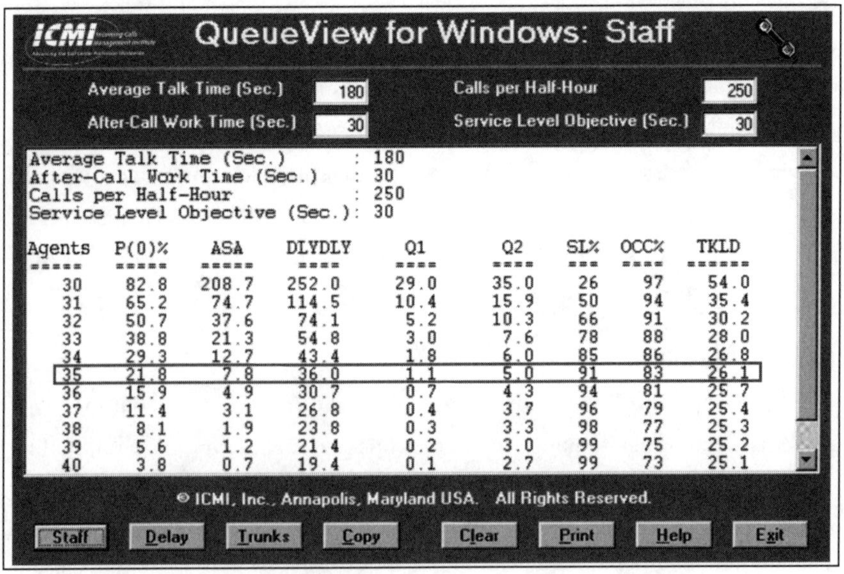

Agents	P(0)%	ASA	DLYDLY	Q1	Q2	SL%	OCC%	TKLD
30	82.8	208.7	252.0	29.0	35.0	26	97	54.0
31	65.2	74.7	114.5	10.4	15.9	50	94	35.4
32	50.7	37.6	74.1	5.2	10.3	66	91	30.2
33	38.8	21.3	54.8	3.0	7.6	78	88	28.0
34	29.3	12.7	43.4	1.8	6.0	85	86	26.8
35	21.8	7.8	36.0	1.1	5.0	91	83	26.1
36	15.9	4.9	30.7	0.7	4.3	94	81	25.7
37	11.4	3.1	26.8	0.4	3.7	96	79	25.4
38	8.1	1.9	23.8	0.3	3.3	98	77	25.3
39	5.6	1.2	21.4	0.2	3.0	99	75	25.2
40	3.8	0.7	19.4	0.1	2.7	99	73	25.1

QueueView screenshots courtesy of ICMI.

Agents: Number of sales or customer service representatives on the phones.

P(0): Probability of delay greater than zero seconds (or the probability of queuing).

ASA: Average Speed of Answer. This is the average delay of all calls, in seconds.

DLYDLY: The Average Delay of Delayed (or queued) Calls, in seconds.

Q1: Average number of calls in queue at any time, including times when there is no queue.

Q2: Average number of calls in queue when there is an actual queue.

SL: Service Level. The percentage of calls that should be answered in the number of seconds specified by the number of agents (shown in the agent column).

OCC: Percent Agent Occupancy. The percentage of time agents will be in either the Talk-Time mode or the After-Call Work mode. The balance of the time they are in the available mode waiting for the next call.

TKLD: Erlangs (hours) of trunk traffic, calculated as (Talk Time + Average Speed of Answer) x Number of Calls in one hour. The answer is converted from seconds to hours and presented as an hour's worth of load for easy table reference.

"No, I'm not angry at you, sir.
I'm angry at the random act of fate
that directed your call to my extension."

© 2001 by Randy Glasbergen, www.glasbergen.com

Erlang Assumptions and Imperfections

While Erlang models are used widely in call centers and are the best basic tool for estimating staff needs, they are not perfectly matched to the real behavior of call centers. Erlang assumes no callers abandon (infinite patience) and no calls are blocked (infinite trunking and port resources). These are not valid assumptions for call centers, although when trunking is sized properly and you have a low abandon rate, it's pretty darn close. If not, Erlang can overstaff. Further, Erlang assumes each agent is dedicated to one shared mix of call types (one skill). Thus, Erlang is not a good model for skills-based environments. Finally, Erlang doesn't match the unique characteristics of some nonphone media. We'll talk more about how today's forecasting and scheduling products handle these imperfections in Chapter 5.

The highlighted row shows that, to achieve 90 percent of the calls answered in 30 seconds, 35 agents are required (actual service level is 91 percent in 30 seconds). With that level of staffing, 21.8 percent of all callers will queue for an agent, the Average Speed of Answer is 7.8 seconds, and the callers who queue wait an average of 36 seconds. Agents stay busy with callers and After-Call Work activities 83 percent of the time; the remaining 17 percent of the time they sit idle waiting for a call. These relationships between staffing, queuing and service level use a specific formula of Erlang known as Erlang C.

Erlang C tables also offer insight into the queuing or delay distribution. For the same set of call parameters and service objective, 47 callers wait five seconds or longer, then six of those callers are answered, leaving 41 callers to wait 10 seconds or longer, then five more of the callers are answered, leaving 36 callers to wait more than 15 seconds and so forth, as shown in Figure 3-2.

Figure 3-2: Relationship of Staffing, Service Level and Delayed (Queued) Call Distribution

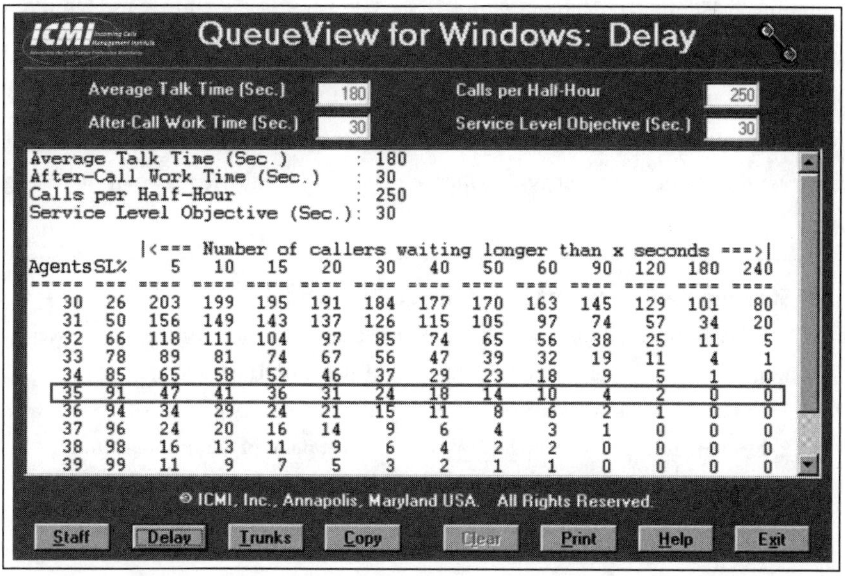

```
ICMI          QueueView for Windows: Delay

        Average Talk Time (Sec.)    [ 180 ]    Calls per Half-Hour              [ 250 ]
        After-Call Work Time (Sec.) [  30 ]    Service Level Objective (Sec.)   [  30 ]
    ┌──────────────────────────────────────────────────────────────────────────────┐
    │ Average Talk Time (Sec.)      :  180                                           ▲│
    │ After-Call Work Time (Sec.)   :  30                                            ││
    │ Calls per Half-Hour           :  250                                           ││
    │ Service Level Objective (Sec.):  30                                            ││
    │                                                                                ││
    │       |<=== Number of callers waiting longer than x seconds ===>|             ││
    │ Agents SL%   5   10   15   20   30   40   50   60   90  120  180  240          ││
    │ ===== ===  ==== ==== ==== ==== ==== ==== ==== ==== ==== ==== ==== ====         ││
    │   30   26  203  199  195  191  184  177  170  163  145  129  101   80          ││
    │   31   50  156  149  143  137  126  115  105   97   74   57   34   20          ││
    │   32   66  118  111  104   97   85   74   65   56   38   25   11    5          ││
    │   33   78   89   81   74   67   56   47   39   32   19   11    4    1          ││
    │   34   85   65   58   52   46   37   29   23   18    9    5    1    0          ││
    │ ┌ 35   91   47   41   36   31   24   18   14   10    4    2    0    0 ┐        ││
    │   36   94   34   29   24   21   15   11    8    6    2    1    0    0          ││
    │   37   96   24   20   16   14    9    6    4    3    1    0    0    0          ││
    │   38   98   16   13   11    9    6    4    2    2    0    0    0    0          ││
    │   39   99   11    9    7    5    3    2    1    1    0    0    0    0          ▼│
    └──────────────────────────────────────────────────────────────────────────────┘
            © ICMI, Inc., Annapolis, Maryland USA.   All Rights Reserved.

    [ Staff ] [ Delay ] [ Trunks ] [ Copy ]      [ Clear ] [ Print ] [ Help ] [ Exit ]
```

Another variation of Erlang, known as Erlang B, provides insight into the required number of trunks for a given scenario. In our example, the Trunk Load (TKLD) of 26.1 Erlangs, or hours, of traffic requires 37 trunks. Table 3-1 shows the relationship of Agents, Service Level, Erlangs and Trunks required.

Table 3-1: Erlang B: Trunking

Agents	Service Level	Erlangs	% Busy	Trunks
30	26	54.0	1	68
31	50	35.4	1	48
32	66	30.2	1	42
33	78	28.0	1	39
34	85	26.8	1	38
35	91	26.1	1	37
36	94	25.7	1	37
37	96	25.4	1	36
38	98	25.3	1	36
39	98	25.2	1	36

To gauge the change in service level, queuing frequency and trunk load with increases or decreases of agent resources, work up or down the Agent and SL% columns in Figure 3-1, Figure 3-2 and Table 3-1. For a given volume and handle time, additional agent resources improve the service level, decrease the probability of queuing and decrease trunking requirements, but at a decreasing rate. The law of diminishing returns is in effect. Fewer agent resources decrease the service level, increase the queuing frequency and increase trunking requirements at an increasing rate.

Six Immutable Laws of Incoming Call Centers

ICMI defines six laws of incoming call centers that convey the relationships between workload, service level, staffing and trunking (based on Erlang tables):

1. For a given call load, when service level goes up, occupancy goes down.
2. Keep improving service level and you will reach a point of diminishing returns.
3. For a given service level, larger agent groups are more efficient than smaller groups.
4. All other things being equal, pooled groups are more efficient than specialized groups.
5. For a given call load, add staff and average speed of answer will go down.
6. For a given call load, add staff and trunk load will go down.

What do these laws mean for call center technology? Here are some implications:

- When calls queue, conditional routing and skills can help find the best available backup resource.
- Virtual centers, remote groups and telecommuting can create larger pools across multiple sites. Converged voice and data networks can deliver virtual centers more cost-effectively.
- When using skills-based routing, oversegmenting skill groups leads to inefficiency (small groups). So skills should be kept simple to maximize agent pools. Similarly, blending media (avoiding media specialization) can increase pool size and efficiency.
- Conditional routing and skills can help to expand the available staff for a given call type.
- Workforce management tools can help forecast, plan, schedule and optimize resource utilization.

These applications will come to life in subsequent chapters.

Technology Implications of Random Call Arrival

What do random call arrival and agent availability, Erlang C and Erlang B mean for call center technology?

• Call center technology managers have to be in tune with their counterparts – the call center operations managers – on planning assumptions for anticipated call volumes, handle times and service level objectives. These plans and assumptions directly drive system sizing requirements as well as the viability of alternative application infrastructures.

• Application infrastructures handle queuing in radically different ways. PBXs and standalone ACDs have internal queue slots and call treatment resources, while a CTI implementation may require one IVR port per call queued. Design is heavily influenced by queuing assumptions.

• Routing, queuing and call treatment consume significant computer processor cycles and queue slots on a voice switch. Technology staff need to periodically monitor processor occupancy and queue capacity on system reports and perform upgrades before a crisis hits.

• Service level, call volume and staffing assumptions drive trunking requirements. If call volumes grow, significant upgrades and additions to the voice switch (cards, shelves, cabinets), as well as additional circuits from your network provider may be required.

• Planning should anticipate the worst to prevent disaster. Worst-case scenarios for call volume, staffing and service level should be used for determining voice switch requirements. Modeling and cost-tradeoff analysis are required. Some insurance capacity is recommended.

Routing Principles: Matching Callers to Agents

Given the random nature of call centers, the question then becomes: What technologies are available to help you make the best match between randomly arriving callers who have unique needs and randomly available agents who have unique talents, skills and abilities? The answer lies in routing and queuing software and hardware.

Figure 3-3: Matching Customers and Agents

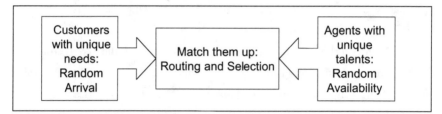

Three Processes to Match Callers and Agents

Call center technology that deals with random call arrival and random agent availability must provide three fundamental functions: 1) call routing, 2) agent selection, and 3) call selection.

Figure 3-4: Three Processes Match Callers and Agents

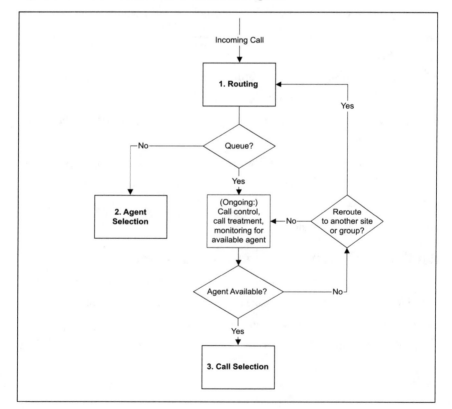

1. **Routing.** The answers to three questions can lead to better routing:

- Who is calling?
- Why are they calling?
- What should we do with this call given what we know about what's happening right now?

The call center can be in two possible situations: No queue (more agents than callers) or queue (more callers than agents). These situations lead to selection – of the agent or the call to be handled.

2. **Agent selection (no queue).** When more than one agent is available, the question becomes: Who is the "best" agent to handle this request? Is it the most idle? Most highly skilled? Least occupied? Or is it the next agent in a simple circular or linear hunting pattern?

3. **Call selection (queue).** When all agents are busy, calls queue. The call may receive call treatment while in queue or the call may be routed to another group or location. But when an agent finally comes available, the decision becomes: Who is the "best" caller to serve from the queue? Is it the caller with the highest priority? Or the one who waited the longest? The caller who is the best customer? The caller who has an outstanding request?

The application logic for these three processes can reside in a variety of places (remember our infrastructure discussion in the previous chapter?). Should this logic reside on your PBX or ACD, a CTI-based application or split between both? Perhaps a Communications Server? Decisions, decisions, decisions.

Various call treatments may be applied during routing or while a call is queued. Call treatment might include music on hold or announcements, or even a busy signal. It might ultimately route to another source, such as voicemail, a voice-response application or perhaps a different group. So a call queued for selection may end up back in a routing process.

Call-Routing Enablers

There are functions in call center software to identify which agents are available, and activities that come before routing a call to identify the "who" and "why" of the call. Think of these as key enablers to routing a call.

Identifying Caller and Call Purpose

A key part of routing is figuring out who is contacting the center and why. There are two types of technologies that can help with identification: information from the network and prompting. There are tradeoffs in the user-friendliness of these options and their effectiveness in various environments. Many callers don't like prompting; however, it is often necessary or more effective in getting the call to the right resource.

Network signals provide information on "who" and "why." The network can pass signals to the switch to use in routing or to display on the phone set, or to use in advanced applications like CTI "screen pops" (more on that in Chapter 6).

• **Dialed Number Identification Service (DNIS)** is a set of digits passed from the network to the switch to identify the purpose of the call based on the number that was dialed. Look at your favorite catalog – chances are that there is one number listed for orders and another number for customer service (returns, exchanges, etc.). Catalog retailers often use DNIS to route the call to the right group of agents – without having to prompt the caller. Another tool for such routing is Direct Inward Dialing (DID). DID is sent for local calls and specifies an extension number. DNIS and DID are used by the switch software to point the call at the proper group or the proper routing path for calls of that type.

DNIS and DID allow a trunk group to serve a number of call types, dynamically allocating trunks to the demand. The result is better utilization of resources (rather than dedicating trunks to certain numbers). Although unique numbers are helpful, overuse can lead to caller confusion and the risk that they will dial the wrong number. So DNIS or DID can be imperfect.

• **Automatic Number Identification (ANI)** is used to identify who is calling or the location from which the call originated. In some countries, ANI is referred to as Calling Line Identification or CLI. ANI is actually the billing number of the trunk on which the call originated.

ANI may work well to identify callers who routinely call from home. Utility outage applications often use ANI. However, if the caller is calling from work, you may receive a number that is not recognized, as the number sent will not be their specific extension, but rather the billing number associated with the trunk they happened to get when they dialed "9" (or some other digit) for an outside line.

Another challenge with ANI is that many companies don't have good phone number databases – they aren't up-to-date, they aren't complete, they only have one field and many customers have multiple numbers (home, office, cell). So ANI, while often useful, is imperfect.

• **Information Indicator (ii) Digits** are included in a special ISDN information field and sometimes used to provide additional context for routing decisions. While ANI/CLI help to identify who is calling, and DNIS/DID help to determine why they're calling, ii digits provide additional caller source information on how they are calling. Examples of source indications include cell phone, hotel or pay phone. This information could be important for a travel assistance service – for example, to route pay phone or cell phone callers to the front of the queue without prompting. It could also be used for fraud detection and high-security screening for credit card authorizations, catalog sales and financial transactions.

• **User-to-User Information (UUI)** is a customized form of network information. The switching devices on either end of an ISDN PRI circuit put some additional information into the D channel along with ANI, DNIS and ii digits. UUI support is vendor-dependent and there are various formats. UUI is commonly used in network-based prompting – for example, a unique number (an account number, case number or claim number) is collected in a network-based IVR and the information is sent along with the voice conversation to the call center. Once at the location, the UUI is displayed on a digital telephone set or delivered to a CTI application for screen pops or data-directed routing.

Prompting Is Often Required

While ANI and DNIS from the network may play a role in routing, because of their imperfections, other options are sometimes necessary. This is when call centers turn to prompting. Prompting is often a key business requirement, for instance: "We need to prompt customers to determine the purpose of their call" or "we need to prompt customers to identify them." Then the fun starts, because there are many potential places to implement prompting:

1. Network. Prompting can be done through a service in the network. With this option, the vendor is a network provider, such as AT&T, MCI, WorldCom or Sprint. They are basically hosting the technology in their network and the call center is paying on a service fee basis (per minute, per prompt) for the prompts. This approach is a good fit for multisite call centers in which different sites handle different call types. By prompting in the network, calls can be immediately directed to the proper location. It is also a good option to consider when trying prompting or when the business philosophy is to avoid acquiring and managing additional technologies.

2. Switch. Switch-prompting is an option for centers that have switches with this capability, but not all switches do. Examples of vendors that provide prompting as a switch-resident capability are Aspect, Avaya and Rockwell. The switch-prompting is generally limited – it is not interacting with a database – but it is good for basic menus and identification. Switch-prompting is tightly integrated with the other switch software, so it's easy to present the collected digits on the agent's phone display or pass the information to a CTI data-directed routing application. It can also help to keep reporting cleaner. If the prompting is extensive, you may want to move it off the switch, as having many prompting port resources there tends to be costly.

3. Interactive Voice Response. IVR is the place for prompting when the goal is to get the customer to self-serve. Banks most often do their prompting in an IVR because the vast majority of callers will successfully self-serve (often 70 to 85 percent). For those who don't self-serve, you can leverage the menus for caller identification and call purpose. When a caller opts out of the IVR ("to speak to a customer service representative at any time, press zero"), the IVR uses the prompt information to point the call to the appropriate routing path in the switch. In some cases, the information collected is passed back to the switch to be used for routing, display or screen pops. We'll discuss this more in Chapters 6 and 8.

4. Voicemail. Voicemail is used in some environments to provide the prompting function. Basic prompting (or automated attendant) is a standard feature of most voicemail systems. In switch environments where the switch doesn't offer prompting and the voicemail is tightly integrated with the switch, it is used for prompting. This option is most often seen in Nortel or Siemens switch environments.

A CTI solution or Communications Server may offer prompting via a voice subsystem or IVR capabilities. In a Communications Server, the prompting is inherently integrated with the routing capabilities. However, an external prompting solution (network, IVR, voicemail) can also be used.

After defining the business need for prompting, call center technologists and business people need to sit down and sort through the options. Which options exist in the current environment? Are port resources available or will additional costs be incurred for prompting ports? What are the tradeoffs of cost, complexity, integration? What other business needs exist, such as self-service or multisite routing? Answers to these questions will define the option that best suits the environment.

Prompting Requires Ports

Get out your Erlang tables! It's time to figure out how many ports you need for prompting (switch, IVR or voicemail). Erlang B calculations are used to determine the number of ports required based on the average hold time and call volumes, and tolerable blocking rate (percent of calls receiving a busy signal).

Identifying Agents and Availability

ACD software enables a business to do those things that are unique to the call center – log agent positions in and out, control agent work states and availability, route and queue calls, and track activity. When you buy ACD software, look for the following fundamental software enablers to identify agents and their availability:

• **Agent Login and Logout.** When agents log in to the ACD, four key events occur. The ACD:

1. Identifies who they are and where they are sitting;
2. Associates the right queues, call types or skills with that position;
3. Monitors work states to determine when the position is available for a call; and
4. Tracks all activity for that position.

The login basically makes the agent identification an active member of application database tables that dynamically update and show the skills and availability of each position. The agent is active until he or she logs out. Because ACD logins are generally software-driven today, they enable shared-seating arrangements or agent mobility, allowing people to work from any position at any time.

• **Agent Work State Control.** Agents use work states to indicate to the system when they are available and ready to take a call, when they are unavailable and, in some systems, the reason they are unavailable. These work states are triggered by pressing a button on a phone or selecting an icon or hitting a function key on a PC (for PC-based softphones).

There are also a variety of agent-activity work states. Examples include inbound ACD call, outbound call, inbound direct-extension call, call on hold, call ringing and call transferring. Every vendor uses different terms for the work states, but most use some form of the following terms for the states agents control directly through buttons on their phone:

Available or Ready: Able to receive a call

After-Call Work or Wrap-Up: Unavailable to take a call and working on activities associated with completing the previous contact, such as data entry.

Auxiliary Work, Unavailable or Not Ready: Unavailable to take a call for non-contact-related reasons, such as breaks, lunch or training.

Unavailable with Reason Code X: Unavailable to take a call for non-contact-related reasons – the reason is indicated by entering a code or pressing a specific button. Examples include training, special projects or handling mail or faxes.

The core ACD software also generates the data that is used in all of the reports. ACD software tracks calls, positions (logins), queues, routing paths and trunks. The software creates messages about activity and passes that information to a reporting tool. More on that in Chapter 5.

Ripple Effect of Work State Use

Work states seem like such a simple function. But there is a powerful ripple effect caused by their proper – or improper – use. The time an agent spends in various states is tracked by reporting tools associated with the ACD. The data generated is passed to the workforce management system for use in forecasting and scheduling. Consistent use of work states is a critical success factor to create valid call center reports, forecasts and schedules.

Your mission: Clearly define when agents should log in and log out (Once per day? Each break? At lunch? For training? Other off-phone activities?). Clearly define the use of unavailable work states. Track and reinforce proper and consistent use. Deviations from the standard practices in your center will create bad data – and bad data in means bad data out, which leads to under- or overstaffing.

On to Routing Technology

That covers the principles behind call routing and the key enablers. In Chapter 4, we'll describe the technology to make it happen.

Points to Remember

• The fundamental call center management challenge is dealing with random call arrival and random agent availability. Erlang calculations reflect this randomness and highlight the relationships between volumes, handle times, queuing, staffing, service level, agent occupancy and trunking.

• The random behavior of call centers has technology implications. Application infrastructures handle routing and queuing in radically different ways. By understanding call center behavior, technologists can more effectively plan and design application infrastructures, system sizing, queuing resources and trunking.

• When a call arrives in a call center, there are three fundamental processes to match a caller with an agent: 1) call routing, 2) agent selection, and 3) call selection. If there is no queue, the decision is which agent should get the call. When there is a queue and an agent becomes available, the decision is which call should be selected.

• Two key enablers come into play in call routing: 1) identify the caller and call purpose, and 2) identify agents and their availability. DNIS, ANI and prompting help identify call needs. Logins and work state control identify agents and availability.

Actions to Take

• Take time to understand the phenomena of randomness and the implications it has for your technology environment. This understanding will enable you to make informed decisions as you plan and design your call center technology (for example, sizing of key elements, appropriate architecture to serve defined queuing needs).

Chapter 4:

Call Center Matchmaking: Routing Callers to the Right Resource

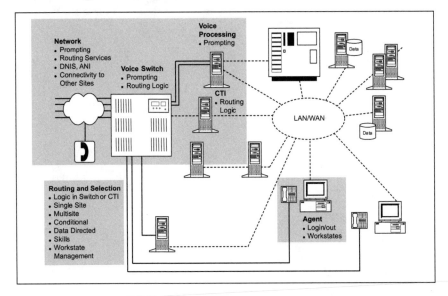

Key Points Discussed in this Chapter:

Single-Site Routing

Routing and Selection Algorithms

Innovative Routing and Selection Schemes

Multisite Routing

The Business Case for "Virtual" Operations

Carrier-, Switch- and CTI-Based Multisite Routing

Remote Agents

ACD Desktop Features

Routing calls to the right resource, as quickly as possible, is the highest goal of a customer-oriented call center – yet it is challenging because of the randomness of call center behavior. Routing can be very basic or highly complex. It can be done in many ways using different tools at different points in time. In this chapter, we'll cover these options for phone calls (we'll address routing other media in Chapter 9).

Note: If you haven't read Chapter 3, and don't understand random call arrivals and their implications, please go back and read about routing and queuing theory and the enablers for routing. You'll get more out of this chapter if you do!

A Spectrum of Routing Possibilities

Call-routing capabilities range from very basic to quite sophisticated. Smaller call centers are more likely to use more basic functionality. However, over the past several years, the vendors have altered their pricing schemes to enable small centers to have very sophisticated routing software, if their business objectives require it. Routing capabilities are often sold as modules or options, and are sold based on the number of licenses required. Thus, a center can purchase the capabilities it needs and grow – in size or sophistication – over time.

Single-Site Routing

Let's first explore the routing and selection schemes for single-site call centers. Figure 4-1 relates these options to the routing and selection framework introduced in Chapter 3.

Figure 4-1: Routing and Selection Algorithms

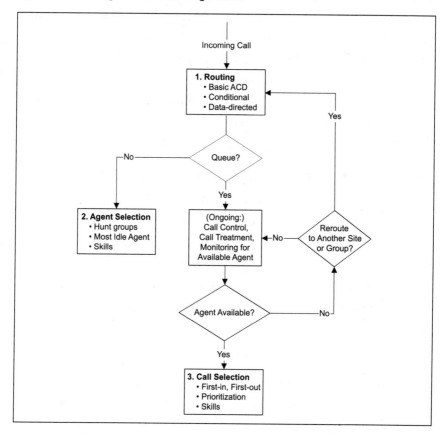

Routing Algorithms

Basic ACD Routing

At a minimum, ACD software provides basic routing and queuing functions. Generally, basic software points a call with a specific DNIS or DID number (or dedicated trunk group) at a queue. The software tracks first-in, first-out order in the queue, delivers announcements at timed intervals and monitors availability so that when an agent becomes available, a call can be removed from the queue and delivered. The routing capabilities of ACD software can also include overflow to other groups or routing to alternative locations or call treatment (e.g., announcements) out of hours. Figure 4-2 shows a sample basic call flow.

Figure 4-2: Basic Call Flow

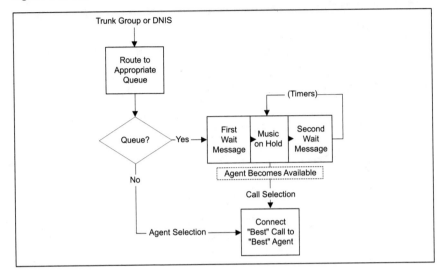

Conditional Routing

Most call centers today leverage conditional routing software. The goal of conditional routing is to route calls to the proper group or treatment based on current conditions. It enables a call center to dynamically respond to changes in resources, call volumes or other variables without manually rearranging things on the fly. The system is already looking for conditions that are pre-programmed and require some reaction. This helps to improve the customer experience and it optimizes the use of resources and, therefore, improves efficiency and costs.

The vendors all use different terminology, but there is a commonality to their architecture for routing software. Figure 4-3 shows the basic framework for this type of routing.

Figure 4-3: Conditional Routing Framework

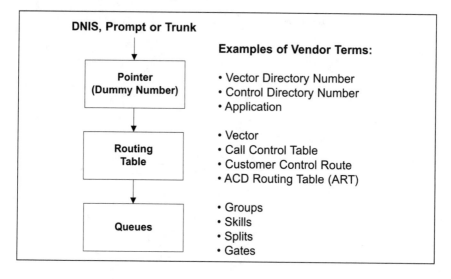

Conditional routing uses routing steps with "if-then" logic. Figures 4-4 and 4-5 show some examples. Using a basic (and proprietary) programming language, routing scripts queue calls to the appropriate group (or groups), play appropriate announcements, and check conditions for other places to queue or route a call. Scripts look at the dynamic databases that reside on the switch (or CTI or Communications Server). The databases track logins, availability, queue lengths and other call center status indicators.

Script conditionals can use:

- Purpose of call – dialed number, response to prompts
- Caller identification – ANI, caller-entered digits, DNIS, Information Indicator
- Time of call – hour of day, day of week, holiday, date
- Priority levels
- Call center status
    1. Staffing (agents available, agents staffed)
    2. Traffic (calls in queue, time in queue, expected time in queue, longest call waiting)

Scripts can also provide call treatment, such as:

- Announcements
- Music
- Busies
- Voice processing – self-service, prompts or voicemail

Figure 4-4: Sample Basic Conditional Routing Path Flow Chart and Script

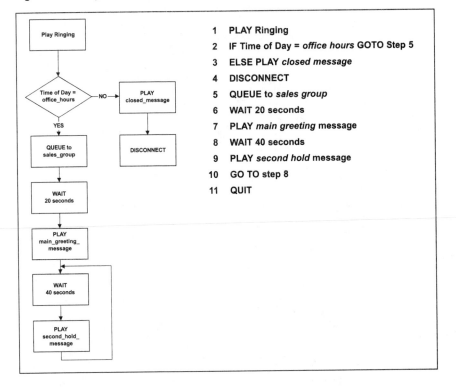

Conditional routing can have loops, "go to" steps and other familiar structures in programming. Routing tables can point calls at resources on that switch (queues, announcements or even other routing paths) or send them across trunks to remote call centers. Figure 4-4 shows a sample conditional routing path flow chart and associated script for a simple route. Figure 4-5 shows a sample flow chart for a complex route that includes prompting and overflow to another group.

Figure 4-5: Sample Complex Conditional Routing Path Flow Chart

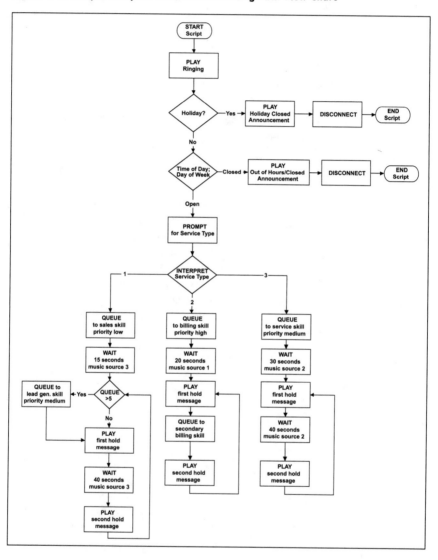

You, Too, Could Develop Routing Scripts...

Call routing is configured through programming tools in the system. The vendors have created their own specific programming language for routing. Most of these languages are fairly intuitive and easy to use. They have a grammar and semantics

Call Center Technology Demystified ■

that must be followed. Many of the products on the market today use a Graphical User Interface (GUI) for programming – drag-and-drop icons, fill-in boxes, etc. Some systems include testing or simulation tools with their routing tools to allow validation of new routes before going into production.

Developing call-routing paths doesn't require a programmer. Rather, it requires someone who knows the business needs, who has a technical bent, who can think through call-flow logic and who gets trained on the specific tool being used. Companies that most successfully apply this technology generally have a resource within the call center (not in IT or telecom) who is responsible for developing, monitoring and updating routing paths. This individual knows the business and works within the operation to make sure the technology is best applied. The technology team should be in tune and available to help, but the technology should be managed by the people closest to the call center operation.

Data-Directed Routing

The next level of routing is a significant leap, as it requires integration with external databases and a clear business strategy (e.g., customer segmentation). Data-directed routing, or customer-specific routing, is generally implemented using CTI (CTI is covered in-depth in Chapter 6). Another data-directed routing option is to use a voice-response application (when the caller identification and call-purpose prompting is done in the IVR).

The concept behind data-directed routing is to access customer information stored in a database and factor that into a routing decision. Following are three examples:

• **Retail or banking:** Is this a high-value or low-value customer? If high-value, let's route them to the front of the queue or to the best agents.

• **Business-to-business:** Is this someone who has been paying his or her bills? If not, and he or she has called on the sales line, perhaps we want to redirect the call to someone who is skilled at collections or payment arrangements.

• **Help desk:** Is this a customer with an outstanding trouble ticket? If so, perhaps we should try to route the customer back to the person with whom he or she spoke last or the agent initially assigned to handle the problem. If that person isn't available, we should route the call to a backup individual or group.

All of these examples show that we are stretching outside the bounds of the basic switch database (which only stores information on the agent positions, queues and other things directly related to the switch). Data-directed routing logic is more complex, but it is more powerful because it takes into account the business relationship with the caller. Data-directed routing is used when call centers truly want to segment customers or differentiate contacts based on knowledge about the individual or their relationship to the company. Thus, it is a fit in environments where there is a CRM strategy or where there is a transformational mindset about implementing technologies such as advanced routing and CTI.

Selection Algorithms

You may recall from Chapter 3 that either agent or call selection has to take place, depending on whether or not there is a queue. There are a variety of selection algorithms, ranging from simple to complex. Here are the key ones you'll encounter.

Agent Selection Algorithms

• **Hunt groups.** The most basic level of agent selection is hunt groups, which really isn't ACD software. Hunt groups put a set of extensions into a circular or linear list. The software then finds the next extension in the list that is available. Generally, call centers today do not use hunt groups for agent positions because other algorithms distribute calls more fairly. Hunt groups usually don't have the associated statistics and management tools needed. However, some centers still set up hunt groups for voicemail or IVR ports.

• **Most Idle Agent (MIA) or Least Occupied Agent (LOA).** Most ACDs use MIA routing – delivering the call to the position that has been available the longest consecutive period of time. Or they use LOA to find the agent who had the most idle time in a defined time period (for example, 15 or 30 minutes, or even an entire shift).

• **Skills.** Skills can play a role in call selection or agent selection. Skills define the types of calls an individual is best equipped to handle and enable individuals to handle multiple call types. Skills mean many different things to different people (including vendors), but true skills-based routing should have these characteristics:

- Allow multiple skills per person.
- Allow prioritization, preferences or competency levels to be assigned per skill, per agent.
- Allow unique skill combinations (that is, an agent doesn't have to fit into an already-defined set or combination).
- Allow a free-seating arrangement (ability to log in to any telephone set).
- Allow a single login regardless of number of skills assigned.
- Allow a single set of work states for all skills (for example, selecting the unavailable work state means the agent is unavailable for calls to any skill).

In a skills environment, agent selection can be derived from skill competency levels. For example, if several agents within the technical support skill are idle, the algorithm selects the agent whose tech support proficiency level is highest (and if there are multiple with that proficiency level, the algorithm selects the agent who also has been idle the longest). The advantage to this methodology is that the caller gets to speak with the "best" resource; the downside is that this methodology might overwork the best people.

Call Selection Algorithms

- **First In, First Out (FIFO).** FIFO is the most basic call selection approach, which is used in core ACD software. It delivers calls to agents in the order in which they arrived.

- **Prioritization.** Conditional and data-directed routing generally enable some prioritization of calls. In either case, calls with certain DNIS or prompt selections, or customer characteristics (based on information in the database), are routed to the front of the queue or with varying levels of priority. Prioritization examples include calls that have come from the IVR, callers who have an outstanding problem or top customers.

- **Skills.** The skills-routing algorithm matches call types with skill groups and skill proficiencies. So when an agent becomes available, the first call that arrived may not be connected first if the agent doesn't have the proper skills to handle the interaction. If multiple call types are queued and a multiskilled agent becomes available, the algorithm may select the call that matches the highest expertise level, across all of that agent's skills, regardless of the caller wait time.

More About Skills

Instead of just allowing agents to log in to multiple groups, skills-based routing enables a truly adaptable configuration of call types per individual. It is software-driven. The login is associated with a set of skills; the login triggers the association of those skills with a given position.

Why Skills?

Using skills introduces benefits at many levels:

- For customers – their calls will be routed to the best-qualified available person to handle their needs, which should also reduce call transfers.
- For agents – it allows for a better career path, as they develop their breadth or depth of skills.
- For managers – they can focus their agents on the proper call types to match their talents, while still leveraging and managing a diverse pool of resources. That translates to better service and better cost management.

Like any powerful technology, there are risks associated with skills routing. A typical flaw in skills implementation is to oversegment the center and classify skills in a very granular manner (the bottom line is, keep it simple). Following are a few challenges with skills-based routing:

- The ability to identify the call type or need (without prompting the poor customer to death) should define your level of skills segmentation.
- Don't oversegment call types. Oversegmentation will compromise economies of scale (remember, smaller groups are less efficient) or will result in calls constantly overflowing to backup groups or lower-skilled resources in order to meet service levels.
- Skills have an operational impact – it's difficult to hire, train, promote and reward people if the number or levels of skills are too high.
- A highly skilled agent may end up in the "hot seat," overwhelmed by a bar-

rage of calls while other less-skilled agents are underutilized.

• Numerous skills are difficult to schedule.

Today, PBX or ACD systems allow hundreds of skills (10 or more skills per person and numerous levels of prioritization) to be configured – and on CTI and Communications Server solutions, it may be unlimited! But that doesn't mean it should be implemented that way (bigger is not necessarily better). Remember, keep it simple to ensure skills are manageable and effective. Examples of skills types typically used in call centers include:

• Languages
• New trainees (e.g., limited set of simpler call types) vs. veterans (breadth or depth)
• Product types
• Customer types

Decisions, Decisions

There are many options for routing calls:
• Basic ACD routing
• Conditional routing
• "Data-directed" routing
• Multisite routing – pre-arrival and post-arrival routing

Call and agent selection decisions can be made with varying levels of sophistication:
• First in, first out
• Prioritization
• Hunt groups (circular, linear)
• Most idle or least occupied agent
• Skills
• Predictive algorithms and other alternatives

Routing can be done in many places:
• Network
• Switch
• CTI
• Communications Server

Architectural Implications of Single-Site Routing Options

Keep in mind that the various levels of routing can be configured in a number of different places: switch, CTI or Communications Server. The architectural tradeoffs discussed in Chapter 2 can help you decide where to put routing. Table 4-1 offers some considerations about the "when" and "where" of routing.

Table 4-1: Single-Site Routing Options, Strengths and Issues

Routing Option	Strengths/Best Fit	Some Issues or Limitations
PBX/ACD	• Value the "five-nines" of reliability • Prefer more traditional approaches – conservative company, like tried-and-true approaches, telecom still strongly influences architectural decisions • Heavily invested in switch-based software and want to continue to leverage it; have people trained on tools, routes developed, etc.	• Often have parameter limits on numbers of routes, paths, skills, priorities, etc. • Requires CTI to provide data-directed routing • Locked into the switch vendor's capabilities
Hybrid	• Similar to CTI (below) • Want to leverage existing switch	• Limits you to the specific switch vendor's capability
CTI	• Like the more open, server-based approaches; want to move intelligence off proprietary switch, but still continue to leverage it as a voice-switching platform • Implementing CTI for other applications, such as screen pops and reporting • Want to route on database parameters external to the switch • Planning for a full multimedia contact center, and want single routing and reporting platform	• Reliability must be assured through redundancy or high-availability configuration • Tools can be more complex than switch-based routing tools • May require significant system integration and custom software development • Announcements and other queue treatment may require an IVR
Communications Server	• Like the more open, server-based approaches • Want to route on database parameters external to the switch • Planning for a full multimedia contact center, and want single routing and reporting platform	• Reliability must be assured through redundancy or high-availability configuration, and available IT support • Scalability is more limited

Innovative Routing and Selection Schemes

ACDs have been around for nearly 30 years. In some ways, calls have been routed and queued the same way for a long time. Sure, technologies like skills- and data-directed routing have been introduced, but the basic concept of queuing a call and delivering it to the best available agent has remained more or less unchanged.

In the last few years, though, there have been several new ideas introduced to the market. This is a good thing – businesses change, customers change (admit it, we all expect more today), and the challenges and needs change. Here are three different ways to look at routing, agent selection and call selection:

• **Pull or take.** Some CTI and Communications Server vendors have introduced a different alternative – present the queue to agents visibly on their PC screen with as much information as is available about the contact, customer and need, and let agents select which contact they want to take next. Basically, the agent makes the selection.

This scenario immediately raises some flags for managers about abuse and concern for the caller who sits in queue indefinitely. However, the software can be programmed with business rules to ensure every call gets handled within a defined period of time (e.g., if a call has been waiting too long, it will just be delivered instead of allowing an agent to choose).

This approach is a good fit for call centers that are truly looking to empower their agents. It gives the agents a sense of control and increased responsibility (and not feeling like they're working in a "sweat shop" type center). The pull-or-take approach can reduce staff turnover and improve productivity. On the other hand, in the wrong culture, it could be disastrous.

• **Predictive routing.** Various vendors have created algorithms for predicting outcomes, such as: Will a specific call meet service level? What is the expected wait time of this particular call? The software then bases its routing and selection decisions on these predictions, often altering the first-in, first-out mentality of the queue to achieve other business goals. For example, a call for a unique skill may be routed ahead of a call for a basic skill if the predictions are that they will both meet service level this way.

• **Weighted factors.** Other algorithms characterize the agent and the call by different levels and weights, such as the cost of resources available to take calls or the potential value of the customer. The algorithm then finds the best match based on the weighting scheme. This introduces a level of complexity, but certainly a level of power in optimizing the bottom line of call center interactions.

Expect more innovative routing schemes to come along – there are new influences, with vendors that have come into the market focused on routing email or other media. And those vendors that have been at this for a while are looking for ways to meet client needs and differentiate their products. Routing calls today requires an open mind!

Multisite Routing

Many organizations have multiple call center sites that operate as a collective pool or a "virtual call center." As with single-site routing options, there are various levels of sophistication available, and a corresponding range of complexity, value and costs. Multisite routing ranges from simple percentage-based network allocations to customer-specific, real-time, event-based routing decisions using CTI.

The Business Case for "Virtual" Operations

There are four key reasons for networking multiple sites.

• **Efficiency.** In Chapter 3, we discussed Erlang C calculations for single-site routing. Erlang calculations demonstrate the pooling principle (larger groups are more efficient and resource utilitzation increases).

• **Flexibility.** Recall that calls arrive randomly and, therefore, volumes are unpredictable, moment to moment. Virtual operations allow greater flexibility to adapt to varying loads. For example, three sites, collectively, can more readily absorb a call spike than a single site could on its own.

• **Disaster recovery.** Disaster recovery prepares you for the unexpected and unplanned, such as hazardous weather conditions, building problems, power outages, strikes/labor unrest, martial law, terrorism, telecom cable cuts, epidemics and system crashes. A well-thought-out multisite strategy allows an organization to rapidly adapt to unanticipated conditions.

• **Consistent customer experience.** A virtual operation is not just a technology implementation. It leads to common processes, metrics and overall customer experience regardless of where the contact is handled.

There are three basic multisite routing technology options:

1. Carriers provide pre-arrival routing, which routes a call before it goes to a site.

2. PBX/ACDs provide post-arrival routing, which routes a call after it arrives at a site.

3. CTI-based applications provide both.

These three technologies can also be combined into other options.

Carrier-Based Multisite Routing

Carrier-based routing is available from Interexchange Carriers (IXCs). IXCs are the telecommunications companies that provide 800-number and long-distance services, such as AT&T, MCI Worldcom and Sprint. Provisioning services from these carriers is essentially outsourcing your multisite routing technology – you rely on the hardware and software capabilities of their network and the carrier manages and maintains the infrastructure. The provider typically charges flat monthly and per-usage fees for these advanced features.

Carrier-based capabilities include:

• **Allocation.** Calls route to various centers with predefined rules, usually on a percentage or threshold basis. For example, in a three-site call center environment with locations in Orlando, Minneapolis and Phoenix, 20 percent of calls route to Orlando, 50 percent to Minneapolis and 30 percent to Phoenix.

• **Area of call origination.** Calls route between centers based on location. For example, East Coast calls go to Charlotte, Midwest calls to Omaha, Mountain states calls to Denver, and West Coast calls to Seattle. IXCs route callers to different locations based on the phone number from which the call originated. The routing can differentiate down to the area code and exchange (the first six digits of the number).

• **Caller identification.** Calls route based on specifically identifying the caller using prompted digits (e.g., account number) or ANI matching. These capabilities are typically used in a customer segmentation routing strategy. For example, send

VIP customers to a center in Cleveland and send all other customers to the Kansas City site.

• **Time-of-day and day-of-week.** Calls route to sites based on the time and the day. This feature is most often combined with one of the other routing capabilities. For example, from 6 a.m. to 10 a.m., Eastern time, all calls route to a center in New Hampshire. Starting at 10 a.m., calls are split 50/50 between the New Hampshire and Oregon centers. Starting at 7 p.m., all calls route to Oregon until 10 p.m. After hours (nights and weekends), all calls route to the outsourcer who provides extended coverage. This feature could even be applied to centers located around the world, which is sometimes referred to as "follow the sun" or "global call routing."

• **Network transfer.** This option provides the capability to transfer the call to another center after it is received by the initial center. This capability is invoked either automatically (prior to agent answer) or manually (after agent answer). With the automatic option, conditional routing logic in the switch or an IVR application plays a short series of touchtone digits back to the network. This signals the network to take control of the call and transfer it to another center. With the manual option, the agent enters a feature access code through the telephone keypad to signal the network. The network then reroutes the call to an alternative call center. Keep in mind that this feature is a post-arrival routing feature, not pre-arrival routing like the other network features.

• **Combinations.** Network features are often combined for routing. Typical combinations are time-of-day/day-of-week routing with various allocation schemes. Network prompting, discussed previously, is also often combined with other options.

• **Real-time management.** Real-time management (or near real-time management) may be an optional capability that your IXC offers. The network carriers provide a dedicated terminal, dial-in access or Web browser access to the network-based routing logic. Your organization designs and changes the routing routines; changes and updates typically take effect in less than 15 minutes. So, for example, when a center needs to hold an all-hands meeting or is hit by a snowstorm or the flu, the allocation of calls to that site can be quickly reallocated to other locations.

Switch-Based Multisite Routing

Voice switch single-site routing can be extended to multisite routing. Examples include Aspect's Network Interflow and InterQueue, Avaya's Look Ahead Interflow and Virtual Routing, Nortel's Network ACD and Symposium Multisite Networking, Rockwell's Virtual Overflow and Siemens' Look Ahead Routing and ResumeRouting Enterprise. Some Communications Servers have similar capabilities.

Figure 4-6: Switch-Based Multisite Routing

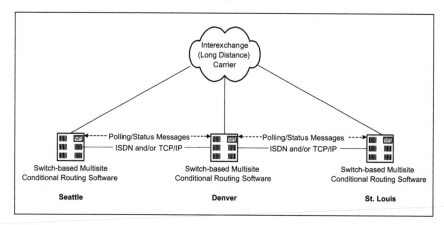

Switch-based multisite routing technology makes extensive use of the conditional routing statements, skills management, scripting tools and logic available in the vendor's single-site routing software. It also leverages intelligent signaling between sites, typically using ISDN and/or TCP/IP. Signaling messages are passed in the ISDN D channel or in TCP/IP-based messages, while the actual voice call is moved between sites on an ISDN B channel, T1 channel or VoIP.

PBX/ACD-based multisite routing uses signaling messages to poll the alternate switches in the organization. The messages can inquire about existing conditions (for example, number of calls in queue, anticipated wait times, agents available, agents staffed), or about ability to take the call.

The decision to reroute the call is controlled by either the sending switch or the receiving switch. When the decision to reroute the call is at the receiving switch, the call is only moved when the "OK to accept" is sent by the receiving switch. It uses its conditional-routing logic to make its decision. When the sending switch controls the decision, it requests information about the status of queues at other locations. Upon obtaining the status information, the sending switch software determines the best site to take the call. For example, in a three-switch network, if a call is received in Denver and there are already 15 calls in queue, the Denver-based PBX/ACD queries sites in Seattle and St. Louis. If Seattle has 20 calls in queue and St. Louis has 10 calls in queue, the Denver switch sends the call to St. Louis because of the shorter queue.

Once the decision is made to move a call, the voice conversation is passed over the network. Private trunks between sites may be used when there is a network in place or the call volume justifies putting in private lines. Alternatively, public network switched lines can be used. Some centers will use packet-based (IP) networks when quality of service can be guaranteed.

The drawback to switch-based multisite routing is that the polling/querying methodology is proprietary to each PBX/ACD vendor; each manufacturer implements this technology in a way that only their products understand. If you have switches from a single manufacturer, consider this option. If you have a mix of switches, you'll have to look at the carrier or CTI-based solutions.

CTI-Based Multisite Routing

Network-based routing primarily addresses pre-arrival routing. PBX/ACD-based routing addresses only post-arrival routing. CTI-based multisite routing addresses both.

CTI-based routing works with a mix of different vendors' PBX/ACDs (for example, Aspect, Avaya, Nortel, Rockwell and Siemens), in addition to a variety of IXCs (for example, AT&T, MCI Worldcom, Sprint). Consider this option if your organization has (or will have) a mix of switch and long-distance vendors. It can also be used in a homogeneous environment. The two most prominent vendors in this arena are Cisco and Alcatel (Genesys Labs).

In addition to pre- and post-arrival routing, this option also delivers advanced reporting, the ability to load-balance traffic among geographically dispersed voice-response units, desktop CTI (softphones, screen pops), and the ability to make data-directed routing decisions across an entire enterprise. So while CTI is the most complex (and costly) option, it is also the most robust and sophisticated.

Figure 4-7: CTI-Based Multisite Routing

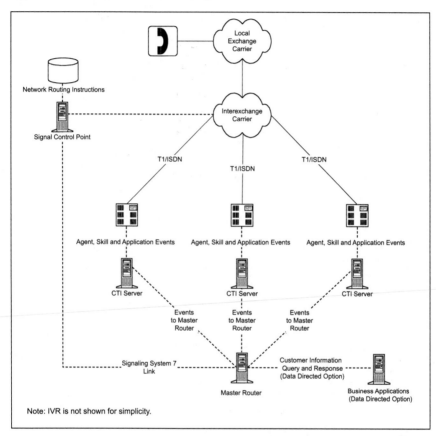

CTI-based routing uses the same underlying CTI capabilities as the data-directed routing application mentioned earlier in this chapter (CTI is described in detail in Chapter 6). This multisite routing alternative uses three key technology elements: CTI event monitoring, CTI control and Signaling System 7 (SS7). CTI event monitoring and CTI control are used for post-arrival routing and all three are used for pre-arrival routing. Following is a brief description of the role of each in pre-arrival routing:

CTI Event Monitoring

CTI monitors state changes of call center resources on the voice switch. The switch real-time events may be provided passively or the CTI server may query the switch for the information. The key types of information monitored are:

• **Agent-related events:** login and logout, work states (available, not ready/unavailable, after-call work/wrap-up, active, etc.)

• **Skill, group or application-related events:** number of calls in queue, number of calls being handled

Signaling System 7

When a caller picks up the phone and dials an 800 number, the call is routed from the local exchange carrier (SBC, Verizon, Qwest, Bellsouth) to the IXC (AT&T, MCI, WorldCom, Sprint). The IXC's Signal Control Point (SCP) queries a network routing database for routing instructions, and the database tells the SCP to get routing instructions from the CTI master router. If the data-directed (customer-specific) routing option is enabled, the SCP also sends ANI and/or network-prompted digits to the master router in the "get route instructions" message.

The link between the SCP and the master router is a special circuit called Signaling System 7. When the SCP queries for the routing instructions, the CTI master router delivers the routing address back to the SCP via the SS7 link (this query and response must be performed in 250 to 500 milliseconds, depending on the carrier). The SCP executes the routing destination, does as it's told, and routes the caller to the "best" call center or even the "best" agent. If the CTI master router doesn't respond quickly enough, the network will follow a default routing path.

CTI Control

CTI can control a call. When CTI is in control of routing, the network or switch is basically asking: "What do you want me to do with this call?" The CTI application gathers the data, applies routing logic, determines the best place to route and tells the switch what to do.

In pre-arrival routing, a master router is in control and talks to the network. Here are the steps:

• The CTI servers provide the event status obtained through monitoring to the master router. The master router maintains a real-time database with the status of agents, skills and applications. Theoretically, this master router is aware of all activity at all call center sites.

• If data-directed routing is enabled, the master router queries enterprise applications for additional information, such as customer segment, sales history, last agent spoken to and order status. Prompted digits or ANI uniquely identify the caller.

• The master router applies business rules to the call center events and business information to determine the "best" destination for a call. The destination options are sites, agent groups or an individual agent.

The CTI-based pre-arrival routing application goal is to get the right caller to the right call center the first time. So why would you use post-arrival routing capabilities if you are using pre-arrival routing? Post-arrival routing applications fit with pre-arrival routing in situations where:

• Lengthy queues exist at all sites when the pre-arrival routing decision executes. The post-arrival routing is a "second look" to see if any sites are clearing their queues quickly.

• Significant traffic is generated by callers who "zero-out" of the IVR for agent assistance. In this case, the pre-arrival routing decision originally looks for IVR port availability, not agent availability.

• Large numbers of transfers and conferences occur between skill groups. At the time of pre-arrival routing, the decision focused on the availability of the original agent or skill group.

Post-arrival routing can be accomplished with a CTI solution or by using a switch-based approach. In a CTI-based post-arrival routing scenario, the switch issues a route request to the CTI master router. Because the master router has enterprisewide "eyes and ears" (event monitoring), it is aware of the availability of resources across the entire enterprise. The CTI master router then issues a route destination to the switch, and the call is transferred. The switch can reroute the call to other sites over private or public facilities. Alternatively, a local CTI server could be queried and it could talk to the other sites or a master router.

CTI is used just for post-arrival routing in many cases (no pre-arrival routing occurs). There are also environments based on "best-of-breed" approaches that use one CTI solution for pre-arrival routing and another for post-arrival routing. As we mentioned before, the post-arrival routing could be done by the switches or CTI. Pre-arrival routing using CTI can be expensive because of the network fees for the signaling interfaces. Therefore, some companies use basic network features, such as percent allocation for pre-arrival routing, and then use the switches or CTI for post-arrival routing. Mix-and-match can sometimes be the right answer, but be sure to recognize the cost and management tradeoffs. This decision is best supported by carefully analyzing the pros and cons tied to your business needs and analyzing the costs of the options.

Architectural Implications of Multisite Routing Options

Earlier, we highlighted the architectural implications associated with single-site routing options. The same thinking applies to multisite routing options, as well. However, the "best fit" and issues for multisite routing have a few more implications.

Table 4-2: Multisite Routing Options, Strengths and Issues

Routing Option	Strengths/Best Fit	Issues or Limitations
Network	• No additional hardware or software to manage and support • Operational costs instead of capital costs • Relatively easy to implement • Good low-cost learning option as a first step • Carrier infrastructure is extremely reliable and robust • Good in combination with other solutions for post-arrival routing	• Very basic multisite routing capabilities; does not provide any automatic adjustment to current call center conditions (staffing level, queue length, etc.) • Service fees may become uneconomical in large volume environments • Lacks control needed in dynamic environments without routing management capabilities • Additional set of management reports to monitor • No visibility between other IXCs and LECs • Provides primarily pre-arrival routing capabilities; take back and transfer is the only post-route option
Switch	• Good option if all switches from same vendor • Provides dynamic routing based on current call center conditions • Uses administrative and management tools of existing infrastructure, leveraging familiarity with the system for each site • May take advantage of existing reporting tools if networked reporting ability provided by vendor • Can be combined with carrier-based services; for example, use carrier-based percentage allocation at the network level (pre-arrival routing) with switch post-arrival routing capability • Good uptime and reliability	• Must have homogenous switch environment • Increases network complexity due to additional private lines and/or switched access between sites • May require significant upgrades, additions, re-engineering to existing infrastructure • Poor design can severely limit scalability due to heavy processor demands • Provides post-arrival routing capabilities only; call must be sent to a site based on network features first (DNIS, prompting, percent allocation, etc.) • Connectivity requirements become complex for more than three sites

continued on next page

Routing Option	Strengths/Best Fit	Issues or Limitations
CTI	• Provides most dynamic routing; can base routing decision on current call center status, as well as information about the customer stored in a database • Can also be used for balancing IVR traffic among multiple sites (pre-arrival routing) • Excellent reporting: can follow call from site-to-site, can combine call information with IVR information and business data, and provides common reporting across a diverse switch environment • Good fit for heterogeneous switch environments (but can also be used in homogeneous environment) • Can be used for heterogeneous network providers (IXCs and LECs) • Provides pre-arrival routing and post-arrival routing capabilities • Very nice fit with other CTI applications (screen pop, soft phones)	• Complex solution; many servers and software modules to manage • Most expensive of the three multisite options; costs include hardware, software, system support and SS7 network charges • Significant new skills, knowledge and system support required • May require significant upgrades/additions/reengineering to existing switch infrastructure • Not as reliable as carrier- or switch-based options

Here's an example to emphasize the challenges of deciding the best multisite routing architecture. Two companies that previously handled different territories were merging and had to develop a plan for creating a virtual center across multiple sites. The three options previously discussed, as well as combinations thereof, offered possible routing solutions. Which is the best candidate? As we've said before, "it depends." Here's how the "it depends" of their analysis netted out:

• For the short term, using some network features (area code routing, prompting) is the best solution. Most calls will be handled in territory for the short term, and not all calls will be handled at all sites. Full virtual networking isn't possible until the computer systems and applications are reconciled or agents are trained on multiple systems. Each company had uniform switch environments prior to the merger, so some switch-based routing can be done within the territory.

• The long term depends on what they do with the diverse switch environment and the likelihood of another merger. While some prefer the simplicity of switch-based routing over CTI-based routing, the design can't be tied to a specific switch vendor if another merger comes along. And switch-based routing means that the switches for half the sites need to be replaced to create a homogeneous environment. That will be expensive.

When the systems are reconciled it will be a good time to implement CTI capabilities, such as screen pops, and explore using CTI for routing, as well. Implementing CTI sooner would result in multiple messy integrations that may then be thrown away when the new system is in place.

Multisite Routing Has Ripple Effects

Organizations that implement multisite routing must assess the impact to other call center technologies, for example:

- **Reporting systems:** Will a new reporting system be required? Can the existing reporting system be enhanced to accommodate multisite routing? Will the old system become obsolete? Will reports be accessed from multiple systems?

- **Workforce management systems:** Can the existing workforce management system handle multiple sites? Does a new interface to a new source system have to be built? Are upgrades or additional software modules required?

- **IVR configuration:** Should you centralize or decentralize? Place the IVRs in front of the switches or behind? (See Chapter 8 for more on these issues.) IVR strategy must be considered at the same time routing strategy is considered.

There are ripple effects to the organization, as well. The move to a multisite routing arrangement necessitates some level of centralized management. The centralized group must control planning, forecasting, reporting, aggregate scheduling and overall design of the routing architecture. The day-to-day operation of the individual centers has some local control of operational practices, but an enterprise-level view of the aggregate activity must be controlled by a central staff. Disaster looms if this tenet is ignored.

Remote Agents

The previous discussion focused on technologies for linking disparate call centers. We now focus on the technologies for linking remote agents into a single (virtual) center where all positions leverage the same switch (PBX, ACD, Communications Server). Remote agents appear no different than onsite agents to the switch, reporting, workforce management systems, quality monitoring and other supporting applications – as well as to the customer.

Remote agents leverage the same core technology infrastructure as the main site and, therefore, are more cost-effective than establishing a second site with a second switch. However, they should not generally be considered a solid business continuity (disaster prevention) strategy since most vendor solutions will lose the remote sites if the main site suffers an outage.

Remote agents come in two forms – groups and single users. Groups are located in satellite, regional or branch offices, while single users are located in a small office or home office (i.e., telecommuters).

Why Use a Remote Site?

There are several reasons to use remote agents. This allows you to:

• Procure, administer and maintain a single technology infrastructure (switch, quality monitoring, workforce management, etc.)

• Expand the labor pool through access to other locations

• Retain experienced agents who are unable or unwilling to commute to the call center location

• Increase the number of agents without establishing another center (save real estate, technology, utility and other costs)

• Provide extended-hours coverage or accommodate other difficult staffing scenarios, such as split shifts, short shifts and part-time shifts.

We've seen many companies that have benefitted from using remote sites or positions. For instance:

• Utilities sometimes have field office personnel who normally handle walk-in traffic (e.g., payment locations) and/or home-based agents who pitch in during an outage. Extreme and sudden peaks can be handled effectively with this expanded staff.

• One firm's call center needed 24x7 coverage but received very few calls during the "graveyard" shift, and no one wanted to work those hours. Offering home-based offices resulted in plenty of volunteers to work the late shift. While certainly not an inexpensive solution, it ensured that a highly skilled and trained individual would be available to handle the unique, complex and critical calls that came in.

• A company wanted its outsourcing partner to be tied more effectively to the main site. A remote cabinet was placed at the outsourcer so their agents could be monitored and calls routed using the same system.

• A company wanted to use disabled workers and others who couldn't easily commute in its call centers. A telecommuting program was established to make these excellent workers part of the call center team.

Recognizing the Operational Challenges

There are a number of technology options for remote agents, but that's the easy part. The real challenges are operational, such as:

• Which agents are eligible?
• What are the rules for the home-office environment?
• How do remote agents get managerial support?
• How do we keep them in the team mindset and in tune with our culture and activities?
• How do we enforce security rules?
• What are the legal ramifications?

Remote Options

Two networking options can be used to connect a remote office or telecommuter to the main site: TDM or IP. Figure 4-8 illustrates the voice connectivity options for a group or single user over IP or TDM. Obviously, you also need data connectivity, which may use the same lines, or a separate connection. High-speed data connectivity is a prerequisite.

Figure 4-8: Remote Office and Telecommuter Options

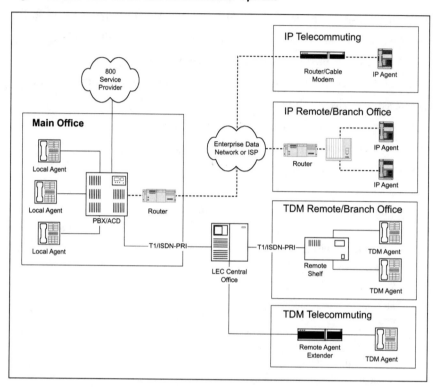

• **Remote office.** This option places a physical cabinet with the necessary ACD/PBX circuit cards at the remote location. Users are generally on the same digital phone sets or softphones as the main site's users. High-speed private lines are generally placed between sites (e.g., T1, ATM).

• **Single agent/telecommuter.** This option extends the voice and data connectivity for a single user. It can use a standard phone, a softphone or a digital phone. To use a switch-specific digital phone, a modem-like device called an "extender" is used in the remote office. Telecommuter positions have various options for the connectivity: analog, ISDN-Basic Rate Interface (BRI), cable modems, Digital Subscriber Line (DSL). Analog is the least desirable because the data speeds are slow. DSL or cable modems optimize performance.

Who to Turn to?

Remote group: Because of the proprietary nature of the hardware and systems communications, remote-site solutions are vendor-specific – get them from your PBX/ACD or Communications Server vendor.

Home office: Vendors generally have their own solutions, which are sometimes proprietary (e.g., if they are extending their digital phone). There are also third parties that sell solutions, often with PC-based softphones.

Table 4-3: Summary of Remote Agent Technologies

Option	Best Fit
Remote office – TDM-based	• Group of 4-8 positions or more* • Traditional ACD/PBX
Remote office – IP-based	• Group of 4-8 positions or more* • Quality of service controls on IP WAN • IP switch or IP-enabled traditional switch
Telecommuter – TDM-based	• Home office • Traditional ACD/PBX • More conservative approach to mixing voice and data
Telecommuter – IP-based	• Home office • Quality of service controls on IP network • IP switch or IP-enabled traditional switch • High bandwidth access like DSL or cable modem available

ACD Desktop Features

Regardless of whether the environment is a single- or multisite environment, calls eventually reach a desktop and an agent asks: "How may I help you?" Following are the desktop features that complete our picture of ACD software. (We had to put them somewhere!)

• **Auto-answer and manual answer.** Auto-answer means that the call is delivered automatically when the agent becomes available and there are calls waiting in queue or when an agent is sitting idle and a call arrives. The agent hears a tone – "zip tone" or "beep tone" – in his or her headset and the call is connected. Manual answer means that a call rings at the phone and the agent must pick up the hand-

---

* Based on comparative costs of multiple telecommuter positions vs. remote staff.

set or select the ringing line to be connected. The answer mode is generally a parameter set for each position or login.

- **Auto-available vs. manual available.** Auto-available means that the position goes to available as soon as a call is disconnected. Manual available means the position goes to an unavailable work state, generally wrap-up, to provide time for the agent to complete data entry or other tasks associated with completing the call. The agent must manually indicate his or her availability by pressing a button (or sometimes it is timer-based). An agent in auto-available mode can still go to wrap-up by pressing a button. Availability is generally a parameter set for each position or login.

- **Wrap-up codes.** Wrap-up codes can be entered via touchtone or by pressing a pre-programmed button. They are entered to capture information about a call – for example, the type of inquiry or type of customer. The use of a code writes data to the ACD reports database. Note that well-configured routing paths can capture much information about call types automatically, and wrap-up codes should be used sparingly so that agents can focus on other tasks. Also, many companies use the PC at the desktop and their business applications to capture this type of information.

- **Auto-greetings.** Auto-greetings are a busy agent's best friend, especially in a call center with high call volumes and short talk times. Agents pre-record their greeting (or greetings, if they are handling a variety of call types). The greeting is played automatically when the caller is connected. Most auto-greetings today use PC-based softphones and record the greetings in .wav files on the PC; some centralize them in a core voice subsystem.

ACD Phone Features and Fashions

The cost of an ACD phone reflects the robust level of features it supports – many programmable buttons, displays, headset jacks and sometimes a ruggedness not common to regular business phones. But it also reflects what the market will bear – call center capabilities often drive requirements and switch selections so the value and, therefore, cost lies with the call center capabilities. This is one of the reasons why alternative architectures have emerged – to combat the $500 to $1,000 phone!

Some of the most valuable features in ACD phones are the ones that give agents feedback about status in the center or information about the arriving call. The figure below shows a sample display. The display shows the type of call (DNIS or prompt mapped to a database entry) and the caller identification through network information or prompted digits that were collected. It also shows the number of Calls in Queue (CIQ) and the time of the oldest call in queue. The phone has lights to show queue status, flashing faster or changing colors as the queue grows. All of this is important feedback to agents so they can make informed decisions about call handling and how to spend their time.

Sample Phone Display

Call to Customer Service	**Sales CIQ: 6 Oldest: 3:24**
Calling From: 303-555-1212	**Customer ID: 555-22-3333**

Some call centers today use "softphones" – PC-based, software-driven phones. Softphones put all the sophisticated functions of the ACD into a graphical user interface. The advantage is that it gives the agent a single system to interface with – the PC – rather than having to jump between the phone and the PC. Softphones can, however, take up a lot of real estate on the desktop screen. In Chapter 6, we'll look at options for embedding softphones into application toolbars using CTI. Some centers are averse to the risk of downtime of the phone because of PC downtime. To address this issue, centers might maintain or buy hard phones as a backup when using softphones.

Points to Remember

- Routing can take place at many levels. The application choices include the voice switch, network service provider and CTI. These options can be combined to optimize your solution.

- Organizations with a single center can utilize basic, conditional and data-directed routing. Businesses with multiple sites have two additional options: pre-arrival routing and post-arrival routing.

- Call selection and agent selection logic are closely related to routing. Call selection options are first-in/first-out, prioritization and skills-based. Agent selection methodologies include hunt groups, most idle or least occupied, and skills-based.

• Remote agents can be in remote groups or telecommuters. They can access the center via circuit- or packet-based connectivity.

Actions to Take

• When designing a routing architecture, be sure to clearly define what technology is routing the call at each point in time. Use call flows to walk through your design. There is significant overlap in the capabilities of the different application sources (network, CTI and voice switch) and the technologies can be combined. Consider scalability, manageability, reliability and support in conjunction with functionality.

• Use cost-analysis and modeling tools to determine the best multisite routing approach when creating a virtual call center environment.

Chapter 5:

Tools for Measuring, Managing and Optimizing Your Center

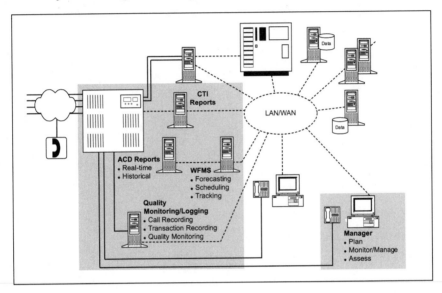

Key Points Discussed in this Chapter:

Call Center Reporting

Building a Reporting Strategy

ACD Reporting Tools

Workforce Management Systems

Basic and Advanced WFMS Tools

Skills and Multimedia Implications

Simulation Tools

Logging and Quality Monitoring Systems

Multimedia and VoIP Implications

Employee and Customer Satisfaction Measurement Tools

There is more to call center technology than the underlying architecture and the latest whiz-bang features. Technology enables centers to run efficiently and effectively, while focusing on business needs. First, though, you have to find the right tools to achieve your business goals, implement those tools effectively and thoroughly apply the capabilities. These principles especially apply to call center management tools.

There are a slew of call center management tools on the market – each with its own purpose for helping to manage the most valuable asset in your center: your agents. Some focus on productivity, others on quality. Together, they help to assess the contact center's performance and enable management to plan for the future.

Call Center Reporting

None of this stuff about reporting and management tools makes sense without the right business context. Traditionally, call centers have focused on a few key statistics that come out of ACD (phone system) reports, for example:

- Offered calls
- Handled calls
- Abandoned calls
- Service level
- Talk time + wrap-up time = handle time
- Average speed of answer
- Trunk utilization

Definitions of these and other statistics can be found in the glossary. But we don't want to focus on what the statistics mean – that's not the main message. The message is that, in the call centers of the new millennium, if the ACD statistics are all you care about and the only thing you measure, you'll be competitively disadvantaged. Call centers today need to take a holistic view of performance (pardon the trendy term). Performance is measured for productivity, quality and satisfaction. It's measured across multiple media. It's measured for cost, revenue and other business goals.

The New Story for Your Elevator Ride with Execs

We contend that the "elevator story" of call center performance is changing.

The elevator story is the short, sweet answer to any question of significance (the tale you can tell in the time it takes to ride a few floors on an elevator).Imagine this: You're on the elevator with a company executive who asks you, "How are things going in the call center?" In the good old days (and, unfortunately, even today), your answer might go something like this:

> *"Well, we're meeting our service level target of 80 percent of calls answered in 30 seconds. Our overall handle time is down, thanks to some training initiatives. We blocked less than 1 percent of all call attempts. We've reduced our abandon rate through some improved routing and allocation of resources, making our overall service and customer accessibility much better."*

Sounds pretty good – but it's all about phone statistics. While those statistics are important since agents and telecommunications costs make up approximately 85 percent of a call center's cost structure, it won't do in today's competitive business environment. Here's a potential elevator story for the more enlightened call center:

> *"Well, our cost-per-contact has dropped by 23 percent since we've provided customers with more media choice and control. And 36 percent of contacts were successfully self-serviced through our IVR and Web site. The revenue driven by the call center is up 12 percent thanks to some concerted efforts around our customer relationship management strategy, supported by process changes, training, incentives and the new tools we've put in place to support effective call flows and work flows. And 89 percent of all service issues were corrected within 24 hours. Finally, we've been able to support our growth with the same staff levels while maintaining our quality and customer satisfaction levels."*

That sounds really good – costs down, revenue up, problems solved and happy customers!

Building a Reporting Strategy

So how does someone know all of that before getting on the elevator? Well, it isn't easy. One of the great challenges in call centers today is the vast amounts of data: What to do with it, how to make sense of it, what's important and what's not, and how to make it manageable.

Figure 5-1 illustrates part of the problem – each of those little "cans" represents a database with information about how things are going in the call center. The data is in separate systems and separate databases, with different formats. Different tools are used to access and manipulate it. One customer contact can easily hit eight or nine of these databases, and that's before the customer fills out the customer satisfaction follow-up survey!

Figure 5-1: Report Data Sources in the Call Center

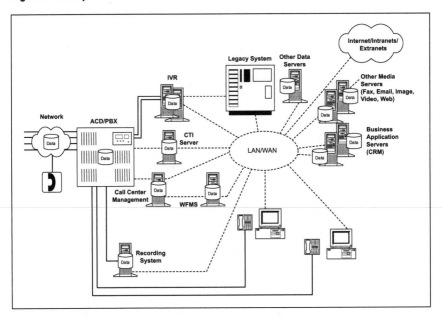

The first place to start, not surprisingly, is with the business drivers: What key metrics will drive the business? What is the business strategy – to drive revenue, control costs, acquire and retain customers or deliver world-class service? What's the mission of the center? From this you build a reporting strategy. Then you can start looking at: Where does the data for the defined metrics reside? How will we access and manage it?

Table 5-1 summarizes the levels of reporting and technology tools that apply for the various evolutionary stages of a contact center.

Table 5-1: Reporting Strategies and Tools

	Stage:			
	Basic	**Emerging**	**Advanced**	**Leading Edge**
Business Position of Call Center*	Necessary	Valued asset	Service differentiator	Strategic value
Management Thinking	"Give me core stats on call-handling performance; I have to manage costs while answering customer calls."	"I need to manage resources to match the work demand. We need to meet productivity and quality goals."	"Our center plays a key role in acquiring and retaining customers, so we need to be able to measure our success in these terms."	"I need to see the contribution the center makes and assess what's working and what's not with our products and in our marketing and business strategies."
Impact on Reporting Needs	Need simple ACD reporting tools	Need a suite of capabilities for planning, tracking and managing	Expands beyond telephony tools to business application tools, CTI and CRM; understanding customers and their interactions (not just call patterns) becomes important	Need to link call center statistics with measures of business performance and sales and service objectives; must conduct more detailed analysis, with technical resources involved
Key Performance Indicators	• Service level • ASA • Handle time	• Quality ratings • Self-service rates • Cost per contact • Schedule adherence	• Business outcomes of contacts, such as sales, saves and first-call resolution rate • Performance per media channel • Customer satisfaction scores • Employee satisfaction scores	• Revenue driven by or protected by the contact center • Contact center contribution to increasing customer satisfaction ratings or customer retention • Campaign success (e.g., new customers, sales)

* From Evolution of Technology-Enabled Center (See Chapter 2)

	Stage:			
	Basic	**Emerging**	**Advanced**	**Leading Edge**
Technology Tools	• Basic ACD reports • Possibly wallboards • Possibly simple forecasting and staffing tool	• Add customization capability (reports, formulas) • IVR reports • Workforce management system • Quality monitoring system (logging system if appropriate) • Simulation tool	• CTI-based "cradle-to-grave" reporting • CRM reports • Reporting capabilities for each media (Web, email, text-chat, Web calls, fax) • Customer satisfaction tool • Employee satisfaction tool	• Integrated reporting system via data warehousing, data mart, CTI, CRM, etc. • OLAP, data mining and other analytical tools

Note that the factors are cumulative across the table. As the positioning grows more strategic, the center must add performance indicators and tools, expanding and integrating the information used. Much of the evolution in reporting strategies reflects the market interest in Customer Relationship Management (CRM). As we'll discuss in Chapter 7, CRM is a philosophy, a strategy, a way of doing business. It's technology-enabled. One of the key technologies that comes into play in CRM environments is the data, reporting and analysis – all tied to business strategy.

To develop a solid reporting strategy, you need to apply strategic planning principles (outlined in Chapter 10). A reporting strategy will require tremendous collaboration between the technology and business staff. It will require some research into the latest tools – this is a part of our industry where solutions are emerging that may help. But you must realize from the start that this is not an easy (or cheap) task, and it is unlikely that you will find an "out-of-the-box" tool that helps you. Why? Every call center is unique in its combination of tools, applications and databases. Call centers are like snowflakes – they might look similar on the surface, but look closer and you'll find that each has its own unique configuration, systems, applications and data.

Reporting Tool Technologies

The reporting tools that are emerging take advantage of today's more open technology architectures. They leverage CTI links, open databases and open interfaces, such as XML (eXtensible Markup Language). XML is a tool generally used with Web architectures for passing data between systems or applications. It provides the data – and data about the data – allowing the two systems to readily pass information and comply with a specification while sending a variety of database fields. Over time, as CRM, CTI and multimedia systems begin to interoperate more openly or merge, we are likely to see richer cross-media reporting tools.

Currently, most companies have to figure out how to extract the information they need from various systems, consolidate it into a single database and manipulate it for true business reporting. An example of the architecture to support this is shown in Figure 5-2.

Figure 5-2: Extracting and Consolidating Report Data

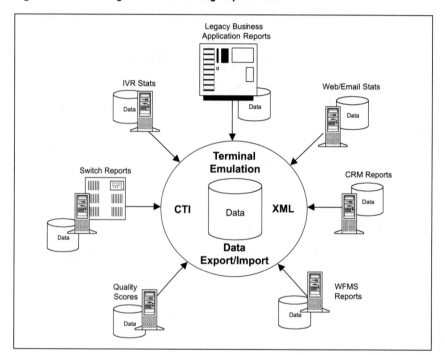

But there is more to the reporting challenge than just data access and extraction, or interfaces and interoperability. The prerequisite is a mechanism – an index, tag or other hook – which can tie the data from different systems together. The linking mechanism needs to be designed into the reporting architecture so that when the data is extracted, it can be used effectively. A call ID provided by CTI messages is an example of a linking mechanism.

Most reporting tools today are either client/server architectures using a Windows client or browser-based tools that access data over the corporate intranet. Some run on Windows, others on Unix, and some vendors give you a choice. Some vendors may supply both the hardware and software for the reporting server and application; some may supply only the software and specify the servers required to host the application and database. They will generally specify minimum configurations for the desktop where client software is loaded.

No Management Tool Is an Island!

"The hip bone's connected to the leg bone…" Remember that song? We could write one like it for contact center technology. Most reporting and management tools are connected to other systems – several of them. Quality Monitoring (QM) and logging connect to the switch, CTI and the LAN. Workforce Management Systems (WFMS) and wallboards connect to the ACD reporting tool and the LAN. Some of these tools may connect to a CTI solution. The QM and WFMS may connect to each other (so quality recordings can be tied to schedules, and maybe even deliver online training at the right times).

Why should you care (besides having to draw more lines in your block diagram)? First, there is a ripple effect of any upgrade. Upgrade one system and you may need to upgrade another – or at least reconfigure and test it. And what about administration and maintenance activities? When you add an agent in the ACD, then you'll need to figure out if you should add them to the WFMS and QM system. In some cases (e.g., a CTI solution or Communications Server with these functions), there may be a single administrative database. Don't forget to figure out the implications of your connections.

Complex Tools Require Specialized Users

As the thinking on reporting tools changes, it creates a side effect: The types of people who use these tools, or the skills they need, change. In the traditional call center model in which ACD reports dominate, there are people within the center who are generally successful at using the tools, generating reports and analyzing the situation. In smaller centers, the supervisors and managers are the users. A larger center is likely to have an operations analyst or other technical support staff who use the reporting and management tools, along with the supervisors and managers. But they generally reside in the center and are not necessarily highly technical people.

But in the new world, the tools and analysis involved are more complex. We're moving away from a basic, shrink-wrapped, one-trick tool (like your ACD reporting system from your switch vendor) to a much more complex system. Users become business analysts or systems analysts, often in the IT department (or less likely, the telecom sub group within IT). They need to work closely with the call center and thoroughly understand it. They use more complex tools, such as Structured Query Language (SQL) and Online Analytical Processing (OLAP) to analyze the data, identify outcomes and work with the call center to apply the learnings to modify processes, call flows, work flows and other activities in the center.

Figure 5-3 shows the evolution of users and tools in call center reporting. We'll dig into these issues more in Chapter 7 when we talk about customer relationship management systems and the accompanying data analysis.

Figure 5-3: Reporting and Management Tool Users

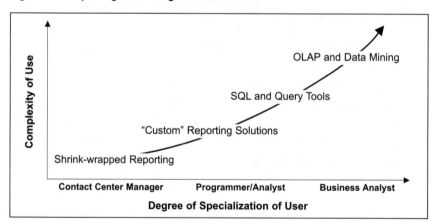

Adapt the Message to the Audience

When considering the various reporting and management tools, keep in mind that this is an area of call center technology for which there will be many different audiences for the output. From the agent to the CEO, and everyone in between, people in an organization want to see data about how the center is doing or how individuals are performing. The tools provide the data. The analysts (or other users of these tools) have to determine what data matters to which audiences, as well as how it can be packaged, delivered or accessed to meet their needs.

That means a variety of options must be at their disposal – from printing a report, to scheduling and printing it routinely, to pulling it up on-the-fly on the intranet. And it must be accessible to the various users in a way that is extremely user-friendly. That's the new reporting world. Table 5-2 reveals the typical audiences, data interests and ideal reporting delivery and formats.

Table 5-2: Report Users and Interests

Factor/User	Agent	Supervisor, Team Leader	Manager, Executive (VP, CxO)
Key interests, information on report	• Calls handled • Talk, wrap, handle time • Quality scores • Comparison to targets, peers • Trends (up/down, improving)	• Calls handled, abandoned • Service Level, ASA • Average talk, wrap, handle time • Quality scores • Customer satisfaction scores • Comparison to targets • Trends (up/down, improving)	• Key Performance Indicators (KPIs) such as Service Level, Quality, Customer Satisfaction, Cost per Contact, Revenue • Comparison to targets or industry benchmarks • Trends (up/down, improving)
Scope	Individual	Group, business area	Overall call center (perhaps broken down by key function, such as sales/service)
Frequency	Daily, weekly, monthly	Daily, weekly, monthly	Monthly summary (perhaps broken down by week), as well as ad hoc access to daily/ weekly reports
Delivery and Format	Ideally online, printout if necessary	Online and printout	One-page printout or email for monthly summary (perhaps delivered at monthly status meeting), as well as reports on request either online or email

Quantity Is Not the Answer

Many call centers' reporting problems are related to management and business vision and direction, not technology. In that case, running lots of reports or generating more data will not help and is likely to hurt. Some centers truly become slaves to their data and reporting tools.

In one situation, a multisite contact center with several hundred representatives had a large staff who just worked on reports, forecasting and scheduling. Over time, it became very clear that they were generating lots of data and reports, but not a lot of value. Things had to change (remember: culture, organization, processes and then technology).

In other cases, centers have invested more in reporting tools or workforce management tools because their performance targets weren't being met – when what they really needed was more agents. Keep in mind, more data or technology is no substitute for proper staffing and scheduling.

ACD Statistics and Reports

ACD statistics and reports are still the lifeblood of the call center. While multimedia is a hot topic, 90 percent or more of contacts are still handled over the phone in most centers. The ACD has the most robust, well-understood and well-used reporting capabilities. It provides a total view of the productivity and performance of call handling. Let's look at how it works.

Information is created about the status and activity of many voice contact elements – trunks, 800 numbers, routing paths, queues, skills, agents, calls. The ACD software – whether it's on a PBX, ACD, CTI or Communications Server – generates information about call center activity. Figure 5-4 illustrates this concept.

The ACD software generates messages to the reporting software where it is written to a database. Today, most systems are event-driven (not time-polling, as some were in the past). Every time a call arrives, gets routed, queues or is placed on hold, it creates a message. Every time an agent logs in, changes work states, hangs up or transfers a call, it creates a message. So lots of data is being generated.

In most cases, the communication between the ACD software and the reporting software is based on TCP/IP. It may use a very proprietary interface (closed to all but the vendor), or it may use a CTI link or other more open interface.

Figure 5-4: ACD Event Messages

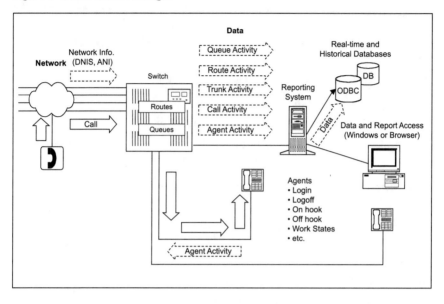

The data is written to a database that is accessed through a reporting application. The database is generally ODBC-compliant, like Oracle, SQL Server, Informix or Sybase. Think of the ACD reporting function as raw data that has formulas applied to it when requested, which are based on queries run by the application software. When a supervisor logs in to the ACD reporting tool and pulls up his or her favorite screen for monitoring real-time activity, it triggers a query against that database and then manipulates the data for presentation.

For real-time reports, the status is updated routinely – usually every five to 30 seconds. Basically, the application requests an update at that frequency. For a historical report, it finds the data for a specified period of time and summarizes, averages or totals as appropriate.

Some systems use separate real-time and historical databases. The more detailed data is summarized or "rolled up" and written to an archived database at certain intervals, such as daily, weekly or monthly. In other cases, the raw data is just stored in a database. When designing a reporting environment, you must define how long you need data and to what detail. While storage is cheap, there are performance tradeoffs when running reports against a large database.

ACD Reporting Tool Capabilities

The ACD reporting tools often offer a choice of sophistication levels. For example, some vendors have low-cost packages with limited standard reports, no customization and limited storage. These packages provide the core information needed to manage the center's resources. They are a good fit for a small center, a start-up center or one with a limited budget. For a larger center (say, 25 seats or more) with more complex and dynamic activities, a more robust tool is needed.

Real-time information from reporting tools can be used to assess problem causes and determine responses or actions to mitigate them. Historical data and reports can be used to monitor productivity and performance of individuals and groups, as well as to plan for the future.

Key Considerations for Selecting an ACD Reporting Tool

Following are a few key things to look for as you define requirements and evaluate options for ACD reporting tools.

• **User interface:** Is it Windows- or browser-based? Is it proprietary software? Does it use its own report customization tool or do you use a standard package, such as Seagate Crystal or Brio?

• **Performance:** How many users can it support at once? What is the refresh rate on real-time reports (for a few users and for lots of users)? How long can the data be stored? How long does it take to run a daily, weekly or monthly report?

• **Features/functions:** What types of graphical reports does it have? What are the standard reports? Does it have a custom report tool (and how easy is it to use)? How much flexibility does it have? How extensive are the real-time statistics and reports? How about historical statistics and reports? Does it have a capability to schedule reports to run routinely? What forms of report output does it offer: files, HTML pages, email attachments or printed?

• **Integration:** How does it link to the switch? Does it have an open interface to pass data to other systems, such as workforce management systems or wallboards?

• **Architecture:** Does the vendor provide all hardware and software, or does it run on a standard platform? What operating system, database and Web server does it use? Do you have expertise in-house in that environment? How is real-time data stored and accessed? What are the data archiving or backup mechanisms and options?

• **Database schema and formulas:** Are the database items and formulas well-documented? Easy to understand? Can you easily customize them to your specific and changing business needs? Can you get access to the raw call records? How long can you store real-time and historical data?

• **Cost:** What is the initial cost, including hardware, software and professional services for implementation, training and start-up? What are the licensing implications as you add users?

Wallboards Offer Data for Real-Time Decisions

Wallboards (also called display boards or readerboards) are fairly common in call centers. Basically, wallboards have a server that receives real-time data from the ACD reporting system through a printer port, terminal port or TCP/IP interaction. The server application then presents that data on electronic displays mounted on the wall or to client software at the desktop or both. The displays may be scoreboard-like displays or television sets. The wallboard output gives call center managers and agents the feedback they need to make real-time decisions: Should I go on break? Should I have additional people log in? Is now a good time to start a training session? Do we need to adjust routing paths or skills assignments? Wallboard systems software also lets you input other messages, such as announcements, status or even birthday greetings. In Chapters 6 and 7, we'll show how much of this type of information is now being delivered to the desktop via CTI or CRM software.

Workforce Management Systems

Workforce management is one of the most critical call center needs: Have the right number of people in place at the right times to handle the workload. At the start of Chapter 3, we talked about the challenge of random call arrivals and random agent availability. Forecasting and staffing are critical because the vast majority of costs to run a call center (60 percent to 75 percent) are labor costs. If you are routinely overstaffed, you will run a very expensive center. If you are routinely understaffed, service will suffer and customers won't be happy. The long-term results of either situation can be disastrous.

Remember that planning call center staff levels should be based on Erlang models. The output of Erlang models shows the number of staff needed to handle a given workload (based on call volume and handle time) at a target service level.

The first step in workforce management is understanding the basic mathematics of call center dynamics, such as the pooling principle, the cost of being short-staffed or how quickly removing a few people from taking calls can kill your service level. (If you need help educating your staff on the mathematics behind call center dynamics, get a basic Erlang calculator like QueueView from ICMI, www.incoming.com, or from Erlang.com and run some models to demonstrate.)

Once the foundation of understanding call center staffing dynamics is secured, you can proceed to figure out what type of workforce management tool is appropriate to address the forecasting and staffing needs in your center. The challenge is that full-blown workforce management systems can cost $50,000 or more. Not every center can afford that, and some may not need the sophisticated functionality these systems provide. So first, let's look at the options and then consider what that $50k will buy you.

Basic and Advanced WFMS Tools

Table 5-3 shows two levels of workforce planning applications. Naturally, the capabilities, sophistication and cost are much greater with the advanced tools.

Table 5-3: Contrasting Basic and Advanced Workforce Management Tools

Approach	Basic Workforce Tools	Advanced Tools
Features	• Erlang modeling of staff levels across daily patterns for a given call load and pattern • Nonskilled environments • Rostering to boost staff based on time lost to nonphone activities • Manual data loading • Perhaps manual scheduling using wizard, codes, tables	• Forecast call loads and patterns based on historical data • Erlang modeling of staff levels across daily patterns • Multiskilled environments • Schedule staff shifts, breaks, lunches, other activities • Track and report results compared to predictions, and adherence to schedules • Direct data feed from ACD reports • Optional capabilities, such as handling multimedia, holiday/vacation schedules, direct CSR access, integration with payroll

Approach	Basic Workforce Tools	Advanced Tools
Pros	• Low cost • Easy to use • Models staffing levels needed	• Robust functionality • Modular – can buy more advanced capabilities as needed • Scalable • Automatic data feed
Cons	• No or limited scheduling; must be done manually • Manual data load or transfer	• High cost • Can be complex to use (require resources and time to use well)
Where and When Used	• Want to do true forecasting • Small (25 or less) to medium-size (25-50) call centers • Limited variability in schedules: limited hours (for example 8-5, Monday through Friday), fixed shifts, or little scheduling flexibility • Call volumes are not highly variable or peaked • Little off-phone time needs to be scheduled (such as training, meetings, or other activities)	• Need true resource management • Medium to large centers (25-50 seats and more) • Dynamic staffing needs: extended hours, diverse shifts, scheduling flexibility • Dynamic call volumes: peak traffic, seasonal volumes • Off-phone tasks such as training, meetings, mail processing, etc., need to be scheduled
Example	• Hills Turbo Tables • ICMI • PRM • Portage	• Aspect (formerly TCS) • Blue Pumpkin • GMT • IEX
Cost	• Up to $15,000	• $20,000 to $25,000 for more basic systems (no skills, single site, etc.) • $50,000 and up (depending on features, size, number of sites) for full-function systems

Low-Cost Forecasting and Scheduling

There are well-managed centers that don't spend thousands of dollars on WFMS. We know of one that handles consumer product questions. This center uses a basic Erlang calculator that costs $50 and a scheduling application based on an Excel spreadsheet that costs $75. It is a small center – their volume is fairly stable and predictable (no seasonal peaks, for example), and schedules don't change much. But the tools do the trick for them. It's a better WFM story than many we've seen where $100,000 systems sit idle or use only a subset of the capabilities because no one knows how to use them.

Figure 5-5 shows the functions of a full WFMS: forecasting, staff modeling, scheduling, tracking and reporting. Two types of inputs are critical to a WFMS: data fed directly from the ACD application (and other media if appropriate), and data entered about the call center operation (growth, shrinkage, shifts, etc.). The outputs include forecasts, rostered staff needs, schedules and reports.

A key item to highlight is the "shrinkage" factors that are input. Shrinkage accounts for time lost to nonphone activities, such as breaks, lunch, training, sick time, vacations and holidays. Shrinkage is a very important element of scheduling, as it can significantly sway the staffing and performance numbers (it is often 30 percent or more).

The output of the WFMS is detailed schedules for each individual, showing when they should work, take breaks and lunch, go to training or meetings, and fit in other nonphone time activities. Other outputs include reports that show true performance against projections, and potential reasons for differences, such as under- or overstaffing compared to the forecast.

Figure 5-5: WFMS Functions

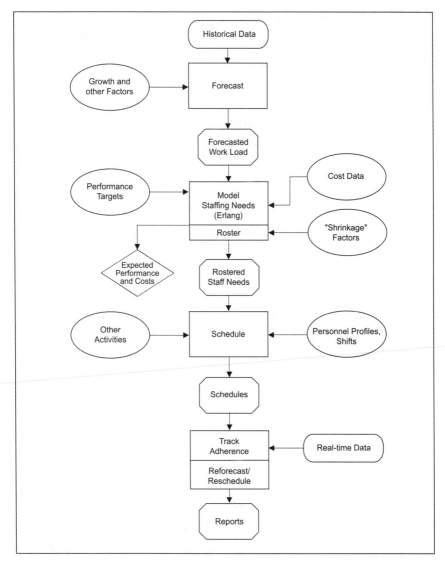

Key WFMS Features and Functions

What should you look for in a WFMS? Following are a few key considerations of the capabilities that differentiate one system from another:

• **Architecture.** Most WFMS today are client/server using a Windows interface.

Many are moving to browser interfaces in an intranet or Internet environment.

• **Erlang model.** While all WFMS use Erlang equations, most modify it to some degree to adjust for the imperfections of Erlang applied to call centers. Erlang tends to overstaff, because it assumes no caller abandons and no blocked calls. Clearly, both of these events occur in most call centers. So the vendors have modifications to Erlang that result in a more accurate prediction of staff levels needed to handle the offered call volume.

• **Skills simulation.** Erlang models have no provision for skills-based routing. They assume a given resource is dedicated to a given function. Skills preclude that; any individual may be available for multiple functions at any given time or unavailable for one function while occupied with another. So forecasting and scheduling in a skills-based routing environment is more difficult. More advanced systems or software options use simulation capabilities to approximate the skills environment.

• **Reports.** Like ACD reports, WFMS reports can be highly flexible. Graphical interfaces and graphical depictions of performance are common.

• **User access.** Some systems today use distributed functionality to enable users to input data and access schedules and reports. There might be full user access for an administrator and controlled access for supervisors and agents.

• **Multisite support.** WFMS can support multisite scheduling for a virtual call center. The forecasting and scheduling functions may be centralized or distributed. You need to determine what operational model will fit, and then find the tool that provides the capabilities you need. Many centers like to forecast and project staffing levels from a central location and conduct the scheduling at a local level. Scheduling is often viewed as a more personal issue, as it often involves people's family needs or other special situations.

• **Optional features.** There are many optional features available on WFMS (which likely add to the cost), such as a direct feed to a payroll system, cost accounting, scenario planning, vacation scheduling, and room and seat assignments for centers with shared desks.

Data is the basis on which all this forecasting and staffing and scheduling takes place. Good data needs to go in, so good data can come out (a more positive view of "garbage in, garbage out"!). This includes data about the staff and their needs (shifts, priorities, skills, etc.) and exceptions, so that when staffing is not as forecasted, the deviations are noted. It includes performance targets and can include cost data, if you want to do some cost-tradeoff modeling. It also includes the data automatically fed from the ACD reporting tool.

Recall that in Chapter 3 we highlighted the ripple effect of not using login/logout and work states effectively and consistently. Here is where it really impacts – misusing work states at an agent desktop hits a technology three steps away (see Figure 5-6). The result could be bad data on which to forecast and determine staffing needs.

Figure 5-6: WFMS Data Flow

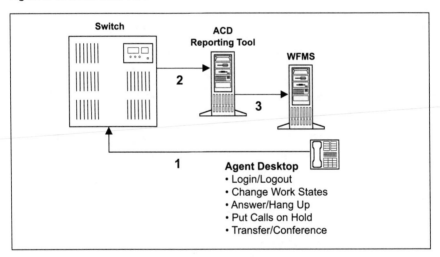

The main users of WFMS are generally technical analysts or other support resources within the call center. Supervisors might also use the system to review schedules and performance against forecasts. In larger centers, it's not uncommon to have multiple people dedicated to managing the WFMS.

Workforce management systems are notoriously underutilized and are famous (or infamous) for turning call center staff into its slaves. Recent improvements in ease of use and function distribution address these issues head on.

Today's systems allow agents to complete some of the data "baby-sitting" tasks.

An intranet- or Internet-based system with browser interfaces and secure permission control can enable each agent to input his or her own requests for time off, check to see if the request went through, view his or her schedule, and even swap shifts with colleagues under approved skill rules. This feature is an excellent example of technology improvements that leverage new architectures, empower the workforce and directly address the pain points of using the tools.

Skills and Multimedia Implications

The Erlang models that are the basis for workforce management tools were designed more than 80 years ago – a time when skills-based routing and multimedia contact centers were not even a glimmer on the horizon. So as we tackle the realities of call center operations today, there is an impact on the essential tools for workforce management.

Most vendors offer a simulation tool for skills environments. These simulators make it possible to forecast volumes and staff needs, and schedule resources in a multiskilled environment. However, it comes at a cost – additional software, greater complexity and more time required to manage and use the system. Most WFMS applications users in skills-based routing environments can attest to the additional burden it puts on them; fine-tuning the simulations to get the most accurate forecasts and schedules takes extra time.

Multimedia adds yet another layer of complexity to this challenge. Media can be thought of as additional skills. For instance, a multimedia agent may have skills for handling phone calls, email and text-chat.

But there are additional challenges. First is the challenge of getting the data feed. The WFMS vendors have partnered with switch vendors – or, at least, they've worked through the challenges of interfacing to the top vendors to get the data they need. Now they must do that with another set of vendors for email systems, text-chat, Web calls or the full multimedia suite (through CTI, CRM or other tools).

The second challenge is defining the real handle time for these alternate media. Because they are more prone to interruptions or multitasking, it is harder to define the true handle time from the raw data. In addition, the statistical behavior of email and text-chat is not yet known (voice call behavior has been studied extensively so it is more predictable).

A third challenge is modeling for multimedia and determining staff levels necessary to meet a totally different set of performance criteria. The "service level" – or response-time commitment – of an email may be 100 percent answered in 24 hours. Erlang models don't work with those kinds of numbers. A text-chat may require multiple interactions, and a text-chat agent may also be handling multiple chats. Erlang equations don't apply in these cases. So the vendors have created (and are still creating) new interfaces and new simulators for these media differences.

The reality today is that all of the problems have not been solved. But that's OK; the WFMS vendors will address these needs. The bottom line is, if you need skills and multimedia capabilities in your call center and you are looking for a workforce management system, you need to dig into these features very carefully. Try to get beyond the marketing hype to the true capabilities. Talk to references and find out what the reality will be in scheduling for this multifaceted contact center environment.

Simulation Tools

Many people confuse simulation tools with workforce management. While they have similarities, they are used to tackle different problems. Workforce management systems forecast workloads, project staff levels and generate schedules. Simulation tools are used to evaluate performance levels under different conditions, model the costs of alternatives, assess alternative configurations or new technology impacts, and conduct sensitivity analysis to determine where to dig further or identify vulnerabilities.

Figure 5-7 shows the basic structure of a simulation tool: agent parameters, configuration data, work volume and call flows are input, then the simulation tool provides anticipated performance levels and other outputs.

Figure 5-7: Simulation Tools

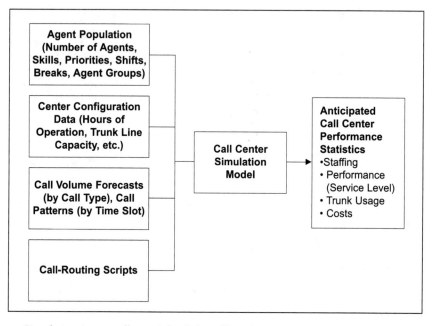

Simulation is generally used for "what-if" analyses, such as:

- What if we change our skills assignments?
- What if we increase or decrease staff levels?
- What if we add self-service options like IVR and the Web?
- What if we run our three sites as one virtual center?
- What if we start handling email and text-chat within our call center?
- What if we alter the prompts to further segment calls and reduce transfers?
- What if we increase the trunks into the center by 24, reducing busies in the network but increasing queue lengths?

For example, we ran several simulations for a call center that was considering a major organizational change while moving to multimedia. The simulations assessed expected performance levels under different staff configurations and contact distributions. It looked at the impact of segmenting by media (voice and email) and by contact type (service, sales). From these simulations, the client could see the expected performance levels and costs of the different scenarios – prior to making technology investments and process changes.

Simulation is also used to pinpoint and resolve problems through "what-if" analysis. For example, if there are a lot of calls overflowing out of the target group into a backup group, the situation can be simulated to see when and why calls are overflowing. Then alternative configurations of staffing or skill levels can be run, perhaps followed by changes to the routing decision tree. The end result: The company can see if overflows can be reduced while still meeting service level and find a solution that works without trial-and-error in the production environment.

How Simulation Is Used

Simulation is used to find answers to more complex questions – those for which analytical modeling capabilities like those provided by a WFMS are not adequate. Simulation models will show the expected performance for an altered configuration or call flow without having to put it into production to find out what happens. This allows centers to determine the best approach and then implement it, reducing risk to operating costs or customer experience.

Call centers with considerable changes, large centers and centers that prefer careful planning over the "just do it" (and hope for the best) approach will find simulation tools highly valuable. And as the previously mentioned "what-if" examples reveal, simulation can be a highly valuable tool for advanced multiskill or multimedia environments.

Simulation is a software-only technology. It is purchased as a standalone tool or, in some cases, comes as a part of the ACD routing software (such as with a Rockwell ACD or Siemens ResumeRouting). Generally, it requires manual data input, although you may be able to export data into a file to import into the simulation tool database.

Warning, Warning!

In our consulting work, we often see underutilized management tools. Organizations are wildly enthusiastic when they purchase them, but then they don't allocate adequate time, personnel and training to use the tools effectively. Or sometimes the person using the tools is promoted or leaves the company, and the tools gather dust. Nobody backfills the position, or if the position is filled, there is no budget to train the new user. Worst case: They bought the technology because it was cool, not because they defined their business needs and goals.

Don't let this happen to you!

- Commit management and staff time to applying the tool.
- Have a plan for staff succession (hint: career path!).
- Budget for training classes.
- Be sure that the technology has a context (strategy, business requirements and process).

Logging and Quality Monitoring Systems

Logging and Quality Monitoring (QM) are related technologies – they both seek to record an event so that it can be played back. They mostly leverage the same basic infrastructure, but they fulfill different business needs.

Logging is used when every call (or contact) needs to be recorded because of risk, liability or government regulations. The recordings are used to verify transactions or to provide proof of a request or agreement. We worked with one financial institution that claims this technology saves them more than $5 million per year in transaction disputes. The recordings must be archived and held for extended periods of time (such as seven years for some financial or insurance transactions), so the recording media is important.

Generally, today only the voice conversation is recorded (not the data screens). In a multimedia contact center, text-chat or email interactions may be recorded, as well. The ability to search for and find a particular contact is key – so the database, call "tags" and retrieval functions are important.

Logging is most commonly found in industries like emergency services, financial services (especially stock and mutual fund trades), insurance and utilities. The business case for logging is generally purely based on risk – the "what-if" of not having recorded conversations as evidence.

Quality monitoring is used to evaluate a sampling of contacts for quality assurance and agent feedback. Random, scheduled, sampled or on-demand conversation recordings make up the base of contacts for quality evaluation. Systems today generally record both the voice and data screens associated with a phone conversation or the data screens accessed during a text-chat or other Web interaction. Archiving is not important; scoring and feedback tools are key (see the item on QM process on page 151).

Quality monitoring tools are used in a wide variety of industries – basically anywhere that people are very focused on customer service and quality. Full-featured systems are rarely used in small centers (fewer than 25 seats), as QM systems are somewhat costly ($50,000 to $100,000 and more).

Quality monitoring is one of the more difficult technologies to build a business case for – at least from a dollar-savings perspective. Companies can justify a QM system on other returns, such as savings compared to manual call observation or recording; improvements to call flows, work flows, systems and applications; and shortened handle times because of training or other action plans that result from quality reviews. The soft benefits include a greater sense of "fairness" among agents due to random call recording, scoring calibration, and better training and feedback since agents can listen to "good" and "bad" calls.

Many QM systems are purchased primarily on the belief that it is essential to assuring customer-focused, quality service. Some organizations are starting to use QM system recordings as feedback for non-call center functions. For example, product managers may use help desk recordings as input for new product functionality, to clarify documentation and improve product quality; marketing managers can review sales recordings for key message development.

It's the Law

Many state laws require notification of call observing or recording. When calling organizations in these states, you may often hear the statement: "Your call may be recorded or monitored for quality purposes." Some states require notification of one party, some require that both parties be made aware. Check with your legal counsel before proceeding.

Figure 5-8: Recording System Architecture

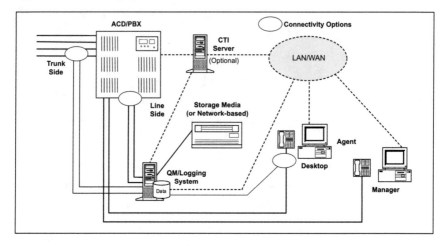

Recording System Architecture

There are four key elements to a recording system:

1. Voice connectivity. There are numerous options for connecting to the voice system to record conversations. The connectivity for a system that is being used to log every call differs from one that is used only for quality monitoring.

For *logging*, there are three options. "Line side" connectivity is the most common. It most easily enables the capture of key data associated with a call. "Trunk side" is used when there are frequently multiple segments to calls (such as IVR conversation, agent conversation and even a transfer to another agent). "Desktop" connectivity is rare today, but may still be used on some older systems. Further considerations include:

• Line side uses connectivity at the line between the switch and the telephone (one connection per agent position). The connectivity is most often in a wiring closet on the floor leading out to the phones. Analog and digital options can be used; a conversion may be required for digital connections as they are proprietary to each voice switch vendor.

• Trunk side uses connectivity where the trunks from the network connect with the switch. Thus, they connect at the demarcation point with the network provider or a wiring rack. The interfaces connect to standard T1 trunks or analog trunks.

Trunk side records only external calls (internal station-to-station calls will not be recorded).

• Desktop is connected to the handset cord or an adapter on the phone. While it is low-cost, it can be readily disconnected by the agent (for a personal call, for example), so with this option you run the risk of not being connected when needed.

For *quality monitoring*, the systems generally take advantage of "service observe" or other features of the phone system. Service observe is an ACD software feature that lets a supervisor port listen in on an agent conversation. By leveraging this feature, a recording system captures a sampling of calls across the center. The QM system software enters the service observation code to trigger the service observation. Thus, the system connects via a set of voice switch ports that are configured as supervisor positions. Some combined logging/QM systems record all calls, and then select a sampling of those recorded calls for monitoring.

2. **Storage media.** Calls are recorded to a storage device. They are initially written to a hard drive. Especially in logging, the calls may then need to be archived to a long-term storage device.

"This séance may be monitored and recorded for quality-control purposes."

There are many options – hard drives, digital random-access storage, digital tapes. Some solutions offer "open storage," which basically allows the center to use whatever storage device it prefers. Under this model, the logging system vendor might not even offer the storage system; rather, they would specify the output and leave it up to the customer to purchase, implement and integrate the storage media of their choice (for example, server farms, optical jukeboxes and storage networks).

The type of storage used can dramatically impact the cost of a logging system. Low-tech approaches, such as Digital Audio Tape (DAT), are a fraction of the cost of the more advanced digital random-access approaches, such as magneto optical. But with lower-cost media, there are corresponding tradeoffs – for instance, accessing specific recordings is not as easy and it may be less reliable.

3. Database. The database captures contact information about the recordings. The data includes information about the contact, such as date, time, connection information (extension, login of agent) and contact information (ANI and DNIS). This information can be used to search for a particular contact. In this case, more data is better! In a QM system, the database also includes all of the scores and notes for reviewed calls, as well as report data for trending and evaluation.

4. CTI. CTI plays a role in many logging and quality monitoring environments. It is used to help gather data associated with a call, such as ANI, DNIS, extension, login and even customer identifiers (account number).

Quality monitoring system vendors are embracing CRM principles, and CTI is one of the enabling technologies to trigger recordings based on values from the agent desktop business application (for example, record 100 percent of "platinum" customer interactions, record all interactions where there is a cross-sell or upsell opportunity). This data is written to the database to aid in search and retrieval of records, as well as associate caller account information with a conversation. CTI is also used to trigger data screen capture.

Beyond these elements, a logging or QM system is a combination of proprietary hardware and software. The hardware includes a server, the cards to interface with the switch and the interface to the LAN for user access. The software includes the applications for accessing calls, scoring and other activities. Table 5-4 covers key functions to help you in defining requirements and evaluating solutions.

Table 5-4: Logging and Quality Monitoring Tool Functions

Function	Logging	Quality Monitoring
Recording interface	• Line side or trunk side (or in rare cases, desktop) • Digital-to-analog conversion necessary?	• Voice switch station ports enabled with service observing

Recording media	• Hard drive for short term
	• Archiving:
	  - Tape (Digital Audio Tape)
	  - Random access digital storage (e.g., hard drive, CD, DVD, ZIP/JAZ, Optical)
	  - Open, network-based
	  - Network-based server store
	  - Centralized storage with remote access for multisite environments
		• Hard drive, generally
		• Centralized storage with remote access for multisite environments
		• (May use archiving if tied to a logging system)

Recording features	• Compression of recording • Triggers for recording (such as DNIS, routing path)	• Scheduled, on-demand, random recording • Sample from logged calls • API for triggering recordings based on business application events and attributes
Searching tools	• Indexing (e.g., ANI, DNIS, login, extension, date, time, caller, ID, length of call, etc.) • Interface (graphical tool for search)	• Interface (graphical tool for search)
Playback capabilities	• Telephone • LAN	• Telephone • LAN • Supervisor and agent functions for review and commentary
Scalability	• Need one port per recorded line or trunk • Scale for center growth or additional sites	• Based on ratio of ports to agents, or estimates based on call volume recorded and stored (Erlang B) • Scale for center growth or additional sites
Redundancy	• Mirrored disks/drives • Hot standby • Power supplies and fans	• Generally not a requirement
CTI-integration	• For capture of data associated with the call (such as ANI, extension, caller identification)	• For capture of data associated with the call (such as ANI, extension, caller identification, business variable) • "Screen Capture" (for coordinated voice and data screen recording) • Trigger recording start/stop

continued on next page

Function	Logging	Quality Monitoring
Database	• For call data	• For call data • For quality scores
Scoring tools/ reporting tools	• Reports on numbers of calls logged	• Customizable scorecards with notation capabilities • Reports on calls reviewed and scored • Customization of scorecards and reports • Trending of scores • Calibration of scorers
Multimedia	• Logging may apply to calls, emails, text-chat, IP calls • Database should allow searching for all contacts with a given ID or other characteristic	• Recording for QM may apply to calls, emails, text-chat, IP calls • Scoring tools must be customized to the particular media
Other	• N/A	• Tie into training systems, coaching tools and HR systems

Screen capture is one of the more popular options in quality monitoring and recording. The ability for a supervisor to observe a screen while reviewing a call can significantly enhance the quality process, and provide important input to necessary improvements in training, processes or technology applications.

However, screen capture adds a bit of complexity to the implementation of the system. It requires CTI, client software at each desktop and a software module on the server for data capture.

Screen capture systems should send only the changes in activity on the screen (not the entire screen repeatedly) to minimize LAN traffic and storage requirements. Desktop software from QM vendors, or even third parties, can also be used for real-time viewing of screen activity while conducting a live service observation.

Multimedia and VoIP Implications for Logging and QM

As with workforce management, the trend toward multimedia contact centers has a significant impact on logging and quality monitoring tools. Logging and QM vendors have well-developed voice switch and CTI interfaces, but now need to interface with a different set of tools and vendors. Or, in some cases, they may use recordings already created within a tool, such as an email system.

Further, the applications must enable a coordinated logging or QM database, while also accommodating the very unique characteristics of each media. For example, quality scores for email or text-chat must consider typing and writing skills. If an agent is handling multiple text-chats, they must be recorded or scored as separate events. Logging and QM vendors are tackling all of these new challenges as they evolve to support a multimedia contact center.

Quality monitoring systems must be IP-enabled to record VoIP streaming voice packets. IP-based QM systems must be able to "sniff" packets passively on a network (in a manner similar to network diagnostic tools), or be compatible with the signaling standard of your VoIP solutions (e.g., H.323, SIP). Ethernet interfaces replace the TDM interfaces on the recording units. VoIP QM still needs to be integrated with CTI to enable recording triggers, reporting and search functions.

Quality Monitoring Tools Need a Good Management Process

Quality monitoring tools are the type of technology that cries out for a good management process. Without a good process, the tool is of little value. Quality monitoring can be done without fancy tools, so a small center or one without the budget for a QM system can, and should, still conduct quality monitoring. Either way, the process is more important than the technology.

Here are our recommendations for a good QM process:

- Define the number of calls (or contacts) monitored per week or month.
- Have a clearly defined scorecard that is objective. Hint: Remove subjectivity and the personality and biases of the scoring person through calibration and by using scores that are binary (yes-or-no or not applicable) or use a very small scale (1-4); a "no" or low score should require a comment or explanation – after all, it's an opportunity for improvement.
- Involve agents in developing the scorecard.
- Maintain a consistent schedule of monitoring and feedback.
- Provide feedback so that agents can create personal action plans for improvement in collaboration with their coach or the quality assurance staff.
- Look at overall operations to identify process improvements, system changes, training needs or other actions that can benefit the entire center.

Employee and Customer Satisfaction Measurement Tools

Tools for measuring customer satisfaction and employee satisfaction should be included as part of an overall performance management strategy. Regardless of size or type of center, satisfaction measurements complete the picture of reporting and management of the center.

Probably the most intriguing technology area here is the ability to leverage the Internet or an intranet for gathering data on customer or employee satisfaction. Email or Web-based forms can be an excellent way to gather information from a customer who has recently interacted with the center. Their interaction is fresh, the feedback can be provided quickly with a few mouse clicks and it is a nonintrusive way to seek their feedback. The Web-based form is superior in that the data can be fed directly into a database for rapid analysis. Even if an email is sent out, it can provide a link to a Web form.

Another technology worth mentioning is an IVR-based survey that a customer participates in at the call's conclusion. When the customer calls the center, they may first go through a menu where they're asked if they would be willing to participate in a satisfaction survey after the call. The IVR port then is conferenced on the call until completion, waiting for the disconnect by the agent. Or the call can be CTI-controlled and be routed to an IVR port upon agent disconnect. Alternatively, an agent could transfer a customer into the system to fill out the survey.

While tools like this are attractive for the immediate feedback they can gather from a customer, the outcomes can be biased toward "good" calls if agents manipulate the system. Ideally, they are tied in with quality monitoring recordings and scores, as well.

Of course there are also good, old-fashioned, low-tech methods of measuring satisfaction. For customers, this includes mailings, phone calls or focus groups; for agents, it could be a form to fill out or interviews. Any approach might be made more valuable and unbiased by using an independent third party that specializes in satisfaction surveys and analysis.

Training and Coaching Tools

With the growth of Internet architectures combined with developing business needs and the focus on people development, a new set of capabilities has emerged: Internet-enabled online training and coaching tools. These products take data about agent performance and create focused training and coaching related to specific needs identified for the individuals or the team. Data (from QM, ACD reports, etc.) is fed in and analyzed, then personalized training is delivered to the desktop. The agent uses a browser to access this information during scheduled training time or perhaps when there is a lull in inbound call volume.

Points to Remember

- The "elevator story" of how the call center is doing is changing. Phone statistics, like service level and talk time, are no longer adequate. Cost per contact, resolution rate, sales revenue, customer defection rate, quality and satisfaction ratings all help to define call center success as the center gains visibility with senior management.

- As the tools for reporting and management in the call center evolve, the user also changes. The operation needs to work with business analysts or others to assess performance – and the audience is expanding to include everyone from the agent to the CEO.

- Workforce management tools are critical for accurately forecasting and staffing to optimize performance and resource utilization.

- Simulation tools can help with "what-if" analysis.

- Quality monitoring tools are used in environments with a major customer focus. Logging tools are used where there is risk exposure, liability concerns or government regulation.

- Other performance and management tools can help to optimize a call center, including wallboards, training and coaching tools, and employee or customer satisfaction surveys.

Actions to Take

• Define your new elevator story. Develop a reporting strategy that is tied to business goals to help you sort through the plethora of tools and determine what you need and how to use the information available.

Part 3: Data and Business Applications

There are two sides to the call center equation: voice and data. And there are two acronyms that every call center professional wants to understand (and many want to buy): CTI and CRM. You can harness the power of these capabilities by applying them effectively and integrating them well with your voice and data environment. Maximize their potential by finding their place within your business and call center strategies.

Chapter 6: CTI: Screen Pops and So Much More

Chapter 7: Information and Applications Bring CRM Strategies to Life

Chapter 6:

CTI: Screen Pops and So Much More

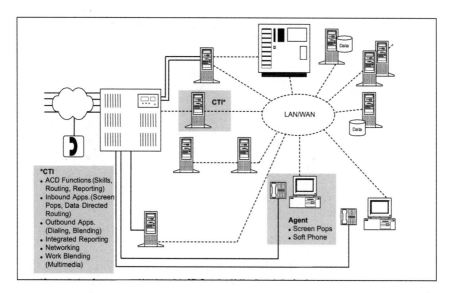

Key Points Discussed in this Chapter:

CTI-Enabled Applications

Inbound and Outbound Applications

CTI Benefits

CTI Architectures

Diverse Switch Environments

Call Flow

"Smart" CTI

CTI Challenges

Key Design Decisions

Quick – what does the term Computer Telephony Integration (CTI) bring to mind? For most people, the answer is "screen pops." Well, yes, CTI allows you to do screen pops – but it can do so much more. CTI is at the pivotal crossroads of key infrastructure decisions and planning for a multimedia contact center environment. In this chapter, we'll show how this robust and complex technology can enable your call center to deliver solid benefits to your customers, operations and your bottom line.

CTI is the integration of the telephone system with the data environment – agent desktop, databases and business applications. CTI leverages customer-centric information to route calls and automates outbound calling for great efficiency gains. It can extend to multimedia routing and queuing, and even VoIP. It integrates with other elements, as well, such as IVR and CRM. And it provides the foundation for multisource integrated reporting. You should think of CTI as an "enabling" technology (you may even hear people refer to it as "plumbing") that supports many applications.

CTI has two fundamental elements:

1. Message exchange. CTI uses links between the phone system and the CTI server to pass messages. It also uses messaging between the CTI server and various other systems, including IVRs, desktops, mainframe or server applications, databases, other media servers, and even workforce management or quality monitoring systems. CTI does two key things with these messages – it monitors and controls. A CTI application monitors the activity around it, requesting and receiving event messages and status from various systems and endpoints. CTI can take control by issuing commands. It might control a call, an agent work state, or an email, text-chat or Web call.

2. Application logic. CTI is more than just the links and messages. The technology must be applied to achieve its value. CTI application logic makes business decisions – which means that someone must decide which screens pop when, what the screens look like, what data is considered in a routing decision and how that decision is made, what data must be collected in report databases, and which outbound calls should be launched and when. These decisions are developed in CTI applications.

CTI also includes integration – the "I" is in "CTI" for a reason. We previously offered an analogy of call centers and snowflakes – because each is unique in its configuration. That is also what makes CTI interesting and often challenging to implement – every call center has different integration elements and issues.

CTI-Enabled Applications

CTI enables a variety of applications through message exchange, application logic and integration. The following list makes it clear that CTI offers much more than screen pops, and it emphasizes the importance of implementing CTI within an overall business, call center and technology strategy. Your strategy must address whether you are automating or transforming, handling inbound and/or outbound contacts and focusing only on voice calls or integrating other media. In addition, it needs to address your application infrastructure – for instance, how much "smarts" you're putting into CTI as opposed to other systems like the voice switch.

Inbound Applications

• **Coordinated voice/data (a.k.a. "screen pop").** CTI can simultaneously deliver the voice call and data screen to a desktop. This can be done on a direct call delivery, transfer or conference, and in both single-site and multisite environments. Often calls are transferred from the IVR, and the data gathered there (e.g., account number) is used in the screen pop. This CTI function can also enable capturing data screens along with voice for monitoring and recording. Screen pops can shave time off of calls and, therefore, save money.

• **Routing.** As we described in Chapters 2 and 4, CTI can be used for core routing capabilities like conditional and skills routing. In this case, the routing logic basically moves out of the switch and onto the CTI server. The CTI application manages all of the agent work states and skills, queues, call treatment, agent selection and call selection.

Another CTI routing option augments the voice-switch routing capabilities by using customer information. This application is often referred to as "data-directed" routing. It accesses an external database for information, such as customer status (open trouble ticket, overdue shipment, 30 days outstanding) or customer business value (premier customer, to whom they last spoke, what language they speak), and then points the call to the best resource for that customer's needs.

CTI can also be used for multisite routing, enabling a virtual network with pre-arrival routing or post-arrival routing (see Chapter 4).

• **Integrated reporting.** In Chapter 5, we presented the new "elevator story" for call center performance. Because CTI is connected through its monitoring and message exchanges, and creates a unique and ubiquitous contact identifier, it is a central point for data gathering and therefore reporting. It can provide "cradle-to-grave" reports on a call as it moves through the contact center, including: What happened in the voice switch? IVR? Business application? Quality monitoring evaluation result? Customer satisfaction survey? It can tie business outcomes to contacts, regardless of media, to show what's working and what isn't. CTI links productivity measures like talk time to business results like sales revenue and trouble-ticket closure, which helps to define the new business-oriented elevator story.

• **Desktop softphone.** CTI can move the telephone functions to the PC. Login/logout, telephone keypad (for dialing), work state control, hold, conference, transfer, status indicators, telephone directories, availability, current statistics and reports all can be placed in a graphical user interface on the PC. The softphone can either be a separate application window or it can be embedded into a toolbar in a desktop application. The advantage of softphone is the agent's attention stays 100 percent focused on the device where the customer and business information resides – no more back and forth between the PC keyboard and the telephone keypad.

• **Web and multimedia integration.** Today, CTI can be a multimedia routing, management and reporting engine. In Chapter 9, we'll discuss various ways you can Web-enable the contact center – email, text-chat, Web calls, collaboration. A CTI solution can be the platform for delivering these functions (it can also be done through standalone or pure Web capabilities, but more on that later). CTI can also combine various media into a common queue for routing and delivery to the properly "skilled" agents.

CTI Integration with Other Applications

CTI can integrate with other applications in the call center besides the voice switch and the business applications:

- **Interactive voice response:** to use the information customers enter into the IVR and to provide information to the IVR for caller or application identification.
- **Workforce management systems:** to pass the historical reporting data for forecasting and scheduling and to pass real-time data for tracking adherence.
- **Quality monitoring and logging tools:** to capture additional data about the call, such as account number, agent ID or extension, to enable easy call retrieval.
- **Online training:** to monitor queue status or agent availability and provide real-time training updates during lulls in call volume.

Outbound Applications

Outbound dialing is another key application CTI can enable. And it's not just for telemarketing and collections. Contact centers that place new customer "welcome calls," or those that encourage proactive or follow-up contact with existing customers should consider outbound applications when implementing CTI.

- **Directory dialing.** Directory dialing allows automated calling from a list that resides in a local or centralized database. For example, a utility call center agent could pull up a list of all customers who started service in the previous month, select a name, click "dial" and the system would automatically dial the number.

- **Preview dialing.** Preview dialing automatically provides a screen to an agent to allow him or her to "preview" customer information before launching the call. The agent views the information and the call is dialed either after a set amount of time or when the agent triggers it by clicking a button or icon, or pressing a function key.

In preview-dialing applications, the agent generally listens when the call is dialed and performs the "call classification," which indicates the outcome of the call: busy, ring/no answer, network intercept, answering machine or live answer. The agent enters the classification into a data field associated with the contact so that it can be redialed later, if necessary. Preview dialing is a great fit when there are callbacks or other situations for which the agent needs time to review past contact notes or customer profile information.

• **Predictive dialing.** These are the calls most of us get at dinner time. After you say "hello" two or three times, someone comes on the line and mispronounces your name. The system has predictively dialed a number of calls greater than the number of agents. The predictive dialing application then listens to the outcomes. It automatically classifies the calls – busy, no answer, even answering machines – and delivers only the live ones to available agents.

The algorithms for predictive dialing are quite sophisticated, using historical data on connect rates, talk times and agent availability to try to match live calls with available agents. If it's done well, the customer hardly notices; if it's done poorly (or cheaply), the customer ends up waiting for an agent. The user of a predictive dialer sets a pacing algorithm for how aggressive they want to be in dialing calls and minimizing agent idle time. As a rough guideline, this application tends to be cost-justified with 12 or more full-time outbound agents. Predictive dialing can have tremendous ROI in the right environment.

• **Power or progressive dialing.** Power or progressive dialing is a variation on predictive dialing, with varying definitions from vendor to vendor. Generally, with power or progressive dialing, calls are not launched until an agent is available – so they predict customer availability, but not agent availability.

• **Call blending.** CTI has monitoring and control capabilities – call blending is a great example of an application that leverages both. The idea behind call blending is to have agents handle both inbound and outbound calls, taking advantage of lulls in inbound call volume to make outbound calls. The CTI application monitors the inbound volume, agent staffing levels and performance. It takes control and assigns blended (or "swing") positions to outbound calls when the volume is low and performance is easily met. It continues to monitor the inbound side and reassigns agents to inbound call handling when the volume picks up.

If you'll recall from our previous Erlang C discussion, adding just a few agents makes a huge difference in performance (as measured by service level). Again, sophisticated algorithms come into play that balance the need to meet inbound service levels with the desire to make outbound volume commitments. Figure 6-1 illustrates the blending concept. This concept can also be applied to multimedia contact routing and management.

Figure 6-1: Call Blending

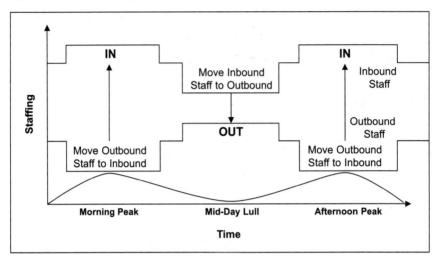

Outbound Dialing Campaigns

Outbound dialing requires a thorough process involving several technologies that define who to call, when to call and what happens if they aren't there, if the line is busy, etc. Figure 6-2 illustrates the process of list and campaign management. A list must be extracted from a database of whom to call (e.g., all customers who are more than 60 days past due, all customers whose warranties will expire in 30 days or less, all customers who just received their first bill). That list becomes part of a campaign. The campaign also defines parameters about the contacts, such as:

• Script – the key marketing or business message

• How many calls to attempt

• Hours to call

• How soon after a busy or ring/no answer to try again

• Outcomes to track

Generally, each campaign is defined in a software application. That application may be part of the CTI solution, the CRM solution or an in-house application. Campaign reports can be generated to show outcomes and measure success.

Figure 6-2: Outbound Call Management

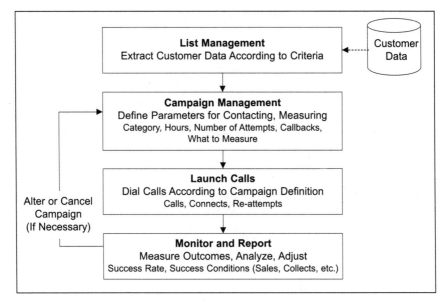

CTI Benefits

CTI has been around a long time... well, more than 15 years. Some thought it might fade into the background as other new hot technologies came onto the scene. Others predicted everyone would be using CTI by now. Many centers still have CTI on their "wish list" because they understand the benefits it can provide. Some companies are rolling out their second-generation CTI solution, taking advantage of the more robust interfaces and applications offered today. And others are implementing CTI as part of a bigger project involving customer relationship management or multimedia. CTI has longevity because it delivers benefits that call centers value, and its value is enhanced in today's CRM and multimedia environments.

A key reason so many people think about – and implement – CTI screen pops is for the efficiency benefit they deliver. Screen pops are a good automation application – automatically delivering the data screen associated with the caller when the call arrives. That saves seconds on every call with a database match. Hard-dollar paybacks in one to two years are common for screen pops in which the customer can be readily identified and matched in the database using phone numbers or a prompted identifier. But that's not the only benefit of CTI.

Building a CTI Screen Pop Business Case

Here are five steps to building a business case for CTI screen pops:

1. Look at how callers are identified and what the options are (ANI, prompt for account number or other identifier). Make sure the database records are there to match. Estimate how often you'll get the identifier and how often it will match.

2. Conduct time and motion studies to see how long it takes from call arrival until the customer screen is brought up on the PC. Figure out how much time you'll save on calls with screen pops and derive a new "handle time." (If you'll save time on data entry during wrap-up or other steps, note that as well.)

3. Run Erlang models for baseline staffing using current handle times. Then run the models using the projected new handle time applied to the percent of calls you project will match the identifier to the database.

4. The difference in staffing levels (Full-Time Equivalents or FTEs) can readily be translated into annual savings, assuming you've got a loaded cost per agent. Figure 6-3 shows an example where there is projected business growth (and corresponding agent staff increases). The difference in the baseline and the projected CTI scenario is noticeable. The beauty of FTE savings is that they are cumulative and significant. For example, saving six FTEs the first year and four more the second year results in a total savings of $560,000 in two years with a loaded agent cost of $35,000 (no net present value or other accounting methods applied).

5. Capture any critical success factors. For example: "We need to 'train' customers to use their account number to achieve the target hit rate" or "Marketing and other customer communications will promote our new service and stress the importance of knowing your account number."

When does screen pop offer a substantial payback? When you can get a high "hit rate" on customer identification, handle times are relatively short, call volumes are significant and the screen that's popped is a useful one on which the agent will stay for a while (i.e., they don't immediately move to another screen). Environ-ments like this routinely get a one- to two-year payback. Screen pop value is disappointing if your volume is low, you can't often get a match, the time saved doesn't make a dent in the long handle time or the agents still have to bounce around to 10 different screens to serve a customer. That's a situation ripe for transformation, not automation!

Figure 6-3: CTI Screen Pop FTE Savings

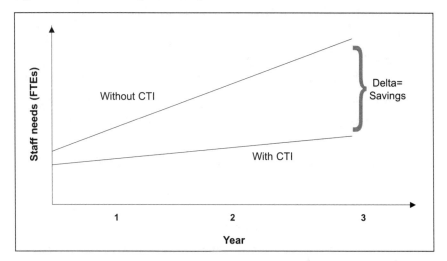

CTI can significantly improve the customer experience. Many companies implement CTI to keep up with or get ahead of the competition. A customer calling a CTI-enabled contact center has shorter waits, gets routed to the right person to handle the need, doesn't have to repeat information and gets more personalized service. That differentiates the company from others and improves the customer experience.

Other companies consider the ability to efficiently and effectively conduct outbound calling to be the greatest benefits of CTI. It significantly reduces cost over manual dialing and can generate more revenue through the additional contacts (e.g., in a telemarketing or collections environment). Outbound applications often achieve hundreds of percent return on investment.

A common CTI testimonial is: "We bought CTI for screen pops. But we really got value in the reporting capabilities." The benefits associated with more detailed and integrated reporting are hard to translate into a tangible business case. The reporting function is harder to implement and isn't nearly as sexy as screen pops (it doesn't show well!). But reporting is where your strategic initiatives will find support, because CTI-enabled systems can link the business outcome (sales made, service completed) with productivity measures (talk time and handle time). If you'll recall from Chapter 1, executives mostly care about the business impact of the call center activities.

A final consideration of CTI benefits is how it will fit with your other call center or business initiatives. CTI provides greater value when it is an enabler for "big picture" strategies in a truly transformational environment. For example, one call center that believed its project was CTI-focused, ended up implementing CTI-enabled CRM. They popped new screens that provided agents with the information they needed 80 percent of the time – all on the first screen. The information included customer profile and relationship information. The center gathered data through the application and leveraged the data in the CRM database to route calls differently. In this example, CTI enabled an enterprisewide customer segmentation strategy.

Companies that have had CTI on a budget "wish list" for years are finally implementing it as the enabler for voice and Web contacts. In this type of case, the CTI solution is the platform for a multimedia contact environment and the business case is truly transformational.

Who Uses CTI?

CTI has not penetrated the market at the rate analysts have projected. Some of the reasons include cost, complexity, cross-department coordination demands and competition for budget dollars. And further, some companies have not thought broadly enough about CTI application opportunities and, as a result, have trouble justifying it. Here are most likely industries and best scenarios in which you'll find CTI:

• **Financial services.** CTI probably has had its greatest success with banks, credit card companies, mutual fund and brokerage houses, and insurance companies. In these types of businesses, customers are well-trained to use account numbers to identify themselves, and often self-serve through an IVR. Therefore, it makes sense to take the next step to CTI. These are also highly competitive industries where service matters. Screen pops, data-directed routing, integrated reporting and outbound applications all fit.

• **High tech.** Many computer, software or other technology firms benefit from CTI. A customer with an outstanding trouble ticket can enter the number and be routed to an appropriate support agent who has knowledge of the situation (and may even be the last person the customer spoke to if he or she is available). Or the customer may be recognized and automatically routed to the properly skilled resources (without having to prompt the heck out of the poor customer).

• **Utilities and telecommunications.** Both utilities (gas, electric, water) and telecommunications companies (including wireless, cable, local and long-distance) can use phone numbers or train customers to identify themselves to use account information for routing, screen pops and other applications. Collections is a key part of the business so there are good outbound dialing opportunities, as well.

CTI is less prevalent in retail or catalog sales today, as many callers are not in the database or not readily recognized (because they're not accustomed to using an account or customer number and it's difficult to match ANI). The travel industry also has hurdles – traditionally, at the start of the call, they are less interested in who you are as an individual than where you want to go. As either of these types of businesses implement CRM strategies, they will benefit more from CTI ("synergy"!). Table 6-1 shows the contrast. The ties between CTI and CRM will be discussed further in the next chapter.

Table 6-1: An Example of Transformation with CTI-Enabled CRM

Without CTI	With CTI-Enabled CRM
1. What: The travel agent, airline or hotel wants to know your travel plans, check availability and find a price. 2. Who: Then, if there is a fit, they'll find out who you are and book it.	1. Who: The travel company wants to know who you are up front so they can see if you're a top traveler. 2. What: Then they route you to the appropriate group or individual, and pop a screen (CTI) with your customer profile, segmentation and scripts for relationship development or upselling (CRM).

CTI Architectures

It's important to be aware of how CTI works so that you can understand and appreciate the complexity and cost that goes with implementing it. CTI enables the exchange of information between dissimilar systems – voice and data systems, proprietary and non-proprietary, circuit-switched and packet-switched, and bullet-proof reliability and accepted failures with rapid recovery. CTI brings these two disparate worlds together.

Today, most CTI solutions are based on a client/server architecture. Figure 6-4 shows the key elements and interfaces for a client/server environment. Figure 6-5 illustrates how CTI messaging occurs between the various systems.

Figure 6-4: Example CTI Client/Server Implementation

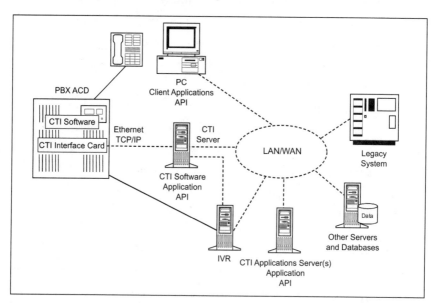

The Future of CTI in a VoIP World

CTI monitors call events and controls calls. In a traditional voice world, those calls arrive on a circuit-switched network. In the VoIP world, those calls arrive in an IP packet stream. CTI in a VoIP world still needs a voice-switch CTI link, and the requirements around planning, integration and testing remain the same. CTI will survive the transition to VoIP, and play a similar role in providing applications "smarts." The question is, will it have a new name?

Following are the key elements of the architecture and communication:

• **Switch.** The switch needs a CTI link, generally software that needs to be turned on (usually a fee-based, licensed right to use) and hardware in the form of a card with an Ethernet port and possibly its own CTI processor. The software enables the switch to send and receive CTI messages. It assigns a call ID or call tag to each call so every message about that call carries the same ID. That way, the CTI server can keep track of the many calls and events occurring simultaneously and ensure that the right screens pop in the right place. (Note: Probe how many links your switch will support. If there are multiple CTI servers, a test bed or lab, or additional applications that need CTI messages, you could require several CTI links to be active simultaneously.)

• **CTI server.** The core software in the CTI server is the traffic cop and translator between the voice switch and other devices. Each switch has its own language for call control messages that is not understood by the data applications, so the CTI server interprets. The CTI server monitors switch resources to track events, calls and agent states. It may also monitor events in other systems, such as the IVR. It assigns its own call IDs to track information about calls and to tie it together as it moves to different places. The CTI server interacts with the switch through its CTI link, with the desktop clients through a client/server exchange, and with other applications and databases as required by the business needs. Standard information exchange, or middleware, tools are used to pass data. Application Programming Interfaces (APIs) are defined for communication between applications. Software "drivers" provide the communications between the CTI server and the switch, much like a driver provides communications between a PC and a printer.

• **CTI applications and databases.** CTI applications and databases can reside on the CTI server or on separate servers. Regardless of where they reside, it operates as a single virtual system using TCP/IP to communicate between the applications and the core server software that translates messages and triggers applications. The application is where the smarts reside and where the power of this technology is applied.

• **Desktop.** The desktop has CTI client software that talks to the CTI server software and to other desktop applications. Again, standard information exchange (middleware) tools are used to pass data. For example, the CTI client software passes the ANI or account number received from the CTI server to the desktop business application so that it can retrieve the customer information associated with that number ("pop").

Figure 6-5: CTI Communications Architecture

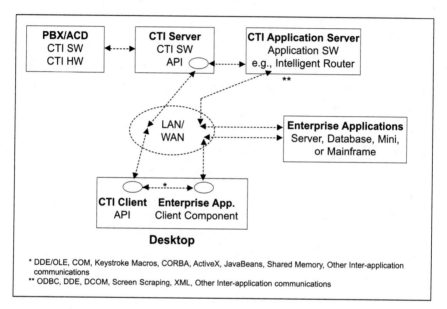

In Chapter 2, we introduced Communications Servers and their architecture. These systems are another way in which CTI might be implemented. In a Communications Server, the CTI functions reside in the server and are somewhat "pre-integrated" with the switch functions, IVR and other elements. Figure 6-6 shows the simplified implementation that results.

Figure 6-6: CTI Communications Server Implementation

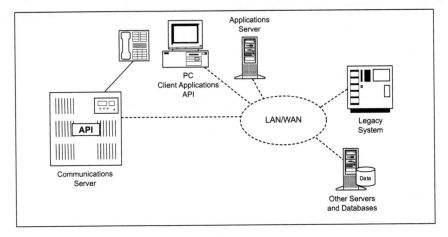

The CTI Market

Three major platform vendors are Alcatel (Genesys), Cisco and Intel (Dialogic). The first two compete head-to-head routinely for robust CTI solutions, multisite and multimedia. These vendors provide full application suites in modularized software packages. Intel's solution is often the plumbing in other CTI and CTI-enabled business application solutions. The voice-switch vendors are also offering CTI solutions that work with multiple switch platforms as they migrate to server-based routing and reporting approaches.

There are also a few application programming interfaces (APIs) for CTI. These are programming environments based on standards. The three you may encounter are:

- **Telephony Application Programming Interface (TAPI):** a Microsoft standard used by many vendors; this is one you're likely to see.
- **Telephony Services Application Programming Interface (TSAPI):** originally an AT&T/Novell (evolved to Lucent to Avaya) standard. You aren't likely to see this one very much these days.
- **Java Telephony Application Programming Interface (JTAPI):** from a consortium of vendors including Sun, IBM, Intel, Avaya, Nortel and Siemens. JTAPI is promoted for its platform independence, in line with Java principles.

Diverse Switch Environments

CTI architectures are generally built with switch-dependent (link-specific) and switch-independent elements, as shown in Figure 6-7. This architecture allows a company to select a single CTI platform to work with diverse switch types, operating independently or as a virtual call center environment. It should also allow you to change your switch and continue to use your CTI infrastructure and applications. Basically, the application can be written to a switch-independent API. The driver software is specific to the switch and its link messages.

Figure 6-7: Multiple-Switch CTI Solutions

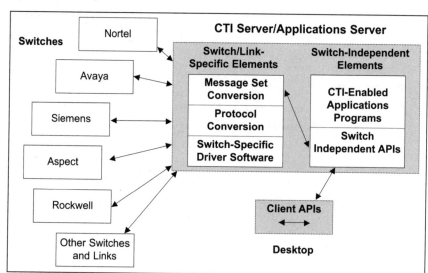

There is a small catch in what appears to be such a beautiful world – all switches and switch links are not created equal. Thus, an application has to adapt somewhat to the unique characteristics (strengths or limitations) of the switch link with which it is communicating. An example is the switch-based prompting that some switches offer and others don't. If you want to take advantage of prompts collected on the switch (such as account number), you will need to adapt the CTI application to work with it.

CTI Call Flow

Figure 6-8 shows a sample call flow using CTI and Table 6-2 provides the details of what is happening at each step. This simplified model illustrates the key characteristics of CTI messaging and call flows. It is not meant to be precise or to represent every message (there are lots!). Also, each vendor's messages are different, but the concepts are the same so use the model to get a feel for what is going on when CTI is at work. Keep in mind:

• The switch passes information on monitored resources (calls, 800 numbers, positions) across the CTI link to the CTI server. Information such as ANI, DNIS, prompted digits, route information, skills, extension and work states is included in the messages. The information can be provided automatically or on request. Remember each message carries a voice-switch call ID.

• The switch can ask the CTI server what to do (e.g., route request) and act based on the command that comes back.

• The CTI server talks to other elements, such as the IVR, business applications and databases, to get the information it needs for popping screens, making routing decisions, creating report data or dialing calls. If more intelligence is moved into the CTI application (e.g., for data-directed routing), it must perform additional queries into other databases or applications. It needs to do this *very fast* (subsecond response time).

• When the call is being delivered, the CTI server sends information to the CTI client software at the desktop. The CTI client software then passes that information to the business application through desktop software exchange mechanisms so it can retrieve the screen.

• The CTI server maintains dynamic databases that map agents, skills, telephone extensions and data locations (IP addresses) so that it can send the right information to the right place at the right time.

• All of the messages going to the CTI server allow it to create reports for integrated reporting.

Figure 6-8 shows a robust CTI application with many different elements of a call flow. Each numbered event is detailed in Table 6-2. The caller is first routed to the IVR and attempts to self-serve. When the caller presses zero to speak to an agent, the CTI application uses the information gathered in the IVR to identify the customer and let the agent know what the customer attempted to do in the IVR.

The example also shows how a customer segmentation strategy comes to life. The call is routed based on CTI application logic and information in a database (a high-value customer with multiple accounts). In this example, skills and work state management, as well as call treatment, is in the switch. The CTI application is providing data-directed routing to augment the routing in the switch (remember routing can exist in multiple places, but only one entity can control a call at a time). Note, too, that this example shows the proximity of CTI and CRM (which we'll discuss more in the next chapter). The CTI application triggers a script for cross-selling as part of the screen that pops. Throughout the interactions, the CTI application creates data for integrated reporting, as well.

Figure 6-8: Sample CTI Call Flow: IVR Integration, Routing and Screen Pop

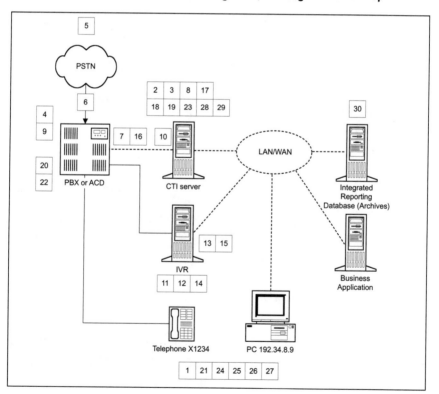

Table 6-2: Sample CTI Message Flow: IVR Integration, Routing and Screen Pop

Step	Action
1	Agent 5678 at telephone x1234 logs into CTI application from PC 192.34.8.9
2	Table in CTI database gets updated with entry: telephone x1234 = PC 192.34.8.9 = agent 5678
3	CTI application logs agent 5678 into telephone x1234 on the switch
4	Voice switch activates agent 5678 skill profile at telephone X1234
5	Caller dials 800 number
6	ANI and DNIS are passed from network to switch via ISDN PRI T1
7	Call ID, ANI and DNIS are sent from the switch over the CTI link to the CTI server
8	CTI server generates a unique contact ID and starts writing switch events into a contact record
9	Caller is switch-routed to a skill group that connects station ports to IVR ports
10	Call ID, skill group number and station number associated with IVR port are sent to CTI server and written to contact record
11	IVR script starts
12	CTI software on the IVR monitors port and application activity (prompts and responses)
13	CTI software on the IVR sends IVR application events to the CTI server for the contact record
14	Caller presses "zero" for assistance, IVR transfers call to routing pointer on switch (to routing script)
15	CTI software on the IVR sends transfer event to the CTI server and it's written to contact record
16	Switch-routing script issues a "route request" message to CTI server (for data-directed routing)
17	CTI server uses ANI and account number to query the business database for customer segment
18	Customer is high-value; CTI server tells PBX to route caller to premier customer service group
19	Call ID and call queued event sent to CTI server and written to contact record
20	Switch selects agent 5678 to receive the call
21	Call gets delivered to telephone x1234
22	Switch sends call ID and call connected event to CTI server and it's written to contact record
23	CTI server looks into data table; associates phone x1234 with PC 192.34.8.9
24	CTI server sends account number to PC 192.34.8.9
25	CTI PC client software triggers business application query with account number

continued on next page

Step	Action
26	PC 192.34.8.9 screen pops with customer record; includes IVR information and scripts
27	CTI client sends business data to CTI server and it's written to contact record
28	Call ends and contact record is closed out
29	Contact record sent to reporting database
30	Contact record is parsed into reporting database for advanced business analysis

"Smart" CTI

In Chapter 2, we set the stage for some key infrastructure decisions you need to consider in your contact center technology environment. CTI is where the rubber meets the road. We're not just pondering some theoretical stuff here, the decisions are real: How much intelligence do you want in the various components of your environment? Telecom and IT people have different histories and think differently.

Some companies are very conservative and cautious, others are more aggressive. Some have very advanced capabilities for routing, management and reporting on voice contacts in their switch already. Others have older switches with few features or want to replace them anyway. All of these factors come into play in defining a CTI architecture and the extent of applications that it will support. Figure 6-9 summarizes the "fit" of various levels of CTI intelligence for different environments.

Note that the "smart CTI" option can also be a Hybrid approach (as described in Chapter 2) provided by the switch vendor with its own outboard server.

Figure 6-9: CTI Intelligence Spectrum

	"Smart" Switch CTI *Augmenting* Switch Only	Balance Switch and CTI Intelligence	"Smart" CTI* CTI *Replacing* Switch Functions
What	• Switch-based call management, conditional routing and work states • CTI for additional capabilities (screen pops, data-directed routing, etc.)	• Switch manages call queuing and treatment but requests routes from CTI • CTI controls data-directed routing but relies on switch for conditional routing and work states	• Switch is in role to "do as it's told" and is basically a voice-switching server • CTI applications control all call management, routing, work states, reporting
When	• Conservative, telecom is comfort zone • Focus on reliability • Have extensive switch features and want to continue to use them	• Find CTI architecture attractive but still want to leverage core switch capabilities • Considering migration to more open and flexible environment	• Don't want to invest further in switch intelligence • Like the openness of CTI architecture • Plans for integrated multimedia environment and possibly VoIP

* Or some refer to it as "Dumb" Switch

CTI Challenges

As realists, we have to point out that CTI has its challenges, regardless of which architectural approach on that spectrum appeals to you. Even though it has been around awhile, the "I" part of "CTI" is still daunting. Following are some of the realities we've encountered while helping clients implement CTI.

Integration Variations and Limitations

When a vendor assures you that they've implemented CTI 500 times, that's great. But even so, your environment will still likely pose some unique challenges – just the variations between switches can present hurdles. Here are some considerations to keep in mind:

• **Nuances of various switch links.** All switch links are not created equal. There are standards, most notably the European Computer Manufacturers Association's (ECMA) Computer Supported Telephony Applications (CSTA). However, not everyone complies with the standards and there are various interpretations of them. Further, the big vendors tend to have their own proprietary but published links. Thus, a CTI solution has to adapt to the differences between links and message sets, depending on the switch they are talking to. These differences impact the vendors developing CTI platforms, as well as application developers (whether it's a software vendor, systems integrator or in-house).

• **Limitations of switch links and what they support.** In general, the message sets defined for these switch links don't provide all the functionality needed to move *all* the intelligence into the CTI applications (e.g., the far right end of the spectrum depicted in Figure 6-9). The result is workarounds, inelegant solutions and limitations on what can be accomplished in the CTI solution.

In addition, you may still need more robust routing and reporting capabilities than you have in the switch and, thus, have to maintain and manage two worlds. For example, you could use the queue management, call treatment, call selection, agent selection, conditional and skills-based routing capabilities of the switch and the data-directed routing, multimedia and integrated reporting capabilities of the CTI application.

• **"We're not familiar with that IVR/switch/applications vendor."** If you've got an off-beat vendor product, watch out. Top-tier switch, IVR and CTI vendors have interfaces to each other. But if you've got a second-tier vendor product, due diligence is in order.

Be sure to ask if the vendors have interfaces (APIs, drivers or other) to each other. Find out who provides it. Get references of installations with those elements. Otherwise, you'll be the first – and, typically, that's not a good position to be in (at least, not unknowingly). Also, if the vendor creates a driver for your environment, discuss whether it will become a product and/or if they will support it.

Capability Variations

Because of the spectrum of intelligence levels in the CTI, there are key issues about which capabilities should reside there. Make sure that you're in the driver's seat so that you define your approach, not the vendor. Other issues to consider:

• **CTI vendors have *different* philosophies about leveraging switch smarts or usurping them.** Some CTI vendors leverage the investment you've made in your switch routing and reporting capabilities. That's great if you like your switch capabilities and want to use them (and are content with managing both worlds). But it's lousy if you don't like your current switch capabilities or don't want to invest further in them.

Other vendors use minimal functionality on the switch and, instead, use all the smarts of the CTI solution. That's good if you like the architecture, although you may still have challenges because of the limitations of the capabilities offered on the link (as noted above and below).

• **Where to provide call treatment.** Call treatment involves the messages, music or other things a customer might hear before or during queuing. Switch CTI links generally do not give control for call treatment to the CTI application. Your options are to use the switch to queue and treat the call or create a separate queuing device, which is usually an IVR, to hold and treat calls.

With the switch treatment option, you need to administer the switch and CTI applications to work collaboratively. The CTI application has to monitor status while a call is held in queue; the switch may passively send these events or the CTI application may have to proactively interrogate the switch for status. With the second option, you essentially build another hardware platform to perform functions you already have. With the CTI application providing the treatment, one IVR port is needed for every call in queue. Neither option is great.

• **Functional overlap.** If you don't do your homework and don't have an architectural strategy, you can easily invest multiple times in functions such as routing, reporting and even text-chat and Web calls. Some CTI solutions let you purchase modules for the functionality you want. Make sure you think it through and spend your money only where you need additive or replacement functionality.

Is Anybody Listening?

It would be helpful if switch vendors provided more robust CTI message sets to make "smart" CTI a real possibility – for example, by providing the call treatment using the resources on the switch, but controlled by the CTI. Lacking that, it would be helpful if CTI vendors didn't present a solution that expects more than the switch link can deliver and, when it doesn't work right, blame the problem on the switch vendor!

Implementation and Support

Before implementing CTI, you'll need to do your homework on the following issues:

• **Performance.** If you don't consider performance in your CTI design effort, well, problems will surface. For example, screens might pop _verrrryyyy sll-loooooowwwwlllyyy_. A routing decision could time out and default route. You can also end up with delays between the softphone triggered work state change and the indication in the switch (or worse, the softphone and switch will be terminally out of sync), resulting in confusion about which positions are available for a call.

Obviously you don't want these things to happen. It's important to assess performance and fine-tune network capacity, processor speed, databases and more when designing CTI applications. Some environments need to trigger a "pre-fetch" of data from a mainframe or other system. In other words, the application retrieves data in parallel with routing or other decisions so that the data is ready to pop when needed. Testing and piloting are also critical to ensure the CTI solution will perform satisfactorily.

• **The need for upgrades.** CTI vendors can't maintain solutions for every release level from every switch vendor in the market. Similarly, switch vendors don't want to have to keep their systems effectively talking to outdated CTI solutions. This is reasonable. Release-level issues can apply to IVR, desktop and other elements, too.

As you consider CTI solutions, it is critical to understand which release level and software modules you'll need in other elements to communicate effectively with the CTI solution. This vigilance is necessary for the initial implementation, as well as for future releases. This technology can create extensive ripple effects – surprises, in the form of expensive upgrades, are not fun.

• **Internal technology support.** CTI touches everything: telecommunications, voice switch, IVR, business applications, servers and the LAN/WAN. It is truly an integration technology. The more mission-critical applications you put in CTI (like routing), the more important system stability becomes.

The problem is that most organizations have very specialized support teams: One group works with voice switches, another works with the data network, somebody else supports hardware servers, while legacy programmers support the mainframe applications. Here are two technology support issues to consider:

1. Someone in the IT/IS organization has to own the CTI application and infrastructure. Further, very detailed system documentation, troubleshooting procedures, testing, administration, maintenance and escalation procedures have to be put in place and kept up-to-date.

2. We recommend creating a CTI lab with scaled-down versions of all components (especially with complex environments and applications) – switch, IVR, multimedia applications, reporting servers and a desktop that can access all of the business applications. When a CTI deal is on the table, vendors will often provide a second copy of the software for a testing-and-development lab for a low incremental cost.

• **Training.** Even the best architected technical solution that's perfectly aligned with the business needs will do nothing for an organization if its people don't know how to use the technology. We know this sounds obvious, but you'd be surprised at how many organizations skimp on system training for the technology staff and end-user training for the call center staff. Don't be one of them!

Key Design Decisions

Here are some key design decisions (or design "gotchas") that companies often struggle with in their CTI implementations, and ways to tackle them successfully.

1. What role will the CTI play? You'll need to examine the entire customer interaction – and look beyond screen pops. As you begin to define CTI's role, you'll need to design the corresponding infrastructure for reliability and scalability to match. CTI technology can help in four distinct phases of contact, and each needs to be considered when defining requirements:

- Prior to answer (identifying the caller and routing);
- During the interaction (screen pops);
- During wrap-up (updating multiple databases, email/fax confirmation); and
- Post wrap-up activities (trigger a follow-up call, escalation, plug-in to a work-flow routine).

2. What should I use to identify my customers? Will I get a high enough hit rate with ANI? Remember, you pay your carrier for each ANI delivered whether or not it matches something in your database. Will I have to clean up my phone number database? Or do I need to prompt callers? If I prompt them, how often will they "play"? Do we have a suitable numeric identifier that they know or can learn to use? Most companies end up prompting. Some implement a hybrid approach – use ANI if you can, and prompt conditionally.

3. If you use an ANI database, be careful with design. With many legacy applications, it's difficult or costly (and sometimes prohibitive) to develop and maintain an ANI database. Often, instead, the ANI database resides on the CTI server or a separate database server. Each number in the ANI table is cross-referenced to a unique customer identifier (e.g., customer name, customer account number). With this type of implementation, the ANI database "learns" as more calls are processed, dynamically updating the database with new ANIs as contacts arrive and are matched with a customer. But remember, ANI has lots of limitations for matching, so only build this database if you'll have a high (60 percent or more) "hit rate."

4. What should my routing decisions be based on, and where is the data I need? Can I apply my routing logic against the data quickly enough? First, you need the business strategy – then work on the data and design. Some companies end up creating a separate database to house routing decision information to achieve the performance needed (especially in multisite pre-arrival routing scenarios where the time limits are extreme). Of course, then it needs to be routinely updated and synchronized with the main customer database.

5. What is my default plan and backup plan? What happens if screens don't pop? What if the switch doesn't get a response on its route request? What if the link is down? The more smarts you put into your CTI applications, the more important it is to have default and backup plans (and redundant and stable platforms). When the CTI link or application is down, the switch still needs to be able to deliver the call somewhere

6. What screen should I pop, and under what circumstances? If you're popping screens but your agents still have to navigate through 10 screens to get the necessary information to satisfy the caller, the CTI application isn't doing much good. The synergy between CTI and customer information system applications is evident here. If your applications are not going to be replaced, consider developing a "super screen" or "80 percent screen" with a desktop development tool (e.g., Web browser-based technologies, PowerBuilder, Visual Basic). The underlying applications aren't changed, and the development tool can create a veneer to quickly tab between sessions in multiple back-end systems or consolidate information from multiple screens onto a single screen (we'll tell you more about this in the next chapter).

Some CTI implementations pop a preliminary screen with basic information, such as the customer name, ANI or account number, where the customer was in the IVR when they exited to an agent, whether they have gone through security steps (e.g., entered a PIN), and even a little scripted greeting. Clicking "OK" on that screen then takes the agent to the business application screen. Design must also address which screens pop based on how much you know about the customer. For example:

- No identifier or no match – pops a screen ready to enter key identifiers to bring up customer information.
- Multiple matches (e.g., you are using ANI but several customers have the same phone number) – pops a selection screen listing the possible customers.
- Single match but multiple accounts – pops the customer profile and key information about each of those accounts, with the ability to quickly drill down into the appropriate one for the conversation.

• Single match, single account – pops the specific account information.

7. How should we manage work states? A current process (pre-CTI) is that agents become available when they're done with a call, but finish some data entry on a screen while greeting the next caller (they don't use wrap-up). If we do this with CTI, won't the new screen pop on top of (and wipe out) the screen they're finishing? What do we do? While options are vendor-dependent, one possibility is to delay the incoming screen so that it doesn't appear until the agent indicates he or she is ready. Others change their process, requiring the agent to finish before becoming available (and the completion of the wrap-up screen triggers the available state).

8. How should I integrate IVR with CTI? Should these systems talk directly using TCP/IP? How should the transfers be handled? Should I use switch-hook transfers from the IVR that are monitored by the CTI or should the IVR tell the CTI to transfer the call and have it be a CTI-controlled transfer? It's best to tackle these questions by sitting down with the vendors of each element – switch, IVR and CTI – and discussing the options and tradeoffs. Often, the vendors will have preferred methods of handling these issues with each other.

Succeeding at CTI

Balancing the opportunities of CTI with the challenges of implementation can turn any project manager prematurely gray. Take time to do things right from the start. Here are six suggestions:

1. Put together a solid project team with representation from the call center, telecom and IT. Get support from systems integrators or consultants to make the project run smoother. And find an executive sponsor who can help all parts of the organization work together effectively.

2. Develop a business case to be sure that CTI will add value in your environment, you're leveraging its application strengths and you won't be disappointed.

3. Define a CTI architecture that fits with your "big picture" technology strategy. Key issues include: How much smarts will reside on the switch vs. CTI, and is it a multimedia environment?

4. Define the set of applications that make sense for your environment, define phases and don't stop after the screen pop implementation. Get the full benefits of the platform and integration by rolling out additional capabilities.

5. When budgeting, don't forget the cost of your hardware servers, software application licenses, database licenses and maintenance (generally, 17 percent to 22 percent of software costs). Then estimate the big item – integration. For a simple CTI application (screen pops, softphone), add 50 percent of the software costs for integration, at a minimum. For more complex efforts (data-directed routing, IVR integration, integrated reporting), budget one to two times the cost of the software.

6. Recognize that, while there may be packaged applications, modules or suites, CTI doesn't just come out of a box or on a CD. You must define what needs to be integrated. You must design the application logic based on business needs (which screens to pop, routing logic, report needs, etc.). You must determine what data is needed, where it resides and how to get at it.

Points to Remember

• CTI uses message exchange and application logic to bring to life inbound and outbound applications. CTI does enable screen pops… and so much more.

• CTI can usually be justified with a hard-dollar business case. The timing for implementing CTI may be best when multimedia or CRM is also being considered, as these applications extend and enhance the value of CTI.

• CTI architectures are generally client/server-based, or a Communications Server platform may be used for CTI.

• Infrastructure decisions are very real when looking at CTI. You must decide how much "smarts" sit in the switch and how much sit in the CTI application.

Actions to Take

• Carefully define your full set of CTI application opportunities. Optimize your investment by extending its capabilities beyond just popping screens.

• Use the foundation of your strategies and infrastructure decisions to help frame CTI thinking.

Chapter 7:

Information and Applications Bring CRM Strategies to Life

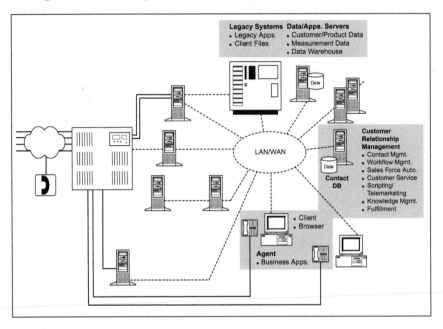

Key Points Discussed in this Chapter:

Information System Architectures

Client/Server Architectures

Web-Enabled Vs. Web-Architected

Desktop Options

Customer Relationship Management

Business Benefits and Addressing Pain Points

CRM Applications and the Desktop

Integration

Data Challenges

Customer Relationship Management (CRM) is a hot topic. People either sing its praises or tout its failures. Articles abound on the power and benefits of CRM, as do articles on the great (and many) CRM failures. So what is it, and why is it so schizophrenic?

Keep in mind that CRM is more than technology – CRM is a strategy, a philosophy, a way of doing business. It's not just a technology, it's not just a desktop thing, and it's not just for call centers. When implemented just as a technology, it is likely to fail. If the only technology used is desktop software applications, it will fall short of its potential. When implemented just for the call center, it will be half-baked. But, when a set of technologies is implemented as part of an overall, enterprisewide CRM strategy with corresponding cultural, procedural, organizational and operational changes, it can deliver tremendous benefits. The contact center is a key participant in making that happen, as well as a top beneficiary of CRM capabilities.

We like to compare CRM to the total quality management (TQM) movement of the 1980s and early 1990s. Both are great ideas (after all, who isn't interested in better quality and customer relationships?), but implementing either one the right way changes the entire enterprise. All of the existing operating principles, engrained assumptions, power structures, reporting relationships, processes, politics, information and departmental fiefdoms are changed. It's quite a challenge – and with so many moving parts, it's easy to see how these efforts can derail.

In this chapter, we'll describe the technology that supports CRM in the contact center. We'll start with a primer on information system architectures and options, and the desktop environment in the contact center today. We'll look at what makes CRM an enterprisewide initiative, and describe how it fits with other enterprise systems, databases and processes. Although our focus is the contact center, this is one technology that can't thrive in isolation.

Information System Architectures

It's important to understand the technology environment in which any customer-contact application – CRM-oriented or otherwise – resides. Figure 7-1 shows the evolution of information systems architectures. We'll address these architectures and their roles in the call center, focusing on the client/server and Web architectures prevalent today.

Figure 7-1: Information Systems Architecture Evolution

	Information Systems Evolution		
Time			
1-Tier	**2-Tier** **3-Tier**	**Web-Based** **N-Tier**	
Architecture	• Mainframe/Mini-Computer • "Legacy" Systems	• Client/Server ————▶	• Web-Enabled • Web-Architected
Desktop	• "Green Screens" • Dumb Terminals or Terminal Emulation on PC	• PC with Thick Client • PC with Thin Client	• PC with Thin Client • Browser
Network	• Coaxial Cabling • SNA	• LAN/WAN • Ethernet, Token Ring • TCP/IP, IPX	• Internet/Intranet/VPN • Ethernet • TCP/IP

It's All So Confusing!

There is a language that is unique to the data world, and many call center professionals have trouble speaking it. If you're from the telecom side of the technology world
or if you have an operations background, it's time to brush up on some key terms:

• **Legacy system:** In-place information systems or databases that house core business information, such as customer records. They may be based on long-established technologies (e.g., mainframes, mini-computers), but are still used for day-
  to-day operations.

• **Middleware:** Software that provides the means to access and integrate different
  types of hardware and software within a network. It typically uses open interfaces
  to access and move information. The practice of integrating multiple business
  applications is sometimes referred to as EAI, or Enterprise Application
  Integration. Most middleware architectures are based on object-oriented programming, meaning the programs are built using a modular approach. The term
  "middleware" is often used to refer to an application that gathers data from multiple systems and then performs some type of processing. When you hear someone use the term "middleware," it's a good idea to ask "What does that mean to
  you?" Here are three flavors of middleware to consider:

1. **Software architecture suites:** Microsoft and Sun are both architects of middleware technology suites for the Windows and Java environments, respectively. Examples are Component Object Module (COM), Distributed COM (DCOM), .NET, Active X and the Java suite of technologies.

2. **Frameworks:** Many vendors use a framework to interface with other systems. Component Object Request Broker Architecture (CORBA) is one such framework. Java 2 Enterprise Edition (J2EE), Remote Procedure Calls (RPCs) and Application Programming Interfaces (APIs) are frameworks that are specified by vendors to allow others to interface with their solutions using a defined programming environment.

3. **Vendor-specific tools:** Specific vendors offer middleware tools to help various products talk to each other, creating an interoperable environment. The software suites contain messaging and formatting functions, message queuing and some type of message or integration broker development kits. These toolkits are increasingly being bundled with workflow and business process mapping capabilities. Examples include IBM MQSeries, Vitria BusinessWare, Sybase (former New Era of Networks), Mercator Integration Broker, TIBCO Active Enterprise and BEA Weblogic Integration.

Client/Server Architectures

Most contact center applications today (whether built in-house or purchased from a vendor) use a client/server architecture. A "client" requests action from a "server," which works on behalf of the client. Client/server applications leverage the interfaces possible on Windows or other types of graphical desktops, as well as the processing capability that resides in a PC. In most contact center environments, the client is the PC on the agent desktop. That's where information is assembled and displayed. These desktop clients are connected to servers that store databases and run application programs that perform calculations on the data.

As an example, a client/server banking application manages the presentation of data (e.g., account profile) at the client level (that is, how information is assembled and displayed on the desktop), and requests account information or transactions from the server. The server talks to a mainframe, a database server or other application to retrieve or update data, and presents it back to the client.

The benefits of client/server over the mainframe/mini-computer system environment are many:

- Applications can be added and changed much more quickly.
- Processing is distributed, potentially increasing performance.
- Changes or additions made on one system don't impact all other applications.
- Costs are lower.
- Technology developments can be made more rapidly.
- There are more packaged solutions available.

Tiered Client/Server Models

In every distributed computing model, there are three software functions or layers: presentation, application and data. The presentation layer refers to the piece with which the end-user interacts (often referred to as the desktop or GUI), the application layer refers to the piece where the business rules get implemented, and the data layer refers to the data that is accessed, processed and managed.

There are three key client/server computing models:

- In the **two-tier** model, the software functions are split between two physical machines – the desktop and the server. The desktop handles the presentation while the server handles the data layer. The application can exist solely on the desktop, on the server or split between the client and the server. Two-tier was the first iteration of client/server computing.
- The **three-tier** model creates a more cleanly defined framework: There are very well-defined interfaces between the presentation, application and data software layers. Usually, these three logical layers are deployed on three different physical machines: 1) presentation on the desktop, 2) application on a server, and 3) data on a server. The data may even reside on a legacy system. Theoretically, a change to one layer doesn't affect the other two layers. For example, changing the business rules for automatic escalation of open trouble tickets from 48 hours to 24 hours requires you to only change the software code on the application server (a two-tier model might require you to upgrade the software version on every single desktop PC). The three-tier model was developed to improve the maintainability, flexibility and scalability of the two-tier model.
  - **N-tier** expands the three-tier concept to multiple systems. With N-tier, the application and data layers span multiple systems, while still giving the user a single

presentation. For example, an order-entry application might access two additional systems (manufacturing and inventory) to find production schedules and warehouse information. In this example, seven tiers are used: three from order entry (presentation, application and data), two from manufacturing (application and data) and two from inventory (application and data).

Figure 7-2: Client/Server Architectures

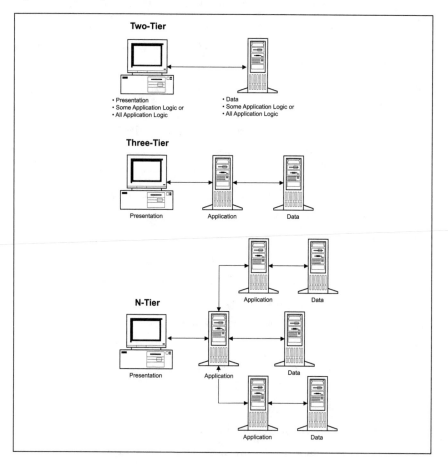

Web-Enabled Vs. Web-Architected

Recently, due to the Web's influence, two data application architectures have emerged. They leverage the Web's standard tools, such as TCP/IP, browsers and Web servers. These architectures can run on private or public networks.

The term "Web-enabled" means that the application works with the Web or a Web server. It is typically a client/server application that has been altered to use a browser-based desktop for the presentation layer, accessing a Web server over TCP/IP. This is a likely path for an established client/server application in which a company has invested heavily and which still has useful life. It will deliver some of the benefits of a Web environment, such as ease of use – for both internal (agent) and external (customer) users – and centralized application development and management.

The biggest challenges are scalability and performance. Performance may be particularly tricky in a Web-enabled application where the client/server application has had extensive application logic running at the desktop. In these cases, applets or JavaScript code may be downloaded to the user desktop to achieve similar capabilities, but the time to download may be slow depending on the connection speed and application size.

Web-architected means that the application was built, essentially, from the ground up to work with the Web. It is based on a browser interface, which can be accessed by internal or external users (over a dial-up, high-speed or LAN/WAN connection). For example, this architecture is often used by vendors selling application services to a wide variety and potentially large number of users (often referred to as Application Service Providers or ASPs). Many vendor packages for CRM and other applications are migrating to Web-architected and, thus, require a significant overhaul of the application software.

The primary advantages of Web-architected applications are scalability and performance. This application architecture makes great sense for contact centers that are moving to extensive Web self-service with assisted service options. It provides the scalability needed to accommodate direct customer access. The agent and the customer can access the same systems, applications and databases via a common interface, thereby optimizing collaboration possibilities. The agent can be located anywhere – main center, remote center or home office. Web architectures are well-suited for CRM applications. Customers can access the knowledge base and self-serve (e.g., enter their own trouble tickets or place orders) and their Web contacts are then visible to the agents who handle subsequent requests.

Desktop Options

The desktop environment for today's contact center is generally a PC. Most centers use a version of Microsoft Windows – usually NT, 98, 2000 or XP. However, what they do within that Windows environment varies greatly. Here are three different scenarios:

1. Thin client. The application software is client/server or Web-based with little or no application software running at the desktop. Thin client is often used to describe browser-based desktops and is frequently used in three-tier systems. Enablers at the desktop include Java and Active X.

In a thin-client environment, maintenance of the application is primarily centralized to the server. The client is "thin" in that it has little smarts (application code) running there, and relies heavily on the server(s) to retrieve, process, update, manage, present and track data. What's the benefit? The Total Cost of Ownership (TCO), which takes into account the cost of equipment acquisition, as well as the support and maintenance services to keep systems up and running, is lower.

Theoretically, thin clients are easier to maintain because most of the software is server-based and only a browser accesses Web-enabled applications. No proprietary clients are installed and maintained at the desktop. Keep in mind that some thin clients are purely browser-based to achieve this server-only maintenance model. Thin clients that act as a graphical front end to another application may have desktop maintenance requirements.

2. Thick client. The application software is client/server, and much or most of the application software runs at the desktop. Programs and data are installed on the workstation, where a significant part of the application processing takes place. The client is "thick" in that it has smarts running there, which can include processing, management and presentation of data.

Thick-client architectures keep processor manufacturers like Intel busy because more robust applications require ever larger and more powerful processors. And thick client means more support costs in your center to configure, upgrade and install applications on each desktop, rather than at a central server.

3. Terminal emulation. Some PCs are configured with a terminal emulation software package (such as Rhumba or Attachmate). In this scenario, the PC is not acting as a PC at all, but rather as a dumb terminal. Centers that use this configuration generally have legacy mainframe applications, but use PCs at the workstation to allow agents to access other Windows applications or use the intranet/Internet through a browser. They may use a mouse for field navigation, but commands are primarily code-driven. In a few large centers, true dumb terminals still exist.

Now Let's Talk about CRM

CRM is a business philosophy that is enabled by processes and technology. Figure 7-3 shows the various pieces of the puzzle. There are three key elements of CRM: marketing, sales and service. Prospects must be found and qualified, converted to customers, and then retained, managed and maximized.

Figure 7-3: CRM Elements

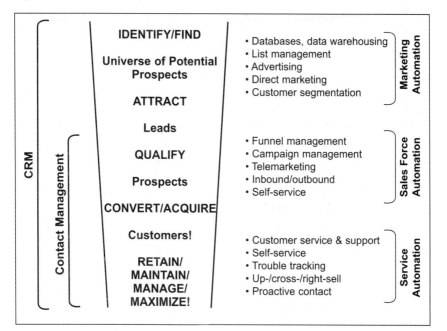

IDENTIFY/FIND **Universe of Potential Prospects** **ATTRACT** **Leads**	• Databases, data warehousing • List management • Advertising • Direct marketing • Customer segmentation — **Marketing Automation**
QUALIFY **Prospects** **CONVERT/ACQUIRE** **Customers!**	• Funnel management • Campaign management • Telemarketing • Inbound/outbound • Self-service — **Sales Force Automation**
RETAIN/ MAINTAIN/ MANAGE/ MAXIMIZE!	• Customer service & support • Self-service • Trouble tracking • Up-/cross-/right-sell • Proactive contact — **Service Automation**

CRM Business Benefits

What's the business philosophy behind CRM? Acquiring customers is an expensive proposition for most businesses. Think about the expenses incurred for prospect lists, lead generation, advertising, promotions, setting up dealer networks and building a sales force. When you factor in all of these costs, you'll find that many customers are unprofitable when first acquired. In fact, first-year acquisition activities can be thought of as an investment for subsequent years' returns.

According to Frederick F. Reichheld, author of *The Loyalty Effect*, most businesses lose customers at the rate of 10 percent to 30 percent each year. Think of the wasted customer acquisition expenditures. Reichheld's research indicates that a 5 percent increase in customer retention yields a 25 percent to 95 percent increase in profitability, depending on the industry.

If the customer can be retained beyond the first year, sales from the second year and beyond often yield profitability. Subsequent years' incremental sales activity can be thought of as the return on investment. In addition, once the relationship is established, it may be easier to sell additional products and services to the existing customer base through upsell and cross-sell activities. Plus, sales cycles are theoretically shorter and advertising and promotions expenditures are smaller, as the business does not have to establish credibility with the customer.

Customer segmentation is another key element of a CRM strategy. Typically, a company's customer base will follow the Pareto Principle, or the 80/20 rule: 20 percent of a firm's customers will generate 80 percent of its profits. The goal is to identify the extremely profitable customers and do everything possible to retain them and maximize their value.

CRM: It's Not Just a Call Center Thing...

CRM initiatives are often associated with call centers. Although CRM principles add value in the call center, the real power gets released in a bigger enterprisewide initiative. CRM also gets implemented in field sales, field service, billing, branch offices, dealers, distributors, marketing and promotions, as well as the Web. All business functions that interact with the customer are ideally included in a CRM initiative.

You can think of these top-level customers as the "platinum" segment. The next segmentation set is comprised of those customers in the middle tier, or the "gold" segment – whom you can turn into platinum customers with very targeted marketing, sales and service activities. The same concept applies for customers in the "silver" tier (whom you can grow into gold customers). For those customers in the gold and silver tiers who can't be enticed into incremental sales, the challenge is to develop cost-effective service options. So relationships for the different customer segments are managed in different ways according to defined business rules.

What's Your Mantra?

The first step for companies pursuing CRM is to define a strategy. A "mantra" can help to keep everyone focused on the goals of the effort. For example, the mantra for one bank that implemented CRM was: "Increase wallet share." They never lost sight of that goal. Its call center implications were substantial – the focus was not on cutting talk times or reducing headcount, but rather on driving revenue by increasing the number of products and value per customer.

Most successful CRM environments have a sales or revenue element to them. The opportunities to drive sales or retention through CRM is significant. However, a CRM strategy can also be created in a pure service-oriented environment. For example, a utility company that is not yet deregulated could implement a CRM strategy that uses the power of CRM to streamline interactions with customers, resulting in better service for customers and cost savings for the company. In this scenario, CRM may also help build relationships with the utility's customers for the (possibly deregulated) future – leading to retention and revenue protection.

Business Drivers and Value with CRM

There are different business drivers for CRM with different corresponding outcomes:

- **Drive sales revenue:** Acquire new customers, increase market share, cross-sell and upsell (increasing customer value), focus on high-value customers through customer segmentation. For instance, a bank that implemented CRM to "increase wallet share" also completely changed the focus of its call center metrics. In its revised performance "elevator story," talk times were up, but so were key measures like revenue per customer.

- **Protect revenue:** Retain customers. A retailer that dealt primarily through a distribution network needed to increase distributor retention. Its entire business case for transforming its call center technology environment could be justified by a 5 percent increase in retention rate.

- **Reduce costs:** Streamline service processes, reduce the cost of serving low-value/high-cost customers through customer segmentation. A call center benchmarking study conducted by Prosci revealed that, on average, contact management saved 37 seconds per call for those with a talk time decrease. Knowledge-based applications (which are often part of or integrated with CRM) saved 50 seconds per call on average.

CRM Hits Call Center Pain Points

Part of the excitement surrounding CRM for the contact center is the opportunity to get away from some of the cumbersome applications in use today. Many contact centers labor under "hand-me-down" applications. The applications weren't built for the call flows and workflows associated with the contact center. They weren't designed for the real-time nature of customer contact. CRM offers an opportunity to build flows to match contact needs.

Observe the call handling in your contact center. Table 7-1 presents some of the common problems we've noticed, as well as the CRM opportunities they present.

Table 7-1: CRM Solutions to Today's Problems

Problem Today	Solution with CRM
Agents have to log in to many applications then jump around to many screens (four, seven, 10 and more).	New screens consolidate key information needed for any transaction onto one screen ("super screens" or "80 percent screens").
Trainers complain it takes a long time to train agents because there are so many systems and they have to keep so much information about where to go when in their heads.	Training time is reduced; agents are trained on the more intuitive CRM interface, and the workflows help guide them to the right places and trigger them to do the right things (it's in the system, not in their heads).
Agents use paper forms and then someone else enters the data into a database later.	Applications and workflows specific to the contact center interactions are created, along with real-time integration with the appropriate legacy systems.
Agents have to manually look up information (paper- or system-based) about the customer and his or her history, products and services. They apply their own judgment (risking inconsistency).	Information is accessible online with search engines or knowledgebase tools. Workflows and decision systems trigger the appropriate scripts and suggest appropriate actions. Actions and communications are consistent.
Agents put customers on hold or get back to them later after conducting research for the answers they need.	Information is accessible in real-time at the desktop, with easy-to-use tools to guide the agent to the right information.

CRM in the Contact Center

What are CRM's capabilities and roles within the contact center? Figure 7-4 depicts the CRM process cycle as it applies to customer contact. There are three key points: 1) the CRM customer contact process takes place across all media channels, 2) contacts are inbound or outbound, 3) continuous updates to data and modifications to how it is applied drive the process cycle. Each step along the way focuses on data:

- *Gather* data about the customer,

- *Use* data about the customer and appropriate products or services,
- *Create* data about this interaction,
- *Analyze* the data, and
- *Apply* what you learn from the data.

CRM involves information – getting it, using it, creating more and figuring out what to do next.

Figure 7-4: The CRM Customer-Contact Process Cycle

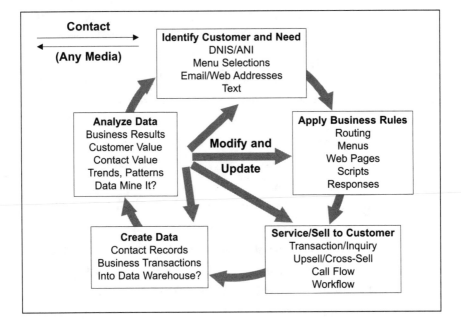

Capability and Application Considerations

CRM technology solutions entail numerous capabilities and applications. Some of these elements may be part of a CRM package, others may be applications that you already have in place and want to integrate with the CRM solution, and some may be critical to your business so you'll want to select the best-of-breed components to integrate. Example capabilities and applications include:

- **Contact management.** This key function is the heart and soul of CRM, allowing you to log contacts, access customer profile data and retrieve contact history. All contacts with a customer (i.e., marketing, sales, service, billing, credit, collections) via any media (phone, Web, email, mail, fax, face-to-face) are logged. This serves two purposes: it creates a single view of the customer and collects data for advanced analysis.

• **Workflow or business rules.** Another fundamental component of CRM is the ability to write business rules or workflows. Where should this contact be routed? What should occur at the desktop based on what we know about the customer? Are there scripts that should trigger? Should other events follow, such as email, calls or mailings? Should the contact be escalated or another group notified after it occurs? This is where CRM draws its power to transform the customer experience and the value derived from customer contacts.

• **Sales Force Automation (SFA).** SFA is one of the key feeder technologies for CRM. It is often thought of as a field sales function, but with contact centers playing a pivotal role in the sales process for many companies, SFA functions have become fundamental. SFA functions track leads or contacts, trigger follow-up contacts, enable win/loss analysis and other evaluations. They can also include scripts and other sales support functions.

• **Service functions.** Help desk tools are another feeder technology for CRM. Help desk functions are a part of service functions. Service functions can include account inquiry and status, billing, shipping and trouble-ticket initiation. These tools can also escalate, track and report on outstanding and closed problems.

• **Knowledge base.** Some CRM systems include an inherent knowledge base with basic functions for online documentation, searches or queries. Others tie into a robust knowledge base or knowledge management system with expert systems intelligence or case-based reasoning. The key elements are the database, search engine and tools for content management. This function is particularly applicable in service environments, but it may also be tied to complex sales environments which need to find the right product to meet the customer needs. A customer interaction can be guided using workflows, scripting and knowledge base interactions.

• **Fulfillment.** Fulfillment can be delivery of a product service, or collateral materials. Materials can be sent via many different channels (mail, email, fax).

• **Scripting.** Scripting is an on-screen agent guide to help manage customer interactions. Scripting can occur on inbound or outbound contacts, and on spoken or written communications. In a CRM environment, scripting is triggered using workflows and intelligently analyzing the customer and business situation. It can be tied to marketing, sales or service steps.

• **Telemarketing.** In a CRM contact center, telemarketing (or "e-marketing" using email) plays a key role. Telemarketing functions within CRM include lead management, campaign management, scripting and reporting.

Beyond these capabilities, when you look at CRM solutions, consider the interfaces and development tools. What will your workflow architects use to develop new business rules? What are your desktop options (i.e., browser, operating system)? What reporting and monitoring tools and capabilities are available? How about optional capabilities, like CTI integration or multimedia (e.g., email, Web integration)?

Business Rules

The business rules running in a CRM environment consist of a set of decisions based on a variety of data. What is currently happening in the center? What do we know about this customer? What is his/her profile? When was our last contact with him/her? What was the outcome? What is his/her preferences for interacting with us (based on observed patterns or what the customer has told us)? CRM first gathers, stores and analyzes this data. Then, business rules are applied to the data and the analysis is used to alter routing paths, present appropriate screens, trigger scripts for upselling, trigger proactive contacts or even dynamically alter self-service opportunities via an IVR or the Web.

The CRM Desktop

You can think of the CRM desktop in the call center as the agent's "cockpit." Agents have the great responsibility of flying customers to their destinations and ensuring that they're satisfied and will want to take another flight in the future. Agents have numerous "gauges and dials" at their fingertips. They have applications that work on their behalf without them having to make specific requests and indicators to tell them if there are any issues that need to be dealt with or opportunities to improve the situation.

Figure 7-5 shows the kinds of things you might find on a call center CRM desktop. Keep in mind, there are different desktop screens for different users (e.g., field sales vs. call center) and different times (e.g., new account, established account, placing order, checking on problem status).

Figure 7-5: Sample CRM Desktop Screen

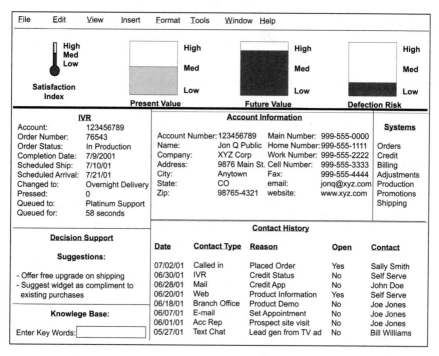

Let's look at an example of how the CRM desktop cockpit works modeled on the bank that uses CRM to "increase wallet share" – meaning enhance relationships with the right customers so that they use the bank for more of their financial services. While a customer might start with a checking and savings account, the wallet-share potential would include products and services such as home equity loans, car loans, student loans, IRAs and even brokerage services for mutual funds, stocks and bonds. Any (and all) of these products can be offered to customers with the right profile, based on business rules evaluating data, patterns and fit.

A business rule checks for certain banking patterns and triggers a script at the desktop prompting the agent to suggest that the customer move into a different account type to save money. Another rule looks at linked accounts for children and suggests reminding the customer that the bank offers car or student loans. All of this is triggered without specific action by the agent as he or she works in the desktop cockpit. The application automatically provides the key information agents need about the customer, triggers gathering of the proper information to populate the databases and suggests the right products to sell ("right-selling") to optimize the relationship with the high-value customer.

CRM: What a Messy Market

The CRM market is a bit messy and certainly crowded. The good news is that, because it is such a hot item, there are many Web sites devoted to tracking this market (a resource list is available at www.vanguard.net). The top player in the market, as of 2002, is Siebel. But there are many others – in fact, too many. These vendors have diverse backgrounds or "heritages" – with legacies that include telephony, sales force automation, help desk tools, e-commerce or specialized software or services. They range from low-end basic contact management applications that cost hundreds of dollars per seat, to full-blown CRM with multimedia and other options that run up to tens of thousands of dollars a seat – and everywhere in between. Finding the best solution to meet your needs takes time. Approach with caution – due diligence is key.

CRM Integration

Much like CTI, CRM is an integration-intensive technology. When purchasing CRM, the key components you'll be buying are client software for the desktops, software on a server, a database and the hardware to house it. Well, that's a start. The real challenge is in the integration steps.

Legacy System Integration

Most CRM solutions need to interface with legacy systems or migrate (or download) data from legacy systems to the CRM database. That's the hard part.

Some CRM solutions are suboptimized because companies haven't taken the time to integrate with the other systems, applications and databases – they are basically standalone systems. While that might be OK for basic contact management, it won't deliver the full power and benefits of CRM.

Implementing an effective CRM solution means that new agents won't have to be trained on all the legacy systems and applications. Plus, call flows and workflows (and therefore talk times) will be streamlined with the new interface to the key data needed. We're moving away from the "hand-me-down" systems that have constrained contact centers for years, and developing screens and flows that match the real-time interaction with the customers. It's a tall order with a powerful outcome. Integration with legacy systems also makes reporting and analysis easier, as the CRM system touches all the key data directly. We'll dig further into this concept shortly.

CRM Integration to Other Contact Center Technologies

Beyond considering which legacy systems and database servers need to be accessed for CRM integration, you also need to consider other contact center elements. The CTI, IVR, QM and Web server may all need to be integrated with the CRM solution. Tying the various systems together is a design issue you'll need to tackle. And besides the initial implementation, be sure to consider ongoing management and maintenance issues.

CRM Integration Methodologies

How is the integration done? With patience and skill. The mechanisms for integration are standard "middleware" tools for desktop, server and database integration. Things like COM/DCOM, OLE/DDE, XML, ODBC databases and SQL queries, MQSeries, J2EE, CORBA, Active X, and even SNA interfaces to legacy systems are used. Some of the switch and CTI vendors are partnering with CRM vendors to create "hooks" into the system, which means there will be standard drivers, or integration software, between top-tier systems. This can ease the integration challenge.

Figure 7-6 shows the integration landscape. There are two middleware elements in this picture – one provides the integration with the business systems, and the other provides the integration with the call center channels and other applications. The vendor-specific middleware tools to which we previously referred (page 194) are the most likely candidates for the business systems side. CTI may play this middleware role on the call center side. CTI's connection with both the CRM application and the call center applications positions it well to provide the integrated data needed for analysis.

Figure 7-6: CRM Integration

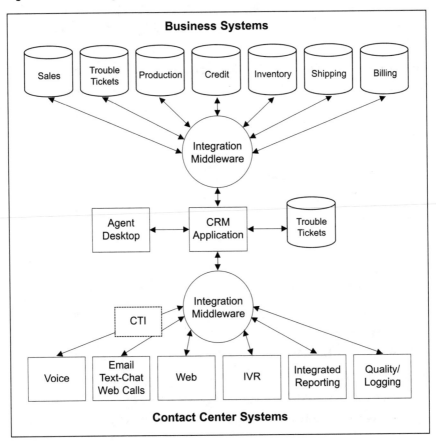

It's important to work with your CRM vendor and their integration partners to define how you will access and update the data you need to use on legacy systems. Be sure to carefully define what new data will be created, where it will reside and how it will be managed and updated. It's likely that the core data you've used for years – customer records, inventory, pricing, etc. – will continue to reside on legacy systems. This is especially true if CRM is being phased in and only parts of the business will use it near-term (while other parts continue to rely on the legacy systems). New data – contact records, outcomes, scripts – will then reside on the CRM database. However, all of it has to be pulled together at the desktop.

The CRM Data Challenge

Harvard Professor Shoshana Zuboff writes about "infomating" in her book, *In the Age of the Smart Machine*. With today's technologies, she points out, when we think we are "automating," we are often really "infomating" – creating data to use for better outcomes. She uses the analogy of the grocery store scanner – do you think it automates the checkout process? Sure, it does. But a larger purpose is to create tons of data about what people (or, specifically, you) buy, when and in what combinations. Did you respond to the ads or buy the items on the end of the aisles? And, if so, did you buy the other items they hoped you would buy, as well? That's what they need to know to optimize grocery selling and maximize customer value.

CRM is not much different. It's about infomating. (It's also about transforming – we're not automating here!) The basic idea is to create lots of data and do something smart with it. Look again at the process cycle in Figure 7-4 (on page 205). A critical component is data analysis and applying what you learn to alter the business rules.

CRM Data Analysis

The steps for analyzing data in a CRM environment further emphasize the transformational nature of CRM. Remember the discussion in Chapter 5 about reporting strategy and the changing elevator story? Those changes highlight the beginning of the transformation on how we use data in the contact center and who analyzes it.

CRM really brings that issue to the forefront. This is not analysis of ACD stats and the intuitive knowledge most call center managers have about what is happening and why ("Talk time is up because of the new system changes," "We're getting hammered because of the marketing efforts," or "Our service level isn't being met yet, but as these new trainees get up-to-speed, we'll be OK"). CRM data analysis involves analyzing relationships and business outcomes that you previously couldn't have imagined, but which may profoundly change the way you interact with customers.

New tools for data analysis using advanced data-mining techniques provide dramatic new capabilities. For instance, suppose that while using these tools you discover your retention rate is higher when customer contact does not lapse for more than three months. The impact on your business and on what the contact center should do is significant. Putting in place a new business rule that triggers proactive contact with customers you haven't heard from or contacted in two-and-a-half months could lead to increased retention and, therefore, more revenue. No manager would intuitively know that target timeframe and the potential result. This is the power of CRM data, analysis and application.

Not all data elements in the CRM system are needed for analysis and business decision support activities. A subset of the transactional data is extracted from the production (transactional) system and uploaded to a database specifically designed for reporting purposes, and sometimes this data is combined with other data sources (demographics, psychographics, market research and other transactional data). By using a second database specifically for reporting, the production system does not suffer any performance degradation from advanced queries. This multisource, reporting-specific database application is sometimes referred to as a "data warehouse," and the knowledge gleaned from it is known as "business intelligence."

Data Analysis Tools

The data analysis environment probably sounds familiar to you – it was introduced in Chapter 5. Changes in what is reported on and how it's reported are very evident in a CRM environment. The data analysis tools and techniques used on the reporting database include:

• **Querying and reporting:** basic historical reports. Tool examples include Seagate's Crystal Reports, Microsoft's Access, Business Objects and Cognos' Impromptu.

- **Online Analytical Processing (OLAP)**: historical reports with drill-down and advanced manipulation capability. OLAP allows you to look at the data from different views, drill down into increasing levels of detail and analyze trends. Although these details could also be found using multiple queries with a basic tool, OLAP tools stage the data to make responses very fast. OLAP tools let you slice and dice loads of data very quickly. Tool examples include Brio's BrioQuery, Microstrategy's DSS suite, Oracle's Express suite and Arbor Software's Essbase.

- **Data mining:** advanced statistical techniques. These tools make extensive use of predictive algorithms and statistical correlation, and they present findings without having to be specifically asked. Tool examples include IBM's Intelligent Miner, NeoVista Solutions' Decision Series and HNC Software's Database Mining Marksmen.

Data Analysis Outcomes

When you have these types of data analysis tools, you can take reporting and management decisions – and actions – to a new level. Here are some examples:

- **Analyze business outcomes** tied to the skill level of the agent handling the contact. For example you might analyze sales or upsells closed, trouble tickets closed, issues resolved, customers saved and products shipped. You can correlate talk time, as well. This analysis may reveal the value of additional focused training to help agents reach new skill levels and therefore protect or drive more revenue.

- **Analyze relationships** between quality monitoring scores, productivity (measured by handle time), customer satisfaction feedback and business outcome. For instance, if the analysis shows that better quality scores correlate with better business outcomes and customer satisfaction, at the cost of additional talk time, trade-offs need to be made. It may be time to change key performance indicators or scorecards to increase the weighting of quality. And it may be time to build the case for more headcount (justified by increased revenue).

- **Analyze channel use and customer value.** Data analysis may show that customers who tend to use a broader set of channel choices add higher value to the company. This analysis points to the value of aggressive multichannel marketing campaigns that emphasize accessibility, choice and control for the customer.

Best-Fit Scenarios for CRM

Companies that are well-suited to CRM have one or more of the following characteristics:

- Customer contact is frequent and ongoing.
- Relationships with customers are direct (i.e., not via distributor, dealer, etc.) or there are opportunities to build relationships with the distributors/dealers.
- Customers desire and value a relationship with the company.
- The company receives value from interacting with the customer (creates or protects revenue).
- The company competes on sales and/or service interactions (it is a source of competitive advantage).
- Diverse products/services create an opportunity to grow the relationship with the customer.

Following are the industries that typically present a good CRM opportunity:

- Financial services (banking, insurance, investment management)
- Retail
- High tech
- Travel/hospitality
- Telecommunications, cellular, cable, satellite

CRM Alternatives

If all of this CRM stuff sounds daunting or you don't feel that your company fits the CRM mold, don't be disappointed. It's actually quite refreshing to hear managers admit, "CRM isn't for us" or "We're not ready for CRM yet."

Companies that take this stance are taking a hard look at their business and at the whole concept of CRM and critically determining it doesn't fit. We've seen this point of view in companies that don't really want to talk to their customers (yes, such policies should and do exist in some organizations). That doesn't mean they don't provide good service when customers call – they do. But they hope that customers won't call back.

Complaint lines for consumer products are a good example. The customer may have questions or a problem with the product, but once they are placated, the company hopes that's the end of the direct contact with the customer. They do want to capture the information about the interaction to use in product management and quality improvements, so creating a record is important, but developing a relationship with the customer isn't.

Product manufacturers that sell to distributors or retailers often have contact centers for the end customer, but the preference is that the consumer will contact the place where they purchased the product. Government agencies, monopolies and highly regulated companies focus on servicing the need, but are not covering the whole a full CRM application package process from marketing to sales to service – CRM has little applicability in these contact center environments.

So what's the alternative? If you need some of the benefits that CRM solutions offer through contact tracking, scripting, workflows or access to key data on few screens, consider basic contact management solutions or build your own front end. The following examples may help you to get an idea of the possible opportunities:

• A start-up contact center with a small number of agents and a very aggressive schedule to go live couldn't afford the time or money to implement a full CRM solution. The company purchased a *basic contact management system* at a fraction of the cost of a full CRM application package and delivered contact tracking, basic scripting, reports and a good graphical interface to the customer data and information on the products and services being offered.

• A government organization with many different legacy systems is struggling with the cumbersome navigation of all these systems, as well as training and ramp-up time for new staff. CRM is not the answer in this case. However, a *front-end system* built in Powerbuilder or Visual Basic, for example, with middleware linking into these systems would grab the needed data and update it upon completion of the contact. This approach is often called "super screens" or "80 percent screens," because the key information needed for a given contact type is consolidated on a single screen.

The moral of the story is that CRM isn't for everyone. If it's not for you, you can still look at other options to achieve some of the benefits of better desktop interfaces and applications. The key is to understand your business goals, look at how they impact your operations and then determine the capabilities you need. In Chapter 10, we'll look at the issues involved with ASPs, which may be another option for companies that think they might benefit in some ways from CRM, but don't want to tackle the technology themselves.

Keys to Success

So why do we hear so many failure stories about a (technology-enabled) business concept with such potential? The biggest obstacle appears to be a lack of clear strategy and vision driven from the top (or near the top). CRM will not succeed as a grassroots effort. It requires compelling business drivers, as well as commitments of resources and monetary support. It is transformational, which requires companies to take the time to alter their cultures, organizations, processes and more.

To really succeed in the contact center, CRM must become an inherent part of the customer contact process. If you look at the CRM customer contact process cycle in Figure 7-4 (on page 205), you'll notice that CRM is never "done." Creating, capturing and analyzing data are ongoing tasks, as is modifying business rules or workflows. You never stop evolving, adapting to business needs or getting more out of the investment you've made. Successful CRM requires a commitment to this evolution, and putting the right resources in place to manage and apply the technology. Along with the technology efforts, there must be creative marketing, customer segmentation strategies and sales offers for the center to execute.

If you're focused on technology, and just on the contact center, look for more basic capabilities for contact management – tracking, reporting, basic workflows and scripting. Call it what you want, but it will not be full-blown CRM. But if you are serious about business strategies that seek to optimize sales and service for high-value customers or drive down costs by streamlining workflows and altering customer experiences and behavior, CRM will be a good fit. Our advice is to go into it with open eyes, and with the time, resources and money it takes to do it right.

Recipe for CRM Success

Here are a few key ingredients for succeeding at CRM:

- Executive vision and sponsorship.
- A well-defined and communicated CRM strategy – it's not just "a contact center thing"!
- Cross-functional team – contact center, technology, marketing and more – to implement and leverage it.
- Great project management.
- Good vendor partners – for technology solution and implementation.
- Recognition of the need to change processes, organization and culture, and time to review and redesign current environment.
- A plan for change management.
- A phased approach and ongoing evolution.
- Resource commitment to continue to leverage CRM (workflow architects, business analysts).

Points to Remember

- CRM is more than a technology; it's a way of business thinking. Technology alone will not yield CRM success.

- Information systems architectures are migrating from client/server to Web architectures. Along with this transition, the desktop is becoming "thinner" as the applications are server-resident.

- CRM technologies offer a rich set of application possibilities. Contact tracking and workflow (or business rules) are key.

- CRM integrates with many other elements in the call center, including legacy systems and, potentially, CTI and multimedia.

- CRM is about creating data and leveraging it so tools for data analysis play a big role, as well.

Actions to Take

- Make sure your company has a CRM strategy (and a "mantra") before pursuing CRM technology. Align your CRM strategy with your business strategy and call center strategy. Define your technology strategy to make correct information systems architecture decisions.

• When implementing CRM, define the suite of applications that makes sense for your environment. Also, plan carefully for integrating CRM with the rest of your technology.

• If CRM isn't right for your company, pursue other alternatives for benefits in contact-tracking and call-flow optimization.

Part 4: Extending Your Reach

So you say you need to do more than answer the phone? Then give your customers choice and control over their interactions with you. Self-service and multimedia take you beyond the call center to the contact center. With self-service and multimedia strategies as your guide, you can leverage the power of these exciting tools.

Chapter 8: Building IVR and Web-Based Self-Service

Chapter 9: Multimedia: Transitioning from Call Center to Contact Center

Chapter 8:

Building IVR and Web-Based Self-Service

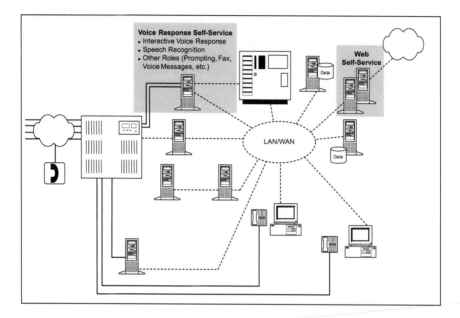

Key Points Discussed in this Chapter:

Building a Self-Service Strategy

IVR Roles and Applications

Automatic Speech Recognition

IVR Integration with the Call Center

Web Self-Service

Self-Service Trends and Directions

IVR and Web-based self-service tools often provide the most compelling business case of any contact center technology – that is, when the technology is applied effectively in the right environment. Live contact handling runs from $3 to $10 per contact and up, depending on the business, complexity and length of transactions. IVR transactions generally cost tens of cents, while Web contacts can be mere pennies. So when "automatable" transactions are identified, the self-service payback time is only months, making it easy to answer the question "why do it?" from an internal perspective.

Of course, the challenge is to do it right. IVR, in particular, has a reputation for being painful from a user's perspective because so many companies have picked the wrong applications or have built bad application logic and scripts. Cartoon fodder – that's what it is. Many of us in the call center profession have had to deal with the wrath of friends and family when they come to understand what it is we really do, and hold us responsible for all of those miserable systems they've encountered!

And while the Web has been less maligned, it's partially because it is less mature and the expectations haven't had as much time to develop and be shattered. Realistically, though, many Web sites don't provide the ease of use and capabilities customers want. While Web-assisted and collaborative service is very cool (and will be covered in-depth in Chapter 9), some of us really want to be able to finish things up on our own, without help. That's a win-win – meet customer expectations while delivering service via a lower-cost channel. When you look at it that way, this self-service stuff can be compelling.

If you look at the question "why do it?" from a customer's perspective, it cannot be answered with a financial business case. While self-service is readily bashed and many talk about "just wanting to talk to a person," the reality is that today's customers expect choice. Their desire can be expressed as: "Let me get service when and how I want it. Web or IVR, I want applications that are usable, and I want to succeed on my own terms."

Here's a good story about a bank that was having stability problems with its IVR. When the system was down, calls were routed directly to an agent. Here is how a telling conversation went:

Surprised at hearing an agent greeting, the customer says: "Um, I was call-ing to use your automated system."

Agent: "I'm sorry sir, but the system is down. How can I help you today?"

Customer: "Thanks. But I'll call back when it's working again." Click.

Wow, the customer reached a pleasant, helpful agent and yet decided to call back later. The customer had lost his choice and control.

The Service Spectrum

There are different degrees of self-service. There is assisted self-service and there is integrated service; there is the phone and the Web. Figure 8-1 illustrates this spectrum. Self-service is generally the lowest-cost approach because the customer never has to speak to an agent. Assisted service gives customers the additional choice and control they sometimes need to complete transactions or find all of the information they need. The service is optimized if, when the caller needs assistance, advanced technologies are used to integrate the IVR events with the agent desktop events, or to enable the agent to collaborate with the customer on the Web site as they chat or talk.

The type of service you offer needs to be a part of your overall strategic planning and, certainly, your self-service strategy. Be sure to consider cost, complexity and integration with other elements. (We'll tie the self-service information in this chapter into the Web-assisted world in the next chapter.)

Figure 8-1: The Service Spectrum

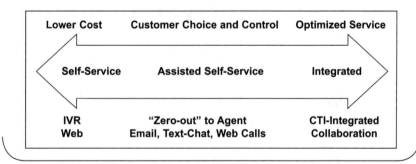

Lower Cost	Customer Choice and Control	Optimized Service
Self-Service	Assisted Self-Service	Integrated
IVR Web	"Zero-out" to Agent Email, Text-Chat, Web Calls	CTI-Integrated Collaboration

In this chapter, we'll look at the technology to deliver effective self-service, including IVR architectures, Automatic Speech Recognition (ASR) and key technologies for Web self-service. However, probably most important are the hints and tips on how to do it right – that doesn't depend on the technology, it depends on you.

Building a Self-Service Strategy

Media silos are a critical flaw in many contact centers today. In the worst case, one technology team "owns" the IVR, another owns the Web, neither group talks to the contact center, and agents don't have a clue what the customer can do with the IVR or Web. In the best case, these groups work collaboratively to create a common experience for the customer, and agents act as the biggest promoters of self-service tools. To create a best-case scenario, the contact center needs to play a pivotal role in developing the self-service strategy and must collaborate with IT, telecom and marketing staff.

Key Steps to Building a Strategy

Here are the key steps to building a self-service strategy.

First, Identify Opportunities:

• Look for opportunities to move high-volume, low-complexity contacts to self-service channels. Use input from customers, agents and benchmarking to identify applications that are suited to self-service. As one example, look for inquiries or transactions that don't require detailed interpretation or explanation, such as requests for account balances.

• Define measurable objectives for your self-service strategy. For example, "Lower the average cost per contact to $2.45 by increasing successful self-service from 30 percent to 40 percent."

• Determine where you want to drive contacts and develop a plan around that. Is the Web the preferred technology for your customer base, application types or cost structures? Are the users mobile, which would make the phone more accessible than the Web? What kind of marketing incentives and promotions will you use? All of these factors can influence the behavior of the customer (natural or encouraged).

- Map self-service applications to the most appropriate channels. Concentrate on developing "quick hits" for the IVR (e.g., transfer funds), while putting more complex and visual applications on the Web (loan modeling). Think about whether or not speech recognition will deliver significant gains in self-service over the phone, beyond any that touchtone provides.

Next, Design Consistent Interfaces:

- Create consistent user interfaces across all channels. Use the same phrasing, same type of information, in the same order, whether it's the IVR, Web or live handling. Develop cross-channel marketing and branding, as well.

- Develop a security strategy that's consistent across channels, too. Don't make customers remember different user IDs and PINs for different channels. And don't require folks to identify themselves if they're only looking for general, nonsecure information.

- Leverage technology and efficiency of scale wherever possible. Ensure that Web and IVR teams work together to identify data requirements, resolve issues with host access and build the core applications that you'll offer across media. Ideally, the two applications will use common interfaces to back-end systems and access and update a common database in real-time.

Third, Maximize the Benefits:

- Save and use information that you collect from customers. After they've identified themselves, don't ask for the same information again.

- Develop strategies to retain customers and increase loyalty through the use of self-service. This requires commitment and a regular feedback loop to evaluate what's working and what's not. Incorporate continuous improvement into your self-service strategy.

- Make sure self-service gets the visibility it deserves and is part of sales and marketing plans for new products and services. Consider incentives for agents to help with promotion and customer coaching.

Got a Self-Service Mantra?

Consider these mantras in your self-service strategic planning:

- **Give customers choice and control;** put them in the driver's seat. Let customers choose when and how they interact with you. Let them decide when self-service is right and when assisted service is necessary. Depending on the caller's situation, the same caller will have different preferences at different times. For example, a customer needs to contact your company for some routine product or service information. First, he contacts you while he's at the office, which has high-speed Internet access and a fast PC. In this case, the Web is a great option. Later on, the same customer is on a business trip, in a hotel. It's after business hours, and he wants to see if an order shipped. In this situation, the IVR is a great option. The same customer finally receives the shipment, but an important item is missing – that's a great time to speak with a live agent.

- **Extend access** to the contact center through extended hours and media. Define the right media and the right hours of service to match customer expectations. Ultimately, you can provide 24x7 access through some form of interaction. Self-service is often a good option for customers during late hours, when the center isn't staffed.

- **Create a common look and feel** across IVR, Web and voice channels. Use common applications and common terminology for live contacts and self-service so customers feel like they are always interacting with the same company.

Other Key Elements to Get It Right

Beyond creating a strategy, four other key elements play a role in successful self-service:

1. **Identify the right applications for the right media.** Not every business needs to offer every application on every media. Many companies offer too many and overly complex applications for the media (especially touchtone IVR), resulting in very little bang for the buck, or worse, becoming a potential turnoff to customers. Focus on the truly automatable applications where the media interface and complexity of applications are a good fit. Recognize that there are unique advantages (and disadvantages) to each media, and the applications need to be matched to the media.

For example, 401k companies sometimes include applications on the IVR to rebalance the account (reallocating the percentages across different funds). While it is possible because it is numeric, it is a complex application involving many steps. It may also require fund numbers. The result can sound pretty ugly on an IVR with touchtone and would likely be used very little – although the design and development effort to create the application will be substantial. On the other hand, this application would be extremely effective on the Web since customers can view their allocations, and can easily and quickly reallocate.

2. Design applications using best practices with the user in mind. Script and call-flow development is an art and a science, so experience helps (it's not as intuitive as you think, which is why there are so many bad ones out there!). Start with call observations and agent focus groups, and whenever possible, conduct customer focus groups. Use best practices, including:

- Keep the user interface consistent. Always phrase each activity in the same way, and speak the action before the keystroke.
- Help callers feel successful – use positive feedback; blame mistakes on the system, not the callers.
- Talk to callers, don't write to them. We speak very differently than we write. Always read your script aloud before it is recorded and test it with a mix of people. And make sure the script doesn't include internal jargon!

3. Conduct usability testing to validate applications, logic and scripts. Usability testing lets users put the application through its paces in a simulated or test environment. Agents can help with usability testing, but ideally, it is conducted with real customers who don't know all of your internal jargon. Create sample inquiries and transactions for the users to try out, and seek specific feedback. Examples of feedback to seek in usability testing might include:

- Did you get confirmation of a successful transaction?
- Were the error messages helpful, clear and friendly?
- Were you able to easily navigate back to the main menu?

4. Track, report, analyze and optimize applications. Once an application is implemented, monitor it for what works and what doesn't. Exit points, hang ups or disconnects, application usage, self-service success rates and customer comments are all evidence to consider. The statistics to report on must be defined for monitoring in the application logic. The reporting needs in your self-service strategy should be tightly tied into your overall reporting strategy (as discussed in Chapter 5).

IVR Roles and Applications

Now that we've covered the importance of a cohesive self-service strategy, let's look at IVR. It can play many roles in the contact center: a prompting machine, a fax machine, a self-service machine.

If you'll recall from Chapter 3, we said that IVR can serve as the prompting vehicle to identify who is calling a center and why. It is the best and most likely candidate for prompting when there is an attempt to encourage customers to self-serve. Send them to the IVR first, and see if they'll take care of themselves – if they need assisted service, use the information they provided to route them to the correct agent group.

Fax is generally a function offered on an IVR when customers routinely request detailed specification sheets, records, forms, instructions or other text-intensive materials. "Fax-on-demand" is one choice from a main menu; alternatively, the fax application has its own local or 800 number. The customer might select a document from a menu of choices, or enter codes that were previously supplied through a mailing or a faxed list. Some applications enable customers to receive a fax of their last statement or recent account charges (e.g., with a bank or credit card company). The customer enters the fax number to which they want the documents faxed.

Most IVR platforms offer fax cards as an option. Fax is used for government, manufacturing and distribution, financial and healthcare applications.

Interactive IVR Has a Special Role

Noninteractive roles can be filled by other technologies (voicemail system, prompting on switch, fax server), if desired. The interaction with a database to complete inquiries and transactions is what differentiates IVR. Callers enter touch-tone digits on their telephones or use automatic speech recognition (ASR) to indicate their unique identifying information and service requests. They receive information back – spoken, faxed or even emailed.

The power of IVR to offload routine tasks is incredible: Many banks have 75 percent or more of their contacts handled fully in the IVR. No human thought is required to provide a bank balance (and who would want to do that all day anyway?). In other industries, the percentages may be much lower, but the business case is still compelling. Insurance companies might get only 30 percent to 35 percent of insured customers to self-serve, but they may routinely get providers to complete their transaction through self-service. If you were an insurance company, wouldn't you rather have your agents talking to insured members than providers? Utilities may normally achieve 10 percent to 30 percent self-service rates, but when there is an outage, that percentage may jump to between 60 percent to 80 percent, aiding tremendously in handling the skyrocketing (and often unanticipated) volume.

Good (and Bad) IVR Applications

Applications that are well-suited to IVR have the following characteristics:

• *Inquiries* **that are numeric and frequently accessed.** Account balance or order status are excellent examples. Another success story is locator services based on zip code or phone number. The customer has or can be readily trained to use a simple identifier that matches information in a business database: phone number, account number, social security number, etc.

Note: Non-numeric inquiries, such as inventory checks against alphanumeric item numbers (such as WBE-145) can be accommodated with some user coaching if using touchtone, but are generally less successful. They are a better candidate for ASR.

• *Transactions* **that are numeric and not overly complex.** Account balance transfer at a bank is good, while reallocation of funds percentages on a 401k is generally too cumbersome. The ability to easily identify the customer as well as the accounts or other entities in the transaction is key. In general, most applications should be no more than three menus deep and four choices across (or it should take less than a minute) to get to the item of choice. There are certain situations in which these guidelines can be exceeded, but the general calling public tends to get anxious with longer menus and lots of layers. Too many will nudge people to push zero to get to an agent, which is not the desired result.

• **Basic information that can be delivered in 30 seconds or less.** Any longer than that and callers will tune out and end up wanting to talk to someone. If the information needs to be written down to be useful, it must be very concise, and the customer should be offered the chance to hear it again. Or better yet, direct them to the Web, a handbook or other source for the information.

There are key flags that identify poorly suited applications:

• Making it easy for customers to uniquely identify themselves compromises security. For example, if information needs to be secured but customers don't call routinely, setting up a PIN may be ineffective.

• The transaction requires a signature.

• Talking to a live agent may positively change the outcome of the interaction, such as account closures in which an agent might be able to offer customers other options to retain them.

© 1996 by Randy Glasbergen, www.glasbergen.com

"To find out if you're someone who could benefit from our Memory Improvement Seminar, please press 59736222582095217059."

• Complex transactions that require too many steps or require the customer to do too much work to succeed (e.g., use code sheets, write things down, etc.).

IVR Architecture

Figure 8-2 shows the architecture of an IVR platform. Keep in mind, this could be a standalone unit or an inherent part of a Communications Server platform. Most IVR solutions are based on either Windows NT or Unix; some vendors offer a choice. Linux is an option from some vendors, as well.

Figure 8-2: IVR Architecture

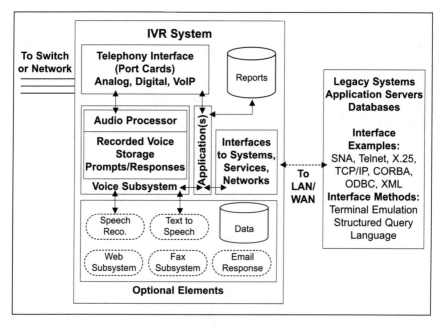

The key architectural elements are:

• **Telephony interface.** Analog, digital (T1) and now VoIP connections terminate in cards on the IVR. Most solutions today will use T1 for cost efficiencies and signaling capabilities. Recall that each T1 has 24 channels (U.S.) over a single connection. Because of this efficiency, the supporting hardware in the voice switch and the IVR unit requires only one slot, and fewer slot requirements translate into fewer servers (which saves money!).

Additionally, ISDN signaling can be used to quickly set up and tear down connections between devices. For an IVR unit, this translates into higher port availability. VoIP is an option that can be considered when quality of service is assured. Most IVR vendors are developing VoIP capability today, with options being Ethernet cards or TDM/IP gateways.

• **Applications.** The applications are basically programs that tell the system what to speak, what to listen for and what actions to take ("if... then..."). These actions include inquiries or updates to databases. Multiple applications can run on a single platform and are triggered by the port number, DNIS and/or DID digits, or menu selections.

• **Application development tools.** This is the software that builds the application. Most vendors today provide a proprietary scripting tool specific to their IVR systems. These tools are used to develop the application flow and speech vocabularies, and to edit speech. Almost every vendor offers a GUI tool for this purpose.

Visually, these tools are very similar in nature to flowcharting tools. Commands are dragged from a palette (e.g., "answer call," "collect digits," "play phrase," "transfer caller," "query database") and dropped onto an application workspace. Parameters and variables are added to the commands (e.g., hours of operation, specific phrase identifier, extension to transfer to, and database values). Finally, the graphical application gets compiled to a machine-specific format, is uploaded and put into production. The latest direction in voice-application development is to use VoiceXML (which is described later).

• **Voice subsystem.** The voice subsystem contains the audio processor and the recorded messages to speak. Recorded messages for prompts and responses are stored and the application tells the system what to speak when.

Well-designed and developed applications have very natural sounding messages, even though what is spoken is really a set of short messages strung together. This natural sound is accomplished by recording with consistent volume and inflection suited to the messages. For example, numbers should be recorded three times with different inflections used for when they are the first, middle or last digit in a string.

• **Data interface.** While databases can reside on the IVR platform (generally static data or data that is batch-updated), most often, data is in an external system or server. There are a number of interface types and methods to access the data from the IVR. Some systems use a terminal emulation or "screen-scrape" method in which the IVR mimics the actions of an agent on a terminal to access screens and read or insert appropriate data fields. For example, the IVR inputs an account number, triggers a screen retrieval and then reads the account balance field. More systems now are using structured database queries. Data Interfaces include 3270 and TN3270, J2EE, CORBA, Telnet, SQL, ODBC and XML, as well as connectors to popular packaged business applications like Siebel and SAP/R3 (note that the same integration technologies are used in CTI and CRM applications).

• **Advanced and optional capabilities.** Advanced and optional capabilities, such as text-to-speech, speech recognition, fax, Web, email or outbound dialing are generally software modules and sometimes require specialized hardware cards, as well.

VoIP Implications for Voice Response

Voice response must be IP-enabled to interpret VoIP streaming voice packets. Ethernet interfaces (10/100 Mb) replace the circuit-switch interfaces (T1, analog) on the IVR and they must be compatible with the signaling standard of your VoIP switch (e.g., Megaco, H.323, SIP). The applications and application development tools remain largely the same, and VoIP IVRs may still need to be integrated with CTI frameworks.

Other IVR Platform Considerations

If you're defining requirements for an IVR vendor and product selection, the items previously discussed are definite considerations. You should also look at overall architecture, as some systems are built on a very proprietary platform while others leverage standard servers and voice cards (remember, what's your technology strategy?).

Another factor to consider is the scalability and networking capabilities, especially if you have multiple sites and significant application opportunities that will take you beyond a single server. For example, a single system may have a maximum port capacity of 96 ports. The number of ports is a reflection of the number of simultaneous users the system can support. Networking features include reporting, network monitoring, application management and updates.

The final consideration when looking at vendor options is the vendor's capabilities. Since the market is so diverse (see "A Note About the IVR Market," on page 239), you can find vendors that just sell the piece parts (boards, development tools), provide core hardware and software and you develop applications, or deliver a turnkey solution (hardware, software and applications). Which do you want and need? Will you be doing your own development or relying on the vendor? The answer to these questions changes emphasis from critically evaluating the development tools through demos to understanding the depth of the resources the vendor has to provide development support (initial and ongoing). Some vendors even offer starter applications for specific vertical markets.

IVR Location Options

You'll need to decide where the IVR platform will physically reside. IVRs can sit "in front of" or "behind" the voice switch. In a multisite environment, IVRs can be distributed or centralized. Figure 8-3 illustrates some options.

Figure 8-3: IVR Location Options

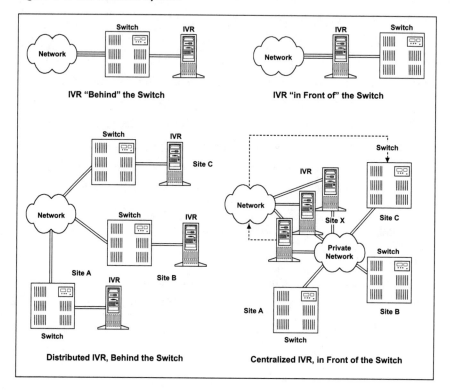

If configured in front, lines from the network terminate on the IVR. If a call needs to be transferred out to an agent, the IVR can route the call to the voice switch, connecting the call through the IVR. Or it may use network features, such as network transfer, in which the call is returned to the network for routing (which frees the IVR port).

When in front, it is generally a situation in which the IVRs are centralized and calls are routed to one of many sites, or a high percentage (e.g., 85 percent or more) of calls complete successfully in the IVR (i.e., callers don't need to transfer out to speak to an agent). We've seen large multisite utilities and financial services with high self-service success rates use this approach.

When the IVR is placed behind the voice switch, the network lines terminate in the switch and the switch connects the call to the IVR. In this scenario, when a call needs to be transferred, it is generally transferred out of the IVR, freeing the port for additional calls.

When Is a Trombone Not a Trombone?

Avoid configurations that use "tromboning" in which the call is looped through the IVR back to the switch. These systems essentially double the port requirements for transferred calls on both the IVR and the voice switch; each transferred call uses two voice-switch ports and two IVR ports. Tromboning is used when the interface and trunk configuration prohibit a transfer between the switch and IVR.

Most call centers place the IVR behind the switch because of switch reliability (callers will get automatically redirected to an agent group when the IVR is down), simplicity of transfer and ease of integration.

A Note About the IVR Market

The IVR market is crowded and messy. It is a flat market, the pie is not big enough for all the players and the slices are just too small. IVRs have basically become commodities in the call center technology realm. So many are trying to be more than just an IVR vendor. They sell CTI, Web capabilities, quality monitoring or logging, and other features. There are turnkey solutions that sell for tens or hundreds of thousands of dollars. But there are also many small systems that are easily built with a PC server, voice cards and a development toolkit. Because there are so many small call centers, this "two guys in a garage" approach to IVR – often targeting specific markets – is not uncommon.

VoiceXML – A New Development

Voice eXtensible Markup Language (VoiceXML) is a relatively new development in IVR architecture. VoiceXML is a standard for voice-application development, much like HTML is for Web-page development. The result is a programming language that is easier to use and vendor-independent. It is used to develop voice-response applications and voice interfaces to Web sites (public or private).

VoiceXML is being promoted by the VoiceXML Forum, an organization consisting of 600 member companies. A similar architecture is being developed and promoted by an organization called the SALT Forum (Speech Application Language Tags), which includes Microsoft as a member. The idea behind these initiatives is to leverage existing Internet infrastructure and developer skills for building voice applications. The VoiceXML forum releases specifications and has the following goals:

• Leverage existing Web infrastructure for voice-application delivery (e.g., TCP/IP, HTTP, Web servers and markup languages).

• Extend the pool of voice-application developers by using existing Web-application development tools.

• Simplify application development with a high-level programming language.

• Separate the application logic from the user interface allowing one application to service several media channels.

• Consolidate Web and voice applications.

• Open up telephony platforms for third-party development.

VoiceXML has three key differences from traditional IVR architectures:

1. It moves the application logic from the IVR system to a Web server.

2. It uses existing data interfaces and moves the external system data interfaces from the IVR to a Web server.

3. It introduces new client software, called a "voice browser." In the VoiceXML world, the voice browser acts as an interpreter between the VoiceXML language and the telephony, playback and encoding capabilities in the IVR – or what might now be referred to as an XML Gateway. Figure 8-4 shows the VoiceXML architecture.

Figure 8-4: VoiceXML Architecture*

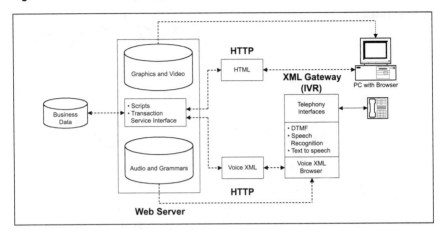

In the VoiceXML world, the IVR system gets decomposed. Systems do not have to be sourced as a proprietary whole, but rather as a series of components (server, XML browser, cards for telephony interfaces and speech recognition, application software, etc.). This decomposition is very similar to the decomposition of PBXs and ACDs we discussed in Chapter 2, in which ACD capabilities formerly embedded in voice-switch-based software are offloaded to servers.

The goals of VoiceXML reflect its potential benefits to you. VoiceXML will benefit companies that choose it over a proprietary vendor language, making it easier to find, develop and retain the skills to write voice applications.

Automatic Speech Recognition

ASR uses a spoken dialog between the caller and the system to enable new applications, as well as making applications that were cumbersome via touchtone downright fun. It is still somewhat expensive, so its early inroads have been in markets where touchtone applications are unable to produce high success rates – primarily travel, brokerage houses and mutual fund services.

The case for speech-enabled applications is compelling here. If you were to contrast this with a bank that is achieving 80 percent success rate with touchtone, the business case for speech will be harder to make, as the incremental gain may be

---

* As described by the VoiceXML forum; www.voiceXML.org

small. We've even seen bank customers reveal a preference for touchtone over ASR in surveys (for security and other reasons).

However, as costs come down and speech applications become more common, companies need to seriously consider this option. Speech has a true "wow!" factor for the caller and, thus, will transform customer expectations.

Speech recognition will serve as a catalyst for change. If you haven't heard an ASR demo, call one of the major airlines' flight arrival/departure status numbers, or go to the Web sites of two major vendors: Nuance (www.nuance.com) and Speechworks (www.speechworks.com). Chances are, you'll say "wow!" when you hear examples of what can be done with speech.

Touchtone and speech applications can reside on the same platform, giving the caller the choice to use touchtone or speech (you've probably heard an application that asks you to "Press or say one..."), or offering some applications in speech only and others in touchtone only. Keep in mind that a speech application should be designed differently from a touchtone application to achieve the benefits of the technology. An application that just duplicates the touchtone interface with speech will not achieve a high return on investment.

Maintaining both touchtone and speech for the same application may become expensive in a dynamic environment. There is a tradeoff though in security; some users prefer touchtone applications because they can enter their account number and PIN without anyone hearing (imagine trying to conduct a financial transaction in a public place). Developing your strategy will ensure that you optimize success while also managing cost of ownership. Consider the applications and the customer expectations, as well as the business case for speech. Then, determine the best approach. Many companies will transition from touchtone to speech through a phased migration of applications.

Speech recognition differs from voice recognition. Voice recognition (or verification) matches a voice print from an individual for security or identification purposes. While this technology is improving and quickly coming onto the scene, it is not generally found in contact center applications today. However, it will help to address some of the security concerns surrounding ASR. For example, a bank customer speaks his name and a password (not his account number and PIN), but the application matches the voice rather than the words themselves to provide security.

Key ASR Capabilities

Here are a few key capabilities to understand concerning ASR technology and applications.

• **Speaker recognition.** Who can speak and be recognized? Contact center applications use speaker-independent technology. The software recognizes many accents and ways of saying the same thing. It doesn't "get to know" the speaking styles of users or require "training" the way speaker-dependent software would. But speaker-independent systems have a more limited vocabulary.

• **Speaking rate.** Today's technology and applications use continuous speech, meaning the caller can speak in a normal manner without having to pause between words or phrases.

• **Speaking format.** There are two key formats – structured, or directed dialog, and natural language. Structured or directed dialog coaches the caller through what to say, with prompts such as: "What type of shipping would you like? You can say overnight, two-day or ground." It recognizes key words or short phrases. Natural language is more wide open, such as: "What type of banking transaction do you need?" It looks for and understands words or phrases ("word-spotting"). Both formats can be used in a single application. For example, an application could start with natural language and use directed dialog when it can't understand what is being said.

• **Other features.** Today's systems support vocabularies of tens of thousands of words. They allow the caller to speak over or "barge in" to bypass prompts.

Several important caveats must be considered with ASR. First, alpha character (letter) recognition is difficult, so alphanumeric codes (those containing both numbers and letters) may be poor candidates for ASR implementation. It's easy to understand why – many letters sound very much alike. For instance, when you spell your name to a live agent, you might say: "That's 'M' as in 'Mary'" or "That's 'F' as in 'Frank.'"

Second, the accuracy can be greatly impacted by the environment. Speaker phones, cell phones, noisy environments (e.g., in a car, at the airport) can all dramatically reduce accuracy. The likely customer situations must be considered when building a business case or designing for ASR.

Speech Architectures

Speech-enabling an IVR platform requires adding hardware and software that is specific to speech capabilities. Speech recognition capabilities can be native to the IVR, or use an external speech recognition engine. Although most IVR vendors offer some type of native speech recognition, the size of the vocabulary tends to be limited and they tend to offer directed-dialog applications. The computational requirements needed for native natural language capabilities simply exceed the computing resources available from the IVR unit. Figure 8-5 shows the external engine approach.

Figure 8-5: ASR Architecture

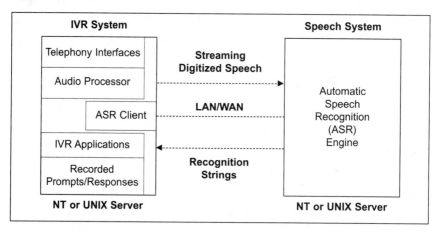

With the external speech recognition engine, the IVR unit and the speech recognition engine act in a client/server relationship. The IVR issues a request for speech recognition services and the speech engine serves that request. More specifically, the IVR collects an utterance from the caller, encodes the utterance into a digital format and streams the digitized speech to the external engine; the engine, in turn, sends a recognition string back to the IVR.

This client/server relationship is necessary because speech recognition algorithms use very complex mathematical formulas to recognize the content and context of spoken words and these algorithms need lots of CPU cycles and memory. By splitting the functions, the combined system responds in a more timely manner. The IVR unit provides the telephony interfaces, application logic, speech phrases, phrase playback and encoding of the callers' utterances, while the speech recognition engine provides the interpretation of the utterances.

Text-to-Speech

Text-to-Speech (TTS) is another specialty feature of IVRs that has improved in recent years. It can sometimes leverage the same hardware (cards) to process voice that is used for ASR. There is also an option to use a client/server architecture, similar to ASR.

TTS is used to speak large and frequently changing vocabularies that are prohibitive to record. For example, an order processing application with thousands of products that change frequently and millions of customers, would use TTS to confirm the products being ordered and the address to which an order should be shipped. Advanced TTS technology uses concatenated human sounds, rather than the computerized voices. Thus, the quality has improved. However, it still doesn't sound as natural as recorded messages.

TTS is a capability whose usability should be tested before being deployed into production. Again, visit a few Web sites to experience the state-of-the-art in this technology (www.nuance.com or www.speechworks.com).

IVR Integration with the Call Center

Realistically, there are many tasks that might start out routine but then lead to questions or at least the need for the human touch. "What do you mean my balance is only $4.23?" "Why hasn't my claim been processed yet?" "Why hasn't my order shipped yet?" "You told me three hours ago this outage would be fixed in two hours!" This is where integrating the IVR with live handling comes into play. There are also other applications for integrating the IVR with the phone system.

For instance, it's possible to:

- **Pass data from the switch to the IVR.** For example, in a multiapplication environment, pass DNIS to the IVR so that ports can be dynamically allocated, resulting in higher utilization of the IVR ports and, therefore, lower costs. (Remember our discussion about Erlang and the efficiencies gained as serving groups get larger? The same concept works for IVR ports. When you can dynamically change the application on a given port to meet the caller need, then all ports are in the same group, rather than having certain ports dedicated to specific applications.) Pass ANI to assist in caller identification and/or reduce prompting.

- **Pass data from the IVR to the switch.** For example, pass the account number gathered in the IVR so the agent doesn't have to ask the customer to repeat the information previously entered. Don't you just hate it when you've interacted with an IVR for five minutes, then transfer to an agent only to hear, "Can I please have your account number?"

- **Enhance caller treatment in queue.** For example, play customized messages based on predicted wait time or the current queue situation or even the caller's favorite music type. Or the caller can use the IVR while waiting in queue, without losing his or her place in queue. When an agent becomes available, the call can be immediately routed.

- **Automate callbacks.** Offer a caller the option to leave a message or receive a callback rather than wait in queue (e.g., after hearing how long the queue time is). The message can then be placed into queue and delivered to the first available agent. Rather than getting a live call, the agent hears the message and is prompted to "Press # when you are ready to return this customer's call."

As with many technologies, the answer to the question "How should I do this?" is "It depends." (But you knew that, didn't you?) The different ways IVRs and switches are integrated is highly dependent on the combination of vendors and products involved. If it is the same vendor or two top-tier vendors that have worked together, they may have standard ways of integrating. If it is a Communications Server, this integration is likely inherent in the product. If you are considering two totally different vendors, you may be quite limited in your options or may have to custom-integrate (because many of the interfaces are still quite proprietary). Here are a few ways the IVR integrates with phone systems (passing data in either or both directions, if needed):

- **Whisper transfer.** The IVR conducts a transfer, but first "whispers" the account number or other information to the agent before connecting the caller. This is sometimes referred to as "poor man's CTI" because the caller experience is similar to a "screen pop," even though it's manual. This option works if there is not a lot of data to pass and if queue times are short or priority queuing can be used on IVR transfers. Why? Long queue times tie up the port, making it unavailable for another call.

- **In-band signaling.** In-band signaling passes touchtones in the same channel as the voice call, prior to opening the voice path to the caller. This option is relatively simple. It works best with short data strings; lengthy data strings take too much time with this method.

- **CTI.** Using a CTI link between the IVR and the switch is a good option if the vendors have developed the link and you have other CTI needs.

- **"Black box."** Third parties have hardware that emulates proprietary phones, reads the display information and converts it to a protocol that can be passed to and understood by the IVR. The call needs to be temporarily terminated on the black box and then transferred. While this sounds a bit strange, it can be a fairly low-cost option to pass information from the switch to the IVR.

Web Self-Service

Clearly, today, the Web is a powerful self-service tool for the contact center. We're not going to present a dissertation on Web-server architectures and interfaces, or developing Web sites and e-commerce and shopping carts – that's a whole book (or several) in itself, and they've already been written. We want to highlight some key ideas about how to optimize Web capabilities for customer contact, and how to bring them into the realm of self-service and customer-contact strategy.

Most companies with contact centers have a Web site that offers customers some level of self-service. The IT department may be in charge of it or it may be outsourced. Marketing, or an e-commerce guru, may play a key role in defining the content, look and feel of the site.

As we highlighted earlier in this chapter, what needs to be "fixed" most often in companies is the level of contact center involvement in the Web site's role. In other words, get involved – this will ensure that the content for self-service is in synch with other customer contact interactions, and the call center is in tune to the Web content in order to leverage and promote it. Collaboration with IT and marketing is important to ensure the Web site plays a significant role in both customer satisfaction and the costs of servicing customers.

An effective Web self-service strategy for customer contact grows out of your overall self-service strategy. So what should be included on the Web site for customer contact? Everything that's on the IVR and more. Here are some examples:

• **Web forms.** Forms may be "ugly" when used on voice response, but they're beautiful on the Web. Filling out name, address and other contact information, and then some characteristics or interests related to the products or services offered is highly efficient and effective.

Note: Too often today, forms turn into emails that get printed and then entered into the system by a human being. What a great way to destroy a business case! Web forms must be integrated with the data systems that will be used for real-time automatic data entry.

• **Models or bookings.** When can I retire? How much house can I afford? What will my electric bills be if I take this new plan or make these changes to my energy consumption? How many flight options are there and what do they cost? These are all excellent Web self-service applications.

• **Orders.** Order applications include being able to select from a wide range of products, entering all shipping and billing information, and getting all of the details on shipping and handling prices. This can be done very effectively on the Web.

• **Multistep transactions.** "I want to check my balance, transfer funds, see my last 10 transactions and pay bills." That sounds like a lot to do, but the Web interface makes it relatively easy to move from one application to the next. Customers might even want to print a few things along the way or save a page as an HTML file.

• **Lengthy information.** Anything that takes more than 30 seconds to speak is a good candidate for the Web. Examples include assembly instructions, detailed product and service offerings, prospectus for financial instruments, legal documents, plan coverage for insurance and loan options. There are many things that can be effectively explained via live handling, but some people prefer to read at their leisure. And a bonus for the company: It costs less for the customer to self-serve than to talk to someone! And in those applications where precise language needs to be conveyed, letting callers read it themselves is a good option.

• **Help.** Static self-help, including a search engine and frequently asked questions, are generally available on good Web sites for self-service. Dynamic self-help may be offered based on the clickstream. This form of help is contextual, meaning inferences are made based on where the user has been and what he appears to be doing.

What You Need to Know About Web Technologies

The typical person who works on call center technologies is not going to specify requirements, evaluate vendors, design Web technology architectures or have to integrate it with legacy systems. There is already a Web server, and its purposes stretch far beyond the contact center. There is a set of Web technologies that make it readily interoperable – it is standards-based, open and highly accessible through the IP networks and browsers that are commonplace.

So what do you need to know? Here are some key terms that may be helpful in your conversations as you seek to *apply* the Web server to your customer-contact needs:

• **Web Server** is the PC that runs your Web capabilities. For customer contact, it's connected to the Internet (an IP network). Browsers access it, and it accesses other systems, databases and applications as necessary to perform the applications defined.

• **Java** is a programming language developed by Sun Microsystems that is very much at home in the Web environment. It is independent of the operating system, network or other characteristics, and is known by the concept: "Write once, run anywhere." JavaBeans, JavaScript and Java Applets can be used to write and run applications in a Web environment.

- **URL,** or Uniform Resource Locator, is the address for a Web page. It is translated to an IP address. For example, www.vanguard.net is a URL. The IP address is the "actual" address of a device on the internet. It is four sets of up to three digits, separated by periods (such as 167.174.27.945). The World Wide Web eases the addressing problem associated with trying to remember strings of digits by enabling us to use www.vanguard.net instead.

- **HTML,** Hyper-Text Markup Language, is a programming language used on the Web to define how to present information on Web pages. The pages it presents are static.

- **HTTP,** Hyper-Text Transfer Protocol, links addresses entered into a Web browser with a Web server, and pulls in the right HTML pages.

- **CGI,** Common Gateway Interface, is a program running on a Web server. CGI scripts are often written in a scripting language called PERL, but can be other languages as well (such as C or C++, Java Script and VB Script). CGI lets you do more dynamic things with a Web page, such as get data or use form input from a customer.

- **XML,** eXtensible Markup Language, is a standard for passing data between systems that includes a description about the data (such as <name> Lori Bocklund </name>). This allows systems to readily pass dynamic information and enables receiving systems to know what a particular data field is so it can deduce how to use, store or display it.

Self-Service Trends and Directions

It's difficult to separate one contact center technology topic from another – self-service is related to CTI for integration with the agents in the center, and with multimedia contact management for Web-assisted service (text-chat, Web calls, email) and collaboration.

Self-service is also becoming closely linked with customer relationship management. CRM data and dynamic, adaptable self-service application code can lead to a personalized self-service experience. Some refer to this as "eCRM," and many think of it as a Web phenomena. However, it can also apply to self-service more broadly. There are a variety of products that analyze interactions, personalization and management of the customer experience.

"Analytics" engines provide software for evaluating Web user paths and outcomes, and reporting on them. Some link to other data outside the Web site, such as marketing demographics or information stored in corporate data warehouses.

Personalization or content-management engines customize the interaction based on what is known about the specific customer, as well as information gathered and analyzed about similar customers. So, when you log on to Amazon.com, suggestions appear of what you might be interested in based on your past buying history, and patterns they see with others who buy similar products. This type of personalization doesn't just occur on retail sites; it's also a good fit for financial services, utilities or travel sites.

In addition, these capabilities can alter how the caller interacts with different media, as well as *what* is presented. Here are a few examples:

• Bob is a valued customer at a bank, but always tries to bypass the IVR menu prompts because he hates "those machines." The application sends notification to the CRM database that he presses zero right away (or waits on the line for a live agent). The CRM analytics software recognizes this trend and flags Bob as a "bypass" customer. The next time he calls from home and there is an ANI match in the database, the CRM application, along with CTI-based routing, indicates the caller should be routed immediately to the premier customer queue with no prompting. Bob is thrilled to go straight to an agent.

• Betty is a customer of the same bank and loves self-service. She routinely uses the IVR to transfer funds between two accounts. As a matter of fact, that's all she ever does. So the IVR application recognizes this trend and starts to provide her with a customized menu that first offers transfers from checking to money market or money market to checking, and then "all other" transactions in case she has a different need this time.

• John frequently books flights online and always likes to check his mileage balance and upgrade coupon availability. The software recognizes this pattern and creates a personalized screen that shows up immediately after login is complete, proactively showing him mileage and coupon balances. Because John is a frequent flyer, he is also offered assisted service on the Web.

• Jane flies twice a year. She is not in any special level mileage level with any airlines. When she goes to book online, the option for assisted service (text-chat or Web calls) isn't always presented to her. If the contact centers are busy, the icons don't appear. When things aren't too busy, Jane sees the option to seek live assistance. (Use this one carefully – it must be tied to a clear customer segmentation strategy.)

Personalizing the self-service experience is the next wave of sophistication for these tools. It is a powerful capability that will transform customer thinking and "raise the bar" for self-service in contact centers of all types. As customers, we'll each have "my Web page" and "my IVR menu" at companies with which we routinely interact. That personalization will tighten relationships and therefore increase retention of high-value customers.

Beyond the application specialization, another key trend in voice-response platforms is the move to IP-based voice. As we described in Chapter 2, because of the business benefits of managing a single IP-based network, voice is migrating to IP. Over time, IVR systems and applications will also migrate to IP. The transition of IVR platforms to IP will be similar to the transition of PBX/ACD systems to IP. Some will use IP cards on the system, others will use an external gateway to convert, while still others will replace their older systems with new IP-based platforms.

Architectures for the Web, as well as Voice XML and ASR, foreshadow an overall trend toward "application server" architectures. These architectures will be discussed more in Chapter 11. Suffice it to say that decomposition (and choice), open platforms, standards and Web-based architectures will ultimately rule!

Beyond Web self-service lies assisted service in a multimedia contact center. In a best-in-class contact center, the surfer who needs assistance can link into the contact center through text-chat, Web collaboration and real-time Web calls. Read on – Chapter 9 covers these topics.

Points to Remember

• A self-service strategy should encompass IVR and Web, and define plans for self-service, assisted service and integration. It also defines applications suited to each media.

• IVR design options today include a choice of platform, development approach and location relative to switches. VoiceXML is the new tool for voice applications design and development.

• Automatic speech recognition enables centers to take phone-based voice applications to a new level of self-service.

• The IVR can be integrated with other call center technologies through a number of options to improve customer service.

• While it is unlikely you will need to design Web technology or select vendors, it is important that you get plugged in to your company's Web site and influence its role in supporting the contact center goals.

• Agents should be your ambassadors to getting customers to use self-service capabilities. They need to understand these systems and help callers know when and how to use them.

• For companies that have well-developed IVR and Web strategies, seamless integration will significantly enhance customer satisfaction.

• Personalized self-service and analytics are the next goals for advanced call centers.

Actions to Take

• Build a self-service strategy that is tied to your other strategies and business goals. It should clearly define the role that IVR and the Web will play. Once you have a strategy, you can define the appropriate technology design to enable it.

Chapter 9:

Multimedia: Transitioning from Call Center to Contact Center

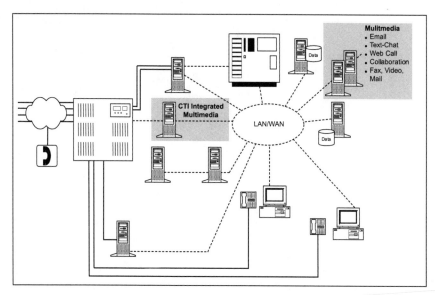

Key Points Discussed in this Chapter:

Web-Based Media Options
Email, Text-Chat, Web Call, Web Collaboration

Multimedia Applications Technology

Integrated Queuing and Routing

Call Flow

Multimedia Considerations
People, Process and Organizational Ripple Effects

Much of the discussion in this book focuses on voice contacts because, traditionally, vioce has been the primary channel for customer interaction. Frankly, it still is for most centers. In this chapter, however, we'll explore newer, additional channels of customer access. Today, we're clearly in a time of transition from a voice-only call center to a *multimedia contact center*.

Figure 9-1: Multimedia Customer Contact

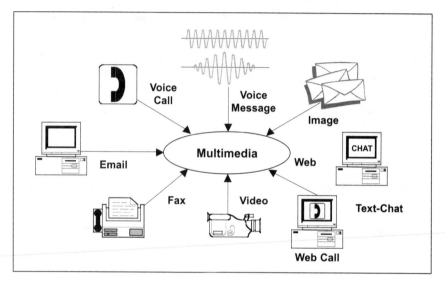

What's driving this transition? The way we communicate is a function of the devices available and the networks we access. Phone calls over the traditional voice network were first. Next, image transmission over the same network (using fax machines) emerged. Email, as a communication mechanism within companies, simmered on a back burner for years. Then along came the Internet. Suddenly, email use exploded – both for person-to-person communication as well as consumer-to-business. "Contact us" buttons appeared on Web sites to support email. Companies realized that there were other, more efficient ways to support Web customer contact – and, thus, text-chat, Web calls and Web collaboration were born.

Here is an important fact of this media proliferation: It's cumulative. Web integration and collaboration doesn't mean you won't have to take phone calls and respond to faxes anymore. It has to be integrated and managed cohesively so that, regardless of which media customers choose, they feel like they're talking to the same company. In this chapter, we'll introduce various media alternatives and then bring it all together with a look at multimedia queuing. Your challenge is to determine which media are needed for your customers and when – sounds like a good time to think strategically!

An Etymology Note

It may not be a phone call in the traditional sense, but customer contacts via multimedia still constitute a "call" to your organization – much like a face-to-face meeting is considered to be "calling on someone." We'll refer to the multimedia user in this same context. In this chapter, the term "caller" is media-independent. It's our industry's tip-of-the-hat to tradition in nontraditional times, and it also reinforces the goal of courtesy, professionalism and responsiveness in all customer interactions.

Web-Based Media Options

The multimedia contact center includes several different types of Web interaction in addition to the potential fax, mail or even video contacts that the center might need to handle. Let's take a brief look at the various types of Web media – then we'll show you how the technology to use them works.

Email

With email, a customer clicking on a "Contact us" email link triggers the browser to open the email client and automatically insert the "To" address in the message. Alternatively, the Web site presents a form in the browser window. The form becomes a *structured* email, so that individual fields can be identified (often by using drop-down boxes). Customers might also originate a free-form email or respond to an email sent from your company. Regardless of how the email originates, the email request is sent to the center for servicing, hopefully, soon. However, it's not a real-time interaction.

Text-Chat

Text-chat, also sometimes called Web chat, is real-time communication. To start the session, the caller clicks on a text-chat link on a Web site and a new frame or window opens within the browser. Once connected to an agent, the customer and agent type and send messages back and forth in this window.

Web Call

To start a Web call, the caller clicks on a Web site link to speak with an agent. The real-time call can be placed over the traditional voice network or VoIP.

• The traditional network call requires a second line to establish the voice connectivity (or the caller must first disconnect from the Web).

• The VoIP approach requires a multimedia PC with speakers and a microphone, as well as some software that is downloaded to, or accessed on, the PC. The call travels through the Internet.

Web Collaboration

Collaboration is used with either text-chat or Web calls to enable the customer and agent to interact on the Web page. Collaboration includes:

• **Co-browsing:** Enables the agent and customer to view the same Web browser screens and either one can control the navigation. It can also include some pointer or "white-boarding" functions (e.g., "You can see here the double-reinforced stitching…").

• **Page pushing:** Enables the agent to send a screen of information to the customer for viewing (e.g., "Here's the performance for that fund for the last three years, Mr. Jones…").

• **Application collaboration:** The customer and the agent can collaborate on a Web-based application. Examples include product configuration in technology industries, and loan applications and portfolio-modeling in financial services.

Real-time Web media are subject to the same challenges as a phone call for queuing and routing to an available agent with the right skills to handle the contact, and treatment in queue (i.e., messages? music?) if no one is available. So you may want to consider one additional capability to be used with real-time Web contacts: Web on hold. While customers are waiting for an agent, they may see the equivalent of queue messages – expected wait time, "thanks for holding" message, or even an advertisement or notice about current specials – which can be provided in a browser frame or text box.

Each of these media options has its place, as well as potential challenges, as you can see in Table 9-1.

Table 9-1: Contact Center Multimedia Options, Use and Issues

Option	Who's Using It and Why	Potential Issues
Email	• Email routing and response systems are appropriate in any industry • Most companies have email coming into the center; if the volume is noticeable, technology tools can help route and respond • Customers are comfortable with email and want to use it • Many interactions don't require real-time response • It allows a center to fill lower call volume times with email handling • It can enable consistent service (both in response time and answers provided)	• Offering email can open the floodgates; it must have proper processes and adequate staff to handle volume • Customers may be unclear in their communications, so it can be difficult to respond automatically or without multiple email exchanges • Servicing time may take longer than a phone call • You risk errors in grammar, spelling and usage (which can be minimized with prepared text) • Some companies require emails to be reviewed for legal or regulatory reasons because they are written communications with customers
Text-chat	• Great fit for tech support or other environments with potential "downtime" in the interaction (not a constant conversation) – can get economies of scale by handling multiple chat sessions at the same time • Allows a customer to communicate with the center while on the Web without needing an extra line • Some customers are very comfortable communicating via typed text	• Still have to staff for real-time response • Communication can be slow – dependent on typing skills • You risk errors in grammar, spelling and usage (which can be minimized with prepared text)
Web call – traditional network	• It has been used by dot-coms, high tech and financial services or retailers with a focus on personalized service • Allows a customer to communicate with someone live to support assisted self-service • Good option for companies that want to offer personalized service	• Some customers don't have a second line (have to hang up Web connection to talk)

Option	Who's Using It and Why	Potential Isues
Web call – VoIP	• In early stages of adoption, but will move fast; early adopters are technology innovators • "Killer application" for Web integration and collaboration services	• Customer may not have configuration needed on PC (multimedia, software) – may have noticeable download time • Voice quality is suspect today

Other Media

There are other types of media that can be used in a contact center, as well, so as you develop your multimedia strategy, don't just look at the Web. Traditional mail can be scanned into an image system and routed to desktops for handling. Faxed letters or forms can be routed to agents. A voicemail message can serve as a placeholder for a call or an outbound call can be queued into the media mix, as well. Or video calls can be routed to an agent with video skills and a video-enabled workstation.

Multimedia Applications Technology

Now that we've introduced each of the multimedia options, let's explore the technologies that make them work for routing, response, management and reporting. First, we need to figure out who's contacting the center and why for each of these media. Table 9-2 lists the tools, starting with the familiar identifiers for voice calls (i.e., ANI, DNIS and prompting).

Table 9-2: Technologies for Determining Who's "Calling" and Why

Media	Who's Calling?	Why Are They Calling?
Voice	ANI, prompted digits	DNIS, prompted digits
Email	"From" address	"To" address, subject line, key words and phrases in body of message
Fax	ANI, OCR/ICR	DNIS, OCR/ICR
Text-chat	Cookies, Web page logins and form-filling	Web URLs, radio buttons, dropdown menus
Web calls	Cookies, Web page logins and form-filling	Web URLs, radio buttons, dropdown menus
Video	ANI	DNIS
Mail	"From" address via OCR/ICR	"To" address, PO Box number via OCR/ICR

Email Response and Management Technology

There is a spectrum of technologies available to manage email in a contact center. If you're just getting started with email, your technology can be as basic as your corporate email system. In a low-volume start-up scenario, you can assign a small group of email agents to a special functional area (e.g., sales, service, billing, lead generation), and have them manually monitor those inboxes. Periodically, the agents will retrieve inbound email, compose the responses and send answers back to customers. If you have a small amount of email traffic and don't need advanced functionality, this option may be all you need.

If you have a high volume of email or your business requires more advanced operations, you may need the functionality of an Email Response Management System (ERMS). ERMS is, essentially, an email ACD – it can be a standalone system or a software module of a broader server-based system. The ERMS application automatically receives or retrieves email from the corporate email server, and then routes and queues contacts to email agent skill groups. Email agents receive email "pops" at their desktops. Like an ACD, these systems track email agent work states and offer a variety of historical and real-time reports.

Figure 9-2: Email Response Management

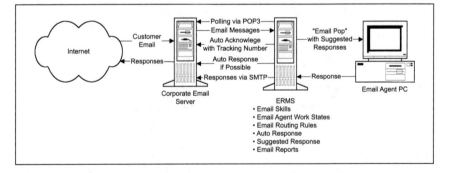

ERMS functionality can include the following elements:

• **Auto-acknowledge message and tracking number.** When an email arrives, the ERMS returns an auto-acknowledgement email to let the sender know that the email was received. The message provides a unique tracking number for the inquiry, and may provide a projected response time. The tracking number serves as a look-up number for status or history for a customer, and links together multiple exchanges with one customer.

• **Interpret caller and call purpose.** ERMS reviews and analyzes the To, From, Subject and Message body. This information is then used to route the email to the correct agent group.

Beware of the Email Death Spiral!

Consider this scenario: A customer sends an email after an unsuccessful Web self-service attempt. The center doesn't respond. The customer sends another email. An incorrect or incomplete response is sent. The customer emails again, asking for clarification. One contact has turned into several contacts. Multiply this by thousands of contacts. All of a sudden, there is a major email backlog and customers are getting restless (and irritated). Agents, under pressure to clear the backlog, try to work faster and more errors ensue. What do frustrated customers do? Of course, they pick up the phone and call.

But the call center strategic plan called for reducing agents by 50 percent because people are now being served by the "efficient" email channel. The call volume didn't drop; in fact, it's up by 20 percent. The voice call and email queues go through the roof, customers are angry, agents are burning out and the CEO is calling. Life stinks!

Moral of the story: Nail down your processes before opening email channels. Don't assume offering alternative media will reduce phone calls on a one-for-one basis. Think of multimedia first as facilitating customer choice and control.

• **Auto-response.** Some ERMS systems have the capability to auto-respond. Auto-response attempts to interpret the question(s) in the email message, apply logic and automatically provide answers. Capabilities range from simple word spotting to sophisticated artificial intelligence engines. In a sense, auto-response attempts to make email a self-service function that requires no human intervention. If the auto-response logic is unsuccessful in finding an answer, the ERMS routes the email to the appropriate agent skill group.

• **Suggested answers.** When the email pops onto the agent desktop, the system offers the agent suggested responses. The agent reviews the options and, if there is a good match, chooses the response with a quick click of the mouse. Or the agent can access libraries of pre-approved text to quickly compose responses.

• **Knowledge base integration.** Agents can find answers more quickly by using a corporate knowledge base, which increases email productivity and quality. With a few mouse clicks, answers are pasted into the response.

• **Fax.** ERMS handles incoming faxes as email attachments. When the email with the fax attachment pops onto the agent desktop, the agent opens the attachment with a fax viewer, composes the response and faxes the answer back. Unique 800 or DID numbers can be used to identify the fax purpose (e.g., 800-555-1111 for sales, 800-444-2222 for service). Optionally, Optical Character Recognition (OCR) or Intelligent Character Recognition (ICR) technology can be used to scan the fax image for content that indicates the fax sender and fax purpose.

• **Encryption and passwords.** These features are used in financial services or other applications where there are security, confidentiality or privacy concerns. When callers receive responses, they enter a user name and password to decrypt the message body.

• **Email systems integration.** ERMS systems typically use two standards to access an email server. POP3 (Post Office Protocol 3) is used to retrieve, and SMTP (Simple Mail Transfer Protocol) is used to send. These are the standards used by all email systems.

• **Common desktop integration.** ERMS can integrate with the regular email client (e.g., Microsoft Outlook, Eudora, Netscape mail, Lotus Notes). Any standard POP3-compliant email client will do (and that's what most everyone has).

• **Reporting modules.** Look for ERMS systems that have an integrated reporting module. Measures should include contacts handled, queue status, response rate, thresholds, handle times and trends. The system should have flexible reporting intervals (hourly, daily, weekly, monthly).

The Challenges with Auto-Response

Here's a example of an actual auto-response message (names have been changed to prevent embarrassment):

"Hi there! I'm the Company X Tech Support automated responder. Since I'm a computer, I can provide the fastest possible response to your question.

If I didn't answer your question, simply respond to this email and it will be sent to one of my human tech support representatives.

Here's what I think the answer to your question is…"

Then the message proceeds to offer eight possible problems and the solutions. Surprisingly, the eight options seem quite unrelated, and then, not surprisingly, none address the issue. This is what might be called the "shotgun approach" to automated response.

When email response management systems first arrived on the scene, auto-response was presumed to be the "killer application." However, over time, the hype quieted. Based on individual experiences, as well as bad press, it became clear that auto-responding to emails is a difficult thing to do. Customers write confusing emails (often filled with poor spelling or grammar), ask multiple questions, don't identify themselves effectively or don't provide enough information. It's hard for the technology to be smart enough to get it right.

This is not to say that auto-response for email isn't possible. It is. But the low success rate may not justify the time and expense it takes to write the business rules and responses. Further, many of those responses still need to be reviewed for accuracy or legal reasons. And finally, if a question is simple enough to auto-respond to, it should also be easy to find the answer through Web self-service!

Text-Chat Technology

When a customer selects "chat" on a Web site, an application is downloaded from the text-chat server using an Active X control or Java Applet. The server queues the chat request to the appropriate skill group (e.g., tech support or product information). If there's no queue, agent selection takes place, and a text message like, "Hi, I'm Lori. How can I help you?" appears on the customer's PC. If there's a queue, a message might say something like, "Thank you for contacting us. Someone should be with you within 30 seconds." Once an agent is available, the customer and the chat agent exchange typed messages.

Here are some key capabilities to look for in text-chat applications:

• **Routing based on caller and call purpose.** Uses the "who" and the "why" to route contacts to the appropriately skilled groups and informs the agent of the caller's identity. The software also monitors and controls agent work states.

• **Prepared responses.** Similar to email suggested responses, a text-chat system may store and provide quick access to common or pre-approved responses. These responses add efficiency, consistency and quality.

• **Multiple chat sessions.** Some systems enable each agent to handle multiple chat sessions simultaneously.

• **Chat transcripts.** After the session is finished, a transcript of the session is sent to the caller in an email. On the agent side, the chat transcript is either automatically or manually copied into the customer contact record.

• **Chat reports.** A text-chat "ACD" tracks chats, service levels, handle times and other key metrics and provides reports on them.

Multiple Chat Session Challenges

Because of the inherent delays in typing and reading on the part of the sender, an agent can chat with multiple customers at once. In a multiple-chat environment, agents have a split screen or a conversation selection window. We've seen up to six sessions being handled by a single agent (but there were considerable delays for the customers). Use of this feature is highly dependent on your business, as well as agent typing and information-processing skills. For example, a high-tech center where customers download software updates may do well with multiple chat sessions. However, a medical advice line would have high risk and little efficiency gained by multiple sessions (there's no conversation downtime in this case).

An undesired ripple effect of multiple chat sessions is that it makes scheduling more challenging – traditional workforce scheduling algorithms assume an agent will only handle one contact at a time.

Web-Call Technology

There are two different methods used to accomplish Web calling. The first option uses the public telephone network for voice and the Internet for data. The second option sends both voice and data over a single Internet connection. Both leverage CTI software, Web-call software and the voice switch.

With the dual connection option, the call can either be an outbound call to the customer or an inbound call from the customer. In the outbound scenario, the caller enters the number where they would like to be called. The Web-call server tells the CTI server to place the call. The CTI server either tells the voice switch to dial the call and then connect it to an available agent, or it sends a message to the agent desktop where the agent clicks on an icon to launch the call. The CTI server and Web-call server synchronize the data stream and the circuit-switched call and the Web page pops onto the agent desktop.

With the inbound calling scenario, after the caller clicks on the "Talk to us now" link, the Web page displays a phone number to call and, possibly, an identifying code. The number dialed and the code uniquely identify the customer. The CTI server and the Web-call server synchronize the separate voice and data paths, and the Web screen pops at the receiving agent's desktop.

The advantages of this dual connection approach are excellent sound quality and a very common voice connection. The disadvantage is the caller needs two lines: one for the Internet and one for voice. Without a second line, the customer must disconnect from the Web before the call is placed, compromising collaboration.

New Technology Terms for the Multimedia World

Here are some technology terms that are important to know in the multimedia world:

- **Cookies:** The little snippets of data that are written to your PC when you visit a Web site (if your browser configuration and/or firewall allow it). They are the secret to personalized greetings on Web sites you visit frequently (i.e., getting that "Welcome back, Dave!" message when you arrive). The Web server reads your cookies to identify who you are – thus, they're like an ANI in identifying Web site "callers."
- **URL** (Uniform Resource Locator): The address for a Web page. It translates to an IP address. When used in multimedia integration, it indicates where the customer is (or has been) on the Web site and what they were doing. It's similar to the information gleaned from an IVR when a caller presses zero for help.
- **OCR/ICR** (Optical Character Recognition/Intelligent Character Recognition):

Read machine-printed or handwritten text. They are used when scanning mail or faxes to interpret address information or other text.

- **Active X controls:** A suite of Microsoft component technologies used in the Web environment for passing information. Active X controls are downloaded to enable an application, such as a Web call.

- **Java applets:** Applets are little applications that run in a Web browser. Java is a platform-independent industry standard architecture that lives in the Web world. So Java applets are little applications that download in a Web environment to provide specific functionality needed. For example, a Java applet can provide text-chat capabilities.

- **Browser plug-ins:** Plug-ins are additional "helper" applications that can run in your browser to more effectively use the Web. Plug-ins are dynamically triggered and the helper application can be downloaded or accessed off a hard drive.

In the single-connect model, both data and voice are sent using IP over the Internet. The CTI and Web-call server requirements and synchronization functions are the same as the dual-connect model. There are additional requirements for the caller, such as a soundcard-equipped PC, headset or microphone and speakers, and a VoIP client application (e.g., Microsoft's NetMeeting). Additional technology requirements for the business include a VoIP-enabled voice switch (IP- or TDM-based, but with IP connections or a gateway). Some vendors offer text-chat as a fallback method when voice quality degrades.

The advantage of the single-connect approach is that the caller needs only one line to connect to the Internet. The conditions for successfully using this approach are consistent quality and customer comfort and familiarity with these types of calls. There is another prerequisite for widespread adoption – the caller's application software needs to be PC-resident or quickly downloadable. Basically, VoIP over the public Internet has to become a mainstream capability for this to succeed.

VoIP innovation is proceeding at a rapid rate, and single-connect Web calling has exciting potential. We expect rapid adoption of this technology once the issues are addressed.

Key Enablers for Text-Chat, Web Calls and Web Collaboration

There are a number of technologies that help to enable text-chats and Web calls, as well as the collaboration that goes with them:

- **Application software.** When a customer clicks on an icon to chat or talk, a server provides them with some additional software. An Active X control, browser plug-in or Java applet downloads to their desktop to enable the interaction.
- **Standards.** We discussed H.323 earlier (see Chapter 2) as a standard for IP communications, including VoIP. It is used in applications for Web calls. Other standards may be used as well, such as SIP. The customer's PC must have a VoIP client, and most today are H.323-compliant. Microsoft NetMeeting and Net2Phone are examples.
- **CTI.** CTI helps tie the call to the Web page the customer is on by a "Web pop" of the page at the agent desktop. It talks to the Web call or chat server to coordinate. It may also play a role in launching an outbound call in response to a Web-initiated request.

Web Collaboration

During text-chat or Web calls, the agent and the customer can also engage in collaboration. Downloaded desktop applications and server coordination make these applications possible.

The Web-call capabilities we've discussed thus far are triggered from the caller being at the Web site and then accessing the call center. It can also go the other way: An agent is on the phone with a customer and asks if they have access to the Web. The customer says "Sure!" and the agent links up with them to begin the collaboration. The caller is uniquely identified on the Web site, the Web-call server talks to a CTI server, and the call and PC screen synchronize.

There is another slightly more intimidating option: The customer is surfing the Web site and an unsolicited message pops up asking if they need assistance. This capability is sometimes referred to as "escort" services and is equated to the tap on the shoulder at a fine clothing store. The service representative is offering assistance when it appears the customer might need it. Additional technologies come into play here, including the analytics software discussed in Chapter 8.

Integrated Multimedia Queuing and Routing

Up to this point in this chapter, we have been addressing email, chat, Web calls and voice calls as separate media applications. With media segmentation, agents are in separate groups with individual applications for routing, queuing and reporting on that media.

Figure 9-3: Media Silos

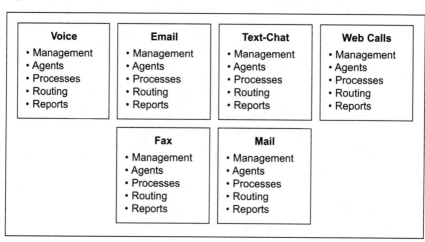

Integrated multimedia queuing and routing helps to break down the barriers between these media silos, creating a cohesive, consistent environment with greater economies of scale. One set of "business rules" manage the routing of contacts to the pool of skilled agents. Customers have a common experience, regardless of media. Agents can handle a variety of media, if properly trained and qualified. Supervisors and managers can use resources more efficiently, and create their reporting "elevator story," which encompasses all media. Of course the technology is only one piece of the puzzle – there are organizational and other barriers to break down, too.

Figure 9-4: Integrated Multimedia Contact Center: Break Down the Silos

All Media

• Cohesive Management
• Pooled but Skilled Agents
• Consistent Processes
• Common Routing Tools
• Common Reports

Four Key Benefits

An integrated multimedia environment has four key benefits:

1. **Efficiency.** As we showed you in Chapter 3, segmenting your agent base leads to lower efficiency and lower occupancy. Breaking down media silos offers the advantage of the powerful pooling principle: Larger groups are more efficient. There is no mystery here – it is a simple extension of Erlang C principles.

2. **Consistency and commonality.** Removing media silos creates consistency in processes, operations, metrics and service. Customers should feel like they're dealing with one company. But to make this happen, you'll also need to break down other silos – organizational (media fiefdoms) and technology infrastructure (databases).

3. **Agent satisfaction.** Agents who work in blended-media environments enjoy the diversity of the workload. Multiple media also create a career path, potentially increasing agent retention.

4. **Technology management.** This may be the most compelling benefit. Without blending media, the business rules for managing contacts need to be written in different places – with different tools, interfaces and reports. That creates an operations, administration and maintenance nightmare that translates to high cost. In a blended environment, a single multimedia routing engine employs one tool, one interface and generates one set of reports.

Integrated Multimedia Business Case Example

The following example shows the business case for multimedia queuing using three real-time interactions. A contact center has three silo applications of traditional voice, chat and Web calls. For the sake of simplicity, assume the following:

- Each contact takes five minutes with a 45-second wrap-up
- The desired service level is 80 percent of contacts answered in 20 seconds.
- In a 30-minute interval, voice takes 1,000 calls, the chat group takes 200 chats, and the Web group takes 100 calls.

To meet the target service level, the voice group requires 202 agents, the chat group requires 44 agents, and the Web group requires 24 agents – a total of 270 agents.

By unifying the queue and blending agents across all media channels, the total agent contact center requirement is 260 people for the same service level. The end result: a headcount savings of 10 agents.

We're not suggesting that all centers should fully blend all agents into "universal agents" or "super agents." That is a daunting (maybe, impossible?) task for many centers. Rather, we want to show the value of applying some level of blending and common management. Most centers will likely expand the "media skills" of their agents over time or enable some to specialize in particular media while others seek diversity. This is not unlike the development opportunities for other skills (e.g., product, customer type, etc.) – either breadth or depth of skills can be valued if managed well.

Multimedia Architecture Options

Now we bring you full circle from our discussion of infrastructure options and tradeoffs in Chapter 2. The various application infrastructure approaches – PBX, ACD, Hybrid, CTI, Communications Server – can be used to deliver multimedia queuing and routing technology. Let's take a look at the architecture options and tradeoffs.

PBX, ACD and Hybrid

The PBX, ACD or Hybrid controls the core call center functionality across all media channels. Nontelephony contacts (email, text-chat, Web calls) access the voice-switch application intelligence through a technique called "phantom" or "ghost" calling. Vendors in this group have enhanced their CTI links so that any nontelephony application can access the queuing and routing logic via a CTI "make call" event.* In this case, the CTI software is pure middleware because the application logic resides on the voice switch.

Once the phantom call is launched, the voice switch thinks that it has a call in queue. When an agent becomes available, the agent phone receives an audible tone and the voice switch sends a "call connected to station" event to the CTI server via the CTI link. The CTI server looks up the IP address of the PC associated with the station, and the CTI server sends the IP address to the multimedia application. The multimedia application then sends the multimedia session to the PC. Because the application logic resides on the switch, the existing voice-switch reporting tool provides reports on all multimedia activities.

Figure 9-5: PBX/ACD/Hybrid Multimedia Queue

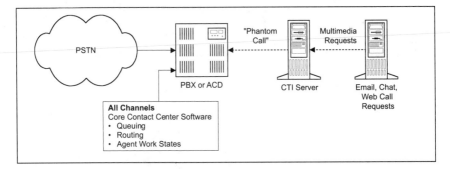

---

* Some vendor implementations actually use phones in closets – they need a true physical call to make the ghost call. So the CTI server tells the switch to launch a call from that phone.

Table 9-3: Advantages and Disadvantages of PBX/ACD/Hybrid Multimedia Architecture

Advantages of a PBX/ACD/Hybrid	Disadvantages of a PBX/ACD/Hybrid
• May be advantageous for environments with minimal nonvoice contacts • High reliability • Familiar environment	• Puts nonvoice functions onto a system optimized for voice (problems may occur; for example, in handling multiple text-chats or in allowing a voice call to interrupt email handling) • Invests further in an architecture that is not in line with industry directions and trends

CTI Blending

With CTI media blending, the voice-switch application logic is used for managing the voice channel, while an external CTI server manages the nonvoice contacts. Essentially, routing, agent work states and queuing are managed in two places. A blending module on the CTI server monitors voice events and other media events. The agent is logged into two applications, and the blending logic changes the work states as needed to deliver contacts.

Figure 9-6: CTI-Blending Multimedia Queue

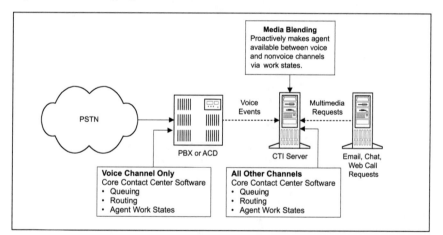

Table 9-4: Advantages and Disadvantages of CTI-Blending Multimedia Architecture

Advantages of CTI Blending	Disadvantages of CTI Blending
• Leverages CTI capabilities while preserving investment in voice infrastructure • Manages voice with tools optimized for voice (PBX/ACD functions) and other media with tools optimized for non-voice (CTI, server-based, IP)	• Creates environment with dual administration and reporting systems

Total CTI

All of the application logic is placed on an external server in a total CTI approach. The voice switch is just one of many servers with which the multimedia routing application must communicate. All routing, agent work states and queuing gets managed in the CTI application.

Figure 9-7: Total CTI Multimedia Queue

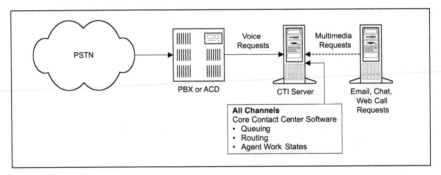

Table 9-5: Advantages and Disadvantages of Total CTI Multimedia Architecture

Advantages of Total CTI	Disadvantages of Total CTI
• Single infrastructure to administer, maintain and upgrade • Common management, reporting and development tools for all media	• Lacks the reliability of the PBX or ACD – if CTI server fails, can't route any contacts, even voice, without substantial backup plan • Significant integration and customization may be required

Communications Server

Many of the Communications Servers were developed with multimedia in mind. As a result, they are more readily adapted to a multimedia environment.

Figure 9-8: Communications Server Multimedia Queue

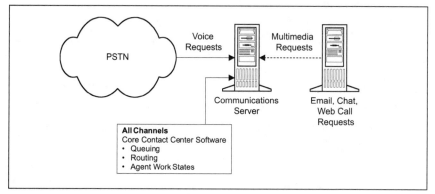

Table 9-6: Advantages and Disadvantages of Communications Server Multimedia Architecture

Advantages of Communications Server	Disadvantages of Communications Server
• Engineered for multimedia from the start • Single infrastructure to administer, maintain and upgrade • Common management, reporting and development tools for all media • Good package for when you need lots of functionality fast • Good for small and medium centers	• Scalability is limited • Generally not as reliable as a PBX/ACD

So What to Do?

Today, most centers that are planning for or implementing universal routing and queuing will use a CTI or Communications Server approach. The key decision factors are based on the overall infrastructure tradeoffs detailed in Chapter 2. It's important to keep in mind that any of these options may use IP as the switching platform rather than traditional TDM-based circuit-switching. IP is more compelling if you're expecting to receive lots of contacts from the Web. In Chapter 11, we'll further address the future directions for this leading-edge technology.

Other Multimedia Technology Considerations

In addition to the applications and network infrastructure decisions, there are additional technology considerations for a multimedia environment.

• **Multiple sites.** In Chapter 4, we discussed various routing options for phone calls across single or multiple sites. If your business operates as a "virtual" call center across sites, it probably needs to be virtual for multimedia, as well.

• **Network security.** New rules for firewalls need to be written to allow new application ports and protocols to pass through to secure networks.

• **Forecasting and scheduling.** If you have an existing WFMS, verify that a multimedia module is available. If you're looking at WFMS for the first time, make sure that multimedia capabilities are on your "must-have" list. And remember, a lot of this media doesn't fit well with traditional workforce management tools and algorithms (see Chapter 5).

• **Simulation tools.** Consider using a call center simulation tool to find system and process bottlenecks prior to procuring and implementing multimedia systems. This approach identifies pain points and tests worst-case scenarios before you introduce the application to the production environment.

• **CTI.** Beyond using CTI as a multimedia queuing engine, you may have other potential CTI applications. Look at CTI as a whole and select a single platform for all applications.

• **Quality monitoring/logging systems.** The premium on QM and logging systems to perform screen capture is very high as contact centers begin handling email, text-chat and Web collaboration. The QM system must receive a CTI event to start and stop screen capture. And the QM system must offer different scoring templates for different media.

• **Knowledge base.** Although a knowledge base is considered key to effectively handling phone calls (e.g., tech support), it becomes critical in the multimedia world. For example, during an email, the agent can quickly search the knowledge base and paste the information into the message body.

• **Reporting.** A decision must be made on whether to implement a new source of reports or integrate multimedia into an existing reporting architecture.

• **CRM.** Agents must have access to all contact records, regardless of the media channels used. So the CRM (or contact management) system must track all contacts on all media. Scenarios like: "I'm calling to clarify some information from a Web chat I had after receiving email confirmation for a Web site purchase," will become common.

Multimedia Call Flow

The following example shows the event flows of a unified multimedia queue for a combined voice and email queue. The universal queuing engine is a total CTI implementation: All application intelligence resides on an external server; the PBX is used only for its switching matrix capabilities. The PBX CTI link sends events only for the voice channel. The CTI server talks to the other media servers, as well (email in this example). Like the call flow example for CTI in Chapter 6, this is only meant to be a representative example, but it should give you a good sense of what occurs in a multimedia-routing environment. Figure 9-9 depicts the devices involved in the multimedia interaction and the message flow, while Table 9-7 describes the call-flow events.

Figure 9-9: Sample Multimedia Call Flow: Voice and Email Queue

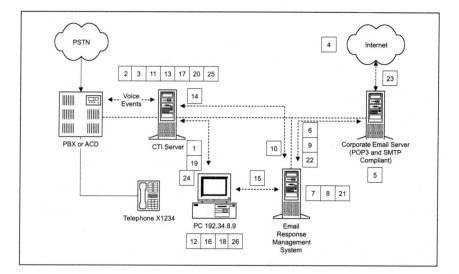

Table 9-7: Sample Multimedia Message Flow: Voice and Email Queue

Step	Action
1	Agent 5678 at telephone x1234 logs into CTI application from PC 192.34.8.9, desktop software notifies CTI server
2	Table in CTI database gets updated with entry: telephone x1234 = PC 192.34.8.9 = agent 5678
3	CTI application activates agent 5678 skill profile including voice and email skills
4	Customer sends email to service@abccompany.com
5	Email arrives in corporate email server mailbox service@abccompany.com
6	Email response system periodically polls mailbox service@abccompany.com via POP3
7	Email response system copies email from corporate email server into its database
8	Email response system deletes message from the corporate email server
9	Email response system sends auto-acknowledgement with tracking number 9876 back to sender
10	Email response system sends routing request for email 9876 to CTI server for email service skill
11	CTI server queues email 9876 request to its email service skill
12	Agent 5678 becomes available and there are no pending voice calls
13	CTI server selects agent 5678 for the next service email
14	CTI server sends message "send email 9876 to PC 192.34.8.9" to email response system
15	Email response system sends email 9876 to PC 192.34.8.9
16	Email 9876 screen pops into client application on PC 192.34.8.9 for agent 5678, desktop software notifies CTI server
17	CTI server updates its work states table that agent 5678 is active in email service work mode
18	Agent composes email response and hits "send"
19	Agent 5678 moves into wrapup work state, desktop software notifies CTI server
20	CTI server updates work states table that agent 5678 is in wrapup mode
21	Email response system updates its database that request 9876 is closed out by agent 5678
22	Email response system sends email 9876 to corporate email system
23	Corporate email system sends response to customer
24	Agent 5678 moves into available work state, desktop software notifies CTI server
25	CTI server updates work states table that agent 5678 is in available mode
26	Agent 5678 waits for next voice or email work item

Multimedia Considerations

Opening a new media channel is like publishing a new 800 number or running a large advertising campaign. You're setting an expectation that an agent will "answer" in a timely way, and the agent will have the skills and knowledge to efficiently and effectively handle the interaction. When opening and promoting a new media channel, you must exert the same managerial attention to strategy, processes and operations as you do for the voice channel. Here are some issues to consider as you embark on a multimedia contact center:

• **Link your multimedia strategy to your business and call center strategy.** What are your business goals (e.g., reduce costs, drive revenue)? What is your overall customer-contact strategy? What media "mix" works best for your particular business, and what are the priorities for rollout? What media apply in which situations, for self-service and assisted service? Define the multimedia strategy in the context of your other plans and consider factors such as customer expectations, competition and business value.

• **Customers want choice and control.** Let the customer choose and control his or her use of media channels. As we described in Chapter 8, a caller's inclination to self-serve changes based on where they are and how urgent the need. This behavior also applies to multimedia. Need some clarifications about some product specifications? Email is great channel. Have a minor technical problem with a product that is still working? Fire up a chat session. However, when a delivery doesn't arrive, the billing problem isn't resolved or a critical product is out of service, a phone call or Web call is likely. The customer gets to choose.

• **A phone call is not a failure.** In our consulting work, we've seen call center strategic plans that called for 90 percent of customer contacts to be handled through the email channel. That's not likely to happen. The nature of business communications is often interactive, requiring discussion and negotiation. Multimedia has its place, but it is not a cure-all. When there is a problem, people still want to pick up the phone and talk to somebody – and that's okay.

What Media When?

Not all media need to be offered on the Web site at all times. If customers are trying to self-serve on a Web-based application and they get stuck, it is a great opportunity to offer assistance through a real-time multimedia application, such as text-chat or Web calls. When there is revenue at risk (for example, order processing via shopping carts) or other time-sensitive applications, assistance can mean the difference between closing the sale or an abandoned shopping cart. For less time-sensitive self-service applications (such as, billing, technical support), an email link may be sufficient.

Transitioning your center to a contact center changes everything. Multimedia contact center technology touches literally every piece of your technology and new processes must be put in place. There are many moving parts involved, so extra vigilance is required. A prerequisite to success is strong leadership to bring together a cross-functional team. Your corporate brand is on-the-line, and teams encompassing human resources, training and development, call center, sales and marketing, and e-commerce must work well with telecommunications and IT to make multimedia succeed.

There will be ripple effects for people, processes and the organization. Let's examine those.

People Ripple Effects

• **Organizational design.** Job descriptions and skill requirements may change with a multimedia environment. Organizational relationships can also change if organizational silos are being broken down with multimedia.

• **Human resources.** The skills needed to work in nonvoice channels are different than those for the voice world. Keyboard and grammar skills are now as important as voice skills. That will alter your HR processes, including how you screen, qualify and promote.

• **Training and development.** You'll have to augment or alter existing training programs and lengthen your ramp-up times.

• **Quality monitoring.** Agent coaching and development managers must conduct grammar and writing evaluation. You'll also need to update evaluation forms.

• **Compensation.** Multimedia can create pressure to raise compensation levels or they may need to vary by media.

• **Agent retention.** For existing employees, the opportunity to learn multimedia skills may help to reduce agent turnover.

• **Existing agent skills and talents.** Agents who are skilled in typing and have an inclination for picking up new technologies enjoy the variety of multimedia contacts. On the other hand, if you have agents who were hired for their phone skills, don't force them to handle multimedia if they don't have the skills or interest. Voice contacts will be the majority of contacts for a long, long time.

• **Depth and breadth of skills.** If you're doing a good job with self-service, then when a customer contacts an agent, it's because they've got a real issue. The easy stuff has been handled. The agents need advanced problem-resolution, conflict-resolution and critical-thinking skills. One company calls these "dragon-slaying" skills. Translation: Recruit and screen for these advanced skills, and emphasize training and development once agents are onboard. And be forewarned – call lengths may increase.

Process Ripple Effects

• **Business rules.** Your multimedia processes and business rules for multimedia contact must be well-defined. Web calls and chat are real-time events, and should be given equal priority to voice. If you've segmented your customer base, multimedia contacts should be aligned with that strategy. Non-real-time contacts are not as clear. Should a high-value customer email be handled before a low-value voice call? Your business strategy and customer contact strategy hold the answer.

• **New measures of accessibility.** Until now, the main measure of call center accessibility has been service level (X percent of calls answered in Y seconds). Service level and Erlang C still apply to real-time multimedia interactions (e.g., chat*, Web calls). But a new measure is needed for non-real-time contacts (e.g.,

---

* Note that Erlang is not good at representing multiple chat sessions per agent.

email, mail, fax) – response time. With response time, the measure reflects a much longer time interval. For example, instead of 80 percent of calls being answered in 20 seconds, the measure becomes 100 percent of emails responded to within 24 hours. Or, all priority email messages are responded to within four hours. You will also need multimedia equivalents for your other key performance indicators, such as handle time or cost per contact. Revisit Chapter 5 and the discussion of the changing elevator story when considering the impact of multimedia on metrics and reporting.

Organizational Ripple Effects

• **Information technology.** IT roles take on new responsibilities in a multimedia environment. They must document troubleshooting procedures, escalation processes and vendor support contacts for a new, highly integrated and complex set of tools. Consider setting up a lab where interoperability and load tests can be performed.

• **Legal.** For email or text-chats that have potential legal ramifications (remember, they're written documents), institute a quality-control or risk-management process in which a supervisor and a lawyer, if necessary, review a response prior to sending it to the customer. There may be pre-approved text that can be sent, as well.

There is another major consideration with multimedia, and that is the question of how to procure and implement this stuff in an already complex technology environment. That's a good question – so we'll address it in a discussion about sourcing options in Chapter 10.

Points to Remember

• The call center is in a state of transition from a voice-only function to a multimedia contact center. Additional contact media include email, text-chat and Web calling. Text-chat and Web calling can be combined with Web collaboration to aid complex interactions.

• Although new multimedia interaction channels are different from the voice channel, similar management vigilance and discipline are required for processes and operation.

• Information contained in email addresses, subject-line headers, message bodies, browser cookies, URL addresses, logins and Web-based radio buttons or drop-down menus aid in answering the questions "who's calling?" and "why are they calling?"

• Multimedia applications can exist as standalone applications, or as part of an integrated multimedia center. Integrated multimedia queuing yields staffing efficiencies, consistency of processes and service, agent job enrichment and a common source of business rules.

• Application infrastructure is the critical enabler for universal queuing and routing. There are three options: 1) voice switch (PBX, ACD or Hybrid), 2) CTI (blending or total), and 3) the Communications Server.

Actions to Take

• Tie your multimedia strategy to other business, contact center, technology and self-service strategies.

• Consider the ramifications of multimedia for other call center technologies – application infrastructure, network infrastructure, reporting, WFMS, quality monitoring, CTI and CRM systems. Integrated multimedia can mean replacing, upgrading or adding modules to any of these components, with multiple integration touch points.

Part 5: Where to from Here?

Once you understand the wealth of technologies available to the call center, it's decision-making time. Then it's time to move into implementation. Here's some input on the planning and decisions ahead.

Chapter 10: Making It Happen: Implementation Considerations

Chapter 11: Perspectives on the Future

Chapter 10:

Making It Happen: Implementation Considerations

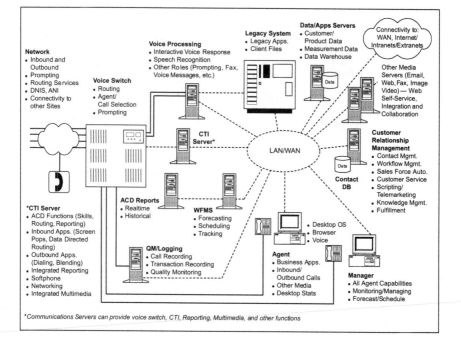

Communications Servers can provide voice switch, CTI, Reporting, Multimedia, and other functions

Key Points Discussed in this Chapter:

Building a Customer-Contact Technology Strategy

Developing a Framework for Implementation

Navigating the Vendor Map

An Overview of Technology Sourcing Options

In previous chapters, we looked at the various call center technologies, from basic to complex. We've discussed the why, what, how, who, when and where of these technologies. Hopefully, this background has helped to provide you with a vision – a strategic, technology-enabled contact center that's focused on your business needs and properly positioned within the organization.

In this chapter, we'll show you how to successfully implement that vision. Implementing call center technology requires a solid foundation – clear context, in the form of a strategy and business requirements, provides a start. Allocating adequate time, resources and money are prerequisites to success. Other critical ingredients include good project management, a cross-functional team of business and technology staff, careful planning, and attention to detail in execution. A final key element is the careful selection of vendor partners.

Keep in mind, successful implementation depends specifically on the decisions made about which technologies will be used, in what order and into what type of existing business and technology environment.

Building a Customer Contact Technology Strategy

In Chapter 1, we discussed the importance of strategy for establishing a context for your technology environment. We also looked at the three levels of strategy: 1) the overall business strategy, which is defined by senior management; 2) the call center strategy, which defines the processes, organizational structure, operations blueprint and metrics that help the business to achieve its strategic objectives; and 3) the technology strategy, which should support the business and call center strategies.

Your technology strategy will drive the right investment choices. It defines an overall picture of what should be implemented when and why. For a new center, or one that is truly transforming, the strategy may cover all or most of the different technology elements discussed in this book. For a center that is currently performing well, but also wants to support changing business needs, the strategy might focus primarily on the advanced elements, such as speech recognition, CTI, CRM and multimedia, along with upgrades to existing infrastructure. The key is the technology strategy should create a vision or blueprint that everyone in the organization can follow. Keep in mind that there will be tradeoffs, because you can't do everything all at once. Deciding what's in, what's not and what are top priorities is the difficult part of developing a technology strategy.

Don't Let this Happen to You!

Why is a technology strategy so important? The lack of one can create numerous problems:

- The technology purchased for the contact center delivers less value than expected (i.e., business cases are not realized).
- The technology is not embraced by users (and, therefore, is not successful) because it is not tied to clear business goals.
- The technology doesn't provide benefits to customers and agents.
- The technology group and business group lack common goals and priorities, and end up working at cross-purposes.
- The contact center's options are limited because the technology doesn't have the flexibility, adaptability or scalability to meet business goals.

In Chapter 1, we presented a matrix to illustrate the relationship between the progression of call center technology and corporate positioning (or strategic value) of the call center. Figure 10-1 reiterates this important relationship and serves as a reminder that, without a solid strategy that is aligned with the business vision, call center technology will be suboptimized. While some companies may make technology investments that exceed the business vision (resulting in underutilized technology), others may see the call center as having a strategic role, yet don't make the necessary investments to achieve business goals (the center lacks the tools to make an impact).

Use the graph to determine where your center is today, and where it needs to be tomorrow. Once those positions are defined, you can begin to define how to get from one place to the other.

Figure 10-1: Call Center and Technology Suboptimization

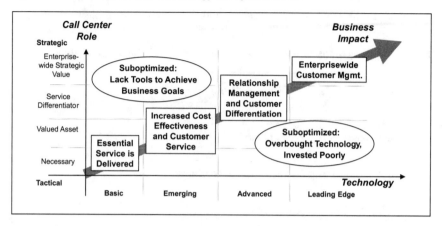

Key Steps to Developing a Strategy*

Now that you know why a contact center technology strategy is so critical, how do you go about developing one? There are three fundamental phases comprised of 10 key steps, as illustrated in Figure 10-2. Keep in mind these are the steps to defining the strategy – not executing it. At this point, you're not defining detailed requirements for specific technologies, selecting vendors or developing call flows or workflows.

Phase 1: Planning

The first phase – the planning phase – is the time to get your act together and prepare the project team for the work that lies ahead. There are four essential steps for planning the strategy project.

• **Form the project team.** The project team should reflect a representative cross-section – vertically and horizontally – of the company and those who influence or who are influenced by call center technologies. It should include representatives from business/finance, the call center (including agents), technology (IT and telecom), marketing and human resources. This diverse team will help to promote enterprisewide thinking and buy-in. You may also want to consider whether vendor partners or consultants will strengthen your team. The best team members are

---

* An article similar to this description of how to build a customer-contact technology strategy first appeared in *Call Center Management Review*, October 2001.

thinkers – people who look for opportunities and embrace change. And, finally, but most importantly, you'll also need a senior-level sponsor or project champion.

Figure 10-2: Key Steps to Building a Customer-Contact Technology Strategy

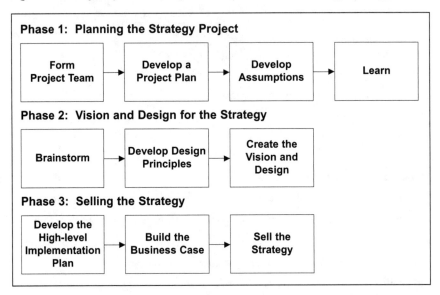

• **Develop a project plan.** The project plan should define the business drivers, scope, duration and depth of the planning effort (and its cost, if necessary), and key objectives. In addition, it should clearly identify your target outcome. For example, a target outcome might be: "Approval by senior management of a three-year contact center technology strategy. The strategy will be supported by a solid business case with a two-year positive return on investment, and increased customer satisfaction."

• **Develop assumptions.** Without a commonly understood set of assumptions, each team member may view the project from a completely different context. Developing assumptions early in the project will ensure your team has a coherent view. Define what is changing and what is not changing. For instance, are certain technologies considered building blocks or is everything fair game? Determine the relative importance of design criteria, such as cost vs. higher customer satisfaction or increased ability to expand the customer base. And last, define the elements of your current operation that are considered to be cherished strengths and, therefore, should not be changed by the strategy.

• **Learn.** Take the time to learn about the technology. Online research and articles can give you the background information for a fundamental understanding. Also, attend seminars and/or conferences, and subscribe to various trade publications (there are many).* You can also read books, engage consultants and, importantly, find out what other call centers are doing through benchmarking and site visits. It's ideal to speak with customers and, certainly, hold agent focus groups to get their input. Research and learning will arm your team with the knowledge of what you need and what is possible.

Phase 2: Vision and Design

In the second phase, you apply what you've learned in Phase 1 and draw on the brainpower of the team to come up with the strategy vision and design. This is the fun part!

• **Brainstorm.** Guide your team through exercises to shape the vision for the future – for customers, agents, managers and supervisors, and the organization. Structure brainstorming sessions to ensure that the team's thinking is not hampered by past decisions, initiatives or biases. Set a ground rule for the sessions: No one is allowed to say "no," "but" or "we've tried that before and it didn't work." Remember, this is the time for everyone to let loose and think about the possibilities.

• **Develop design principles.** Group and analyze the thoughts generated during brainstorming sessions so that you can come up with a few conclusions on what the team was really thinking. During the process, design principles will begin to emerge that will help you to frame the architectural principles. Here are some examples:

> *"We want to give our customers the choice and control they desire, and will do so by offering access via the media of their choice across extended hours."*

---

* Reminder: There is a resource list at www.vanguard.net if you're looking for sources on call center technology.

"We will purchase (not build) applications whenever possible, as it will enable us to be nimble and adapt to changing business needs more quickly."

"We will migrate toward IP-based infrastructure for the lower cost of ownership and to prepare us for a rich multimedia environment. However, we will design carefully and perform rigorous due diligence before implementing to ensure no risk to our mission-critical call center."

"We will use server-based platforms for applications intelligence, migrating away from proprietary platforms whenever possible."

• **Create the vision and strategy.** Finally, you need to create the vision and strategy. During this step, the project team will begin to develop an overall view of the technology environment and the base architecture. The team must determine key technology elements, as well as the features and functions each must deliver. For example, a key element of your vision may be CTI-based routing, reporting and other features. Another step might include Web integration with text-chat, Web calls and collaboration – all managed from the same platform that manages voice calls. Be sure to define the end state, as well as interim phases. List the key benefits that this environment will create and define any supporting changes or other critical success factors for the organization, processes and operations.

Phase 3: Selling

The third phase is more difficult. At this time, all of your ideas are incorporated into a comprehensive story that can be communicated effectively to get the buy-in you need to move forward.

• **Develop the high-level implementation plan.** The vision and strategy you created in Phase 2 should be documented in a plan – not a detailed plan, but one that depicts three to five key phases and the major events that will occur in those phases. You will need to show the timeline – what you will do when – and provide reasons to support it. The implementation plan will also identify critical success factors and key enablers that will ensure the plan's success.

• **Build the business case.** Most companies require a solid business case for technology. You may need to build a hard-dollars case for the overall vision, or you may only need a list of key benefits. It will depend on your particular situation and organization. In our work, we've seen centers justify entire technology strategies based on just one assumption (such as an increase in customer retention), while others have had to develop an evolutionary set of benefits expected to occur over several years with an ultimate payback in labor cost-savings, increased revenue or both. The key is to tie the business case to the key business drivers – and keep it simple and manageable. It will be compelling in simplicity, not in complexity.

• **Sell the strategy.** Finally, your ideas need to be documented in an attractive presentation and delivered. You'll need a thorough, comprehensive version (see the sample outline below), as well as a more concise strategy document (two or three pages long). The story must be crisp – the what, when and why tied to the defined business goals (or key pain points). Remember, you're selling – have your story ready, and your closing line planned.

Outline for a Contact Center Technology Strategy Document

1. Executive summary
2. Introduction (business drivers, mandate, scope)
3. Vision for X-year strategic plan (design principles, description of the technology environment, operation and organization)
4. Business case (hard benefits, soft benefits, costs, cost/benefit analysis)
5. Implementation plan (phases, major events and descriptions, timeline)
6. Critical success factors (resource requirements, operational changes required)
7. Next steps
8. Appendices (assumptions, supporting data)

Building a strategy can be a challenging (and fun) project, and the value is clear. Moving through the phases will help your team bring a diverse set of ideas and projects into a cohesive plan for moving forward toward business goals. It also brings together the cross-functional groups that may have been operating in silos. Through these strategy efforts, companies can move from technology-driven sub-optimization to technology-enabled success.

Developing a Framework for Implementation

Technology implementation is a vast topic that could be a book by itself. We are presuming that readers of this book have had previous experience with technology projects or, if you're on your maiden voyage, you are surrounded by others with experience. All we want to do here is give you a basic framework for implementing call center technology. We'll also highlight a few danger zones where call centers typically run into difficulties, especially with the more advanced technologies. Figures 10-3 and 10-4 illustrate the framework for designing, developing and implementing call center technology.

Figure 10-3: Planning and Designing Contact Center Technology

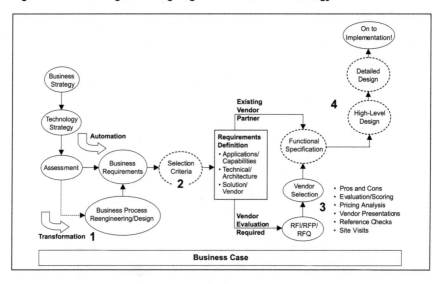

Planning and Design Highlights

The design process shown in Figure 10-3 includes requirements definition, vendor selection and the design steps you need to take before implementation. Here are four highlights.

1. Your path will vary depending on whether you're automating or transforming (see page 11). If you plan to automate, you will move straight to the business requirements that the technology must support. But with transformation, the tech-

nology will be implemented in a different environment, which requires a detour through process reengineering or design. The detour may be brief or highly involved, depending on the degree of change required.*

2. If technology evaluation and selection will be required, define the selection criteria prior to defining technology requirements. These criteria (four to six) define the basis on which you'll make a decision and help to keep everyone on the same page. The criteria will also focus your requirements definition and the questions you'll want to ask vendors. Knowing exactly how you will evaluate vendors will help you to write a more targeted Request for Information (RFI) or Proposal (RFP). Example selection criteria categories (each has a set of defining characteristics) are:

- Features and functionality
- Architecture and technical fit
- Experience, expertise and ability to deliver
- Post-implementation support and partnership
- Vendor positioning and direction

3. If you don't have a solid vendor partnership, an evaluation process will be required. This is a critical process that is often minimized. Many people don't take enough time or commit enough resources to conduct a thorough evaluation. These are big decisions you're making (cost, strategy and infrastructure implications), so it's worth investing a little time. We recommend requesting detailed vendor presentations and demonstrations where you dictate the agenda. Thorough reference-checking and site visits are also key points of due diligence.

4. In a perfect world, you would work through all of the design steps and include all of the documents shown. In the real world, there is generally not enough time. Leverage your partners (consultants, vendors or system integrators) and their experience. Put the burden on them to document (hopefully, they will have shortcuts, such as templates), but retain control of the review and approval.

---

* For help with process reengineering and design, consider working with experts in reengineering or using a toolkit like the Prosci series (www.prosci.com).

System Reliability and Stability

Another key issue to consider about call center technology planning, design and implementation: Call centers are mission-critical and can rarely afford downtime. As the technology in our market continues to rapidly evolve, some companies over-look this important fact. Don't let that happen to you. Be sure that you always keep system reliability and stability in mind as you develop your strategy, timelines, busi-ness and system requirements and proceed to implement the solution. Although the leading edge (or even bleeding edge) of technology is exciting and challenging, it can also be dangerous. Look at solutions that have been proven by others – in the lab, as well as by thorough testing and pilot programs. And finally, once the solu-tion is implemented, it's essential to have properly trained staff and appropriate sup-port functions and processes in place to keep things running smoothly.

Figure 10-4: Implementing Contact Center Technology

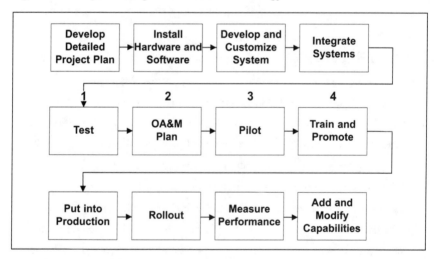

Implementation – Critical Steps

The development and implementation steps shown in Figure 10-4 apply to most technologies. Following are four critical steps to call center technology imple-mentation – ignore them at your own peril!

1. Testing is not fun. It takes time and it requires dedicated, meticulous atten-

tion to detail, but it is critical to success. So take the time to thoroughly test your solution. We highly recommend using a test lab for more complex call center environments and technologies. An effective test plan includes: component testing, integration testing, functional testing, usability testing, load testing and failure/recovery testing. Find the right person within your organization to lead this critical task or bring in outside help, but don't skimp.

2. An Operations, Administration and Maintenance (OA&M) plan is also critical to ongoing success in operating a technology. The OA&M plan should identify the key contacts for help and escalation when things aren't working. It should also include upgrade procedures (i.e., for the technology and other integration elements) and a backup schedule, with clear delineation of responsibilities and ownership.

3. A pilot program is a "must" when implementing anything that creates change for agents or customers. A pilot will expose any unanticipated problems and will help you to fine-tune the solution before going into production. Equally important, piloting tests the people and process sides of the implementation. For instance, do new processes mesh smoothly with the operation? Do callers understand the changes?

4. Training is another critical element. Without proper training, the technology will fail or, at the least, not bring in the anticipated goals or benefits. Develop and deliver specific training for the technology rollout. Training plans should consider end-users (agents and supervisors), as well as the technologists or operations support staff who will administer, manage or maintain the system.

Navigating the Vendor Map

The vendor market is crowded and it's constantly evolving – the players keep changing and the market keeps shifting. But, it's an important element to understanding today's contact center technology. So here are the key concepts that can help you make your way through the market madness – past, present and future.

The Past Defines Us

None of us can deny our heritage, and neither can vendors. The company trying to sell you a voice switch claims their focus is CRM, VoIP and other cutting-edge media. Maybe so – but their heritage may be deeply engrained in circuit-switched voice communications. Or how about the email and Web integration vendor that assures you they can manage all of your media? Possibly – but do they really understand the day-to-day challenges of running a call center that still has 95 percent of its contacts coming in over the phone?

The past is important and you need to understand your vendors' backgrounds. Unfortunately, vendors often will not admit that their heritage influences their thinking and understanding of the call center environment. So, as a buyer, it's up to you to find out where they come from and whether they are truly broadening their scope. It might require a little extra work – you may need to educate them on all of the pieces of your complex contact center environment, and determine how they may fit into it. (If you're a vendor, admit your heritage, gloat about it, but grow beyond it, as well.)

The Present Is Good and Bad (But Not Ugly)

Fortunately, the diverse vendor pasts or backgrounds have helped to create a better "present" for the contact center marketplace. The strength of the "old school" vendors, coming from a solid understanding of the contact center's fundamental challenges and needs (e.g., reliable systems and usable tools for the average supervisor or manager) has been combined with the strengths of the "new school" vendors, whose thinking focuses on the ability to evolve faster with more open platforms and system interoperability.

The bad news is this diversity also means that vendor companies have evolved beyond categorization. It used to be easy to group vendors: ACD/PBX, IVR, CTI, CRM, etc. Today, they defy classification. It's hard to figure out exactly who to talk to when you want to purchase a specific technology, and it's also difficult to comparison-shop. So how do you narrow the field and stay focused on your technology needs? Take the time to conduct research, understand your options, carefully define requirements and stay focused on your business needs. Otherwise, it's easy to become enamored with a technology that you don't really need at the cost of one you do need.

Figure 10-5: Vendor Evaluations Can Be Tough

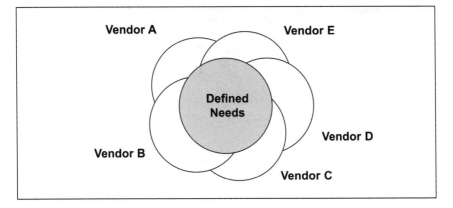

The Future Is Uncertain

We have a headline clipped from a trade magazine that says, "I have seen the future and it is vague." How true. No one knows what tomorrow may bring, so it's best to accept the uncertainty that's part of the contact center technology market. Every day, vendors flood the market with promises of new capabilities driven by the need to move at Internet-speed to satisfy customers and investors, and to keep

up with or get ahead of the competition. The vendors are also continually rein-
venting themselves through acquisitions, mergers, name changes, new product
releases and even self-destruction (some fall as fast as they climb).

What does this uncertainty mean to you? Approach with caution. Unless you
take the time to explore a vendor's future plans, you run the risk of implementing technology that doesn't fit into your plans. Try to hold a candid discussion of
where their products are today, where they're heading, what their business strategy is, and the depth of their partnerships (i.e., just public relations announcement or joint investment and collaborative development?). Find out where
they're investing research and development money and why. Ensure that they
understand your vision and strategy, and determine whether their directions and
plans align with yours.

Suite of Products Vs. Best-of-Breed

There are two strategies to consider when purchasing technology today: Do you want
a suite of products or would you rather take a best-of-breed approach? With a suite, a
vendor – alone or with partners – offers you a set of capabilities that span multiple
business needs. For example, a suite might include CTI and full multimedia contact
routing, management and reporting. The alternative is to select separate best-of-breed
solutions for voice call routing and reporting, CTI, email response management, text-
chat and Web calls, and integrate them. Here are a few of the tradeoffs:

- **Features and functions.** The best-of-breed approach will generally have more
  feature advantages over a suite solution.
- **Speed.** A suite can be deployed more quickly than a set of best-of-breed solutions.
- **Integration.** Suites are typically pre-integrated, at least for basic functionality
  (and more so when all elements come from a single vendor rather than a group
  of partners). With best-of-breed, you or an integrator pull all of the pieces
  together, which takes time and money.
- **Vendor relationship.** A suite basically ties you in with one vendor. Better make
  sure they're a good partner. Best-of-breed means you need to manage several relationships, although your dependence on each vendor is less.
- **Cost.** Consider purchase, integration and maintenance costs – generally, a suite
  will have lower total cost of ownership.

- **Support and maintenance.** Selecting a single-vendor suite creates simpler support and maintenance arrangements than going with the multivendor best-of-breed solution. For instance, if you select a vendor and its partners to deliver a suite, you may be able to get single-point-of-contact support.

The analysis comes down to this: Are the features you may gain from the best-of-breed approach critical enough to warrant the additional effort, time and cost?

Unfortunately, many centers don't develop a purchasing strategy and end up using the best-of-breed approach by default. That leads to overlapping functionality and increased costs down the road. To avoid such costly errors, take the time to define the approach that is best for your center. If neither seems to fit your needs, consider a hybrid purchasing strategy: Use suite solutions if they meet your defined business needs – that will enable your company to move faster and simplify implementation. Consider best-of-breed alternatives when suite solutions don't meet critical requirements.

An Overview of Technology Sourcing Options

Sourcing is defined as the way that you provide a capability. There are three key choices to consider for customer contact technology sourcing:

1. **In-house or in-source.** The technology, processes and operations are set up as an integral part of your call center, using your people and your technology.

2. **Outsource.** A trusted partner provides the technology and people to handle customer contacts.

3. **Application Service Provider (ASP).** A provider of technology services for your call center, using their technology and support resources, and your agents. Often the ASP offers specific functions, such as CRM applications or Web integration and collaboration. Usually an ASP will host the application in a data center, making extensive use of IP networking to your facility. ASPs sometimes refer to their offerings as hosted services or outsourcing.

While those are three main types of setups, there are also variations on these themes. For example, some outsourcers (or service bureaus) offer options such as hosting your people at their call center location, or vice versa – setting up, owning and managing the technology used by your people at your site. And ASPs also offer a wide variety of capabilities, so you may be able to get everything you need from one supplier, or you may need to augment the ASP's capabilities with some of your own, those of their partners or those of other vendors/suppliers. And finally, some vendors and outsourcers also offer hosting services as ASPs.

With any of these approaches, the extent of the technology you can deploy varies widely, from standalone elements, such as email response management or Web integration, to full contact centers with multimedia and CRM. And sourcing decisions range from new centers to long-established centers, to adding a new technology or just evaluating whether or not the current approach is still the best one for your business.

Keep in mind that, regardless of the sourcing choice, the technology has to be integrated with the rest of your environment. Using an outsourcer or an ASP will not eliminate the difficult integration with your legacy systems environment.

And a final note: This landscape is changing rapidly, so you'll need to conduct thorough research on any vendor.* It is particularly important to probe their financial status and their current and/or past partnerships. The fate of the ASP market, in particular, has yet to be determined at this point – it may fly or falter.

Build Vs. Buy

Many contact centers prefer in-house technology sourcing over outsourcing. The key decision then becomes whether to build (e.g., in-house IT or custom-designed systems integrator solution) or buy (e.g., packaged vendor solutions). Most choose to buy technology solutions, especially with advanced applications (e.g., CTI, CRM, multimedia). If you're mired in a build vs. buy debate, here are a few benefits that support the case for buying technology solutions:

- Can you build it fast enough? Vendor solutions come "out of the box" while building your own usually means "from scratch" – which generally takes longer.
- Can you build it good enough? Vendor solutions generally include a robust set of features/functions and toolkits for developing business rules and reports – and they readily integrate with other systems. When you build a solution, you often must compromise on these capabilities, making it difficult and slow to support all the business needs.

---

* Visit www.vanguard.net for up-to-date Web site listings.

- Can you build it cheap enough? Vendors don't like to lose out to a custom solution. Therefore, the market is competitive and vendors are motivated to heavily discount license costs or provide enterprise licenses. Don't be fooled – most "build" approaches cost more than a "buy" when considering all costs (initial and ongoing).
- Can you maintain it if you build it? It's a fast-changing, dynamic marketplace. Your center will always need new functionality. The vendor solutions that you buy will continue to evolve to support their customers and remain competitive. With solutions that you build, it can take a long time to deliver new capabilities. In addition, the business users, not IT, should control screen layouts, business rules, call routing and workflows – and that's more likely with a purchased solution. Finally, custom-built solutions require very well-defined IT processes, documentation and change management – all of which are an inherent part of product solutions, but may be difficult for a busy IT shop to handle.
- Can you retain the staff and skills you need to build and maintain it? Building a solution creates reliance on individuals – while the solution is being developed, as well as when it enters production and maintenance. A vendor solution offers many different potential resources (in-house, vendor or third party) to work on your application.

The Decision Process

Finding the best sourcing approach is similar to the technology selection process. Start by assembling a team of representatives who have a stake in the contact center's success, as well as an understanding of your technology and business goals. Consider including call center staff, visionaries, strategists, marketing staff, technologists and trainers. After the team determines the best sourcing approach for your organization, you can proceed with vendor selection. A fundamental step in the decision process is to develop your business requirements.

Business Requirements

Business requirements will focus everyone involved on a common set of goals and needs. This ensures that your business is the driver (rather than the technology or the vendor's idea of what you should do). Discuss the capabilities you must provide using the customer's experience as a key element.

Here are a few issues to consider when developing business requirements:

• **Media.** Which media do you need to support in what timeframes? What are your customers' expectations? What are your competitors doing?

• **Functions.** What functions do you need to provide? Sales, service, technical support?

• **Coverage.** Do you need to provide 24x7 coverage? What coverage do you provide today, and should it expand?

• **Applications.** What applications (e.g., desktop tools, access to information, creating and analyzing information) do you need to provide? Will you rely on existing applications or will you add new ones? What are the system and database implications? Consider customer relationship management, knowledge base, scripting, contact tracking, fulfillment, database marketing analysis, etc.

• **Growth.** How fast do you expect contact volumes to grow? Will the technologies you're planning (e.g., Web capabilities, speech recognition) offset or add to any of your "traditional" contact volumes?

• **Change.** How fast will changes occur in your company's business? Is your customer base changing? Are your products and services changing?

Outsourcer or ASP Management

Deciding to use an outsourcer or ASP doesn't mean that your organization will have no responsibilities. These vendors need to be carefully managed. A good partnership contract establishes service level agreements, account management criteria (e.g., status meetings and reports) and reporting criteria. An outsourcer is likely to be managed from the operation, while an ASP may be managed by your IT shop with input from the operation. When choosing either of these paths, allocate the appropriate internal resources to work with vendors to ensure success.

Decision Criteria

Decision criteria define the basis on which you'll make a decision about which sourcing approach to use. Consider the following types of criteria:

• **Operations.** What is the operational environment you want? What types of media, functions, applications and hours of coverage are required?

- **Technology.** What does your infrastructure look like – is it leading edge or is it stuck in the 20th century? Does your vision of the future compound the challenges you already face? What infrastructure is needed to meet the business goals, including the media and applications defined in your business requirements? Are you in the process of procuring other technology solutions (e.g., CRM, CTI) with which you will need to integrate?

- **Resources.** What resources do you have now, and what will you need to succeed – both for implementation and maintenance? Consider call center staff and management, technology, HR, training, etc. And don't forget the physical facilities – do you have enough space (or can you get it) for your growing/changing contact center needs?

- **Workload.** Volumes and variability of volumes can be another critical decision factor. Can you project handle times and volumes? Will they grow quickly? Will they present significant peaks, triggered by marketing campaigns, partnerships or publicity?

- **Culture.** Don't forget to consider your culture. Some companies need control of technology, staff or both to deliver the level and type of service and support they desire. Others are willing – even anxious – to focus on core competencies and leave the other functions to partners. Define the approach that fits your organization.

- **Speed.** How quickly will you need to have new functions up and running? What is your anticipated pace of change and growth? Will this be a highly dynamic, rapidly changing environment or one that is fairly stable? If dynamic, do you have the ability to keep up with the changes and the desire to manage it first-hand?

- **Cost.** What are your investment priorities? Do you want capital investments or services (operations costs) paid for on a monthly basis? Consider the cost of technology, resources and ongoing maintenance and support.

- **Core competencies.** Are call center services currently a core competency for your company, or will they be in the future? What about technology implementation, integration, development and management?

- **Future directions.** Can you see ahead to your organization's future needs and operations? Are you choosing a short-term or long-term solution?

Making Your Decision

After defining your business requirements and decision criteria, spend time on education and research – network with colleagues in other companies, leverage vendors, search the Web. Next, apply the decision criteria and compare your business requirements with the options.

Table 10-1 shows a few general characteristics of environments that are well-aligned with the various options. They may help to trigger ideas about what is the best fit for your center. They address the decision criteria previously defined.

Table 10-1: Sourcing Options

Option	Characteristics of a Good Fit
In-house (assuming "Buy" not "Build")	• Call center is key to achieving corporate strategy and is a source of competitive advantage; management feels the need to maintain close control of its operations • Call center is core competency or competency can be developed • Desire to control resources and applications to support customer needs • Have extensive infrastructure to leverage and willing to add what is needed • Have human resources needed – agents, technologists, HR, training, etc. • Prefer hands-on management and administration in highly dynamic environment • Prefer capital investments over long-term operational expenses • Don't have an aggressive schedule for implementation and rollout • Current call center hours of operation match business needs (or can be expanded to match needs) • Volumes and peaks are manageable with resources in-house
Outsource	• Call center is not core competency or focus, and prefer to focus on other areas while leveraging skilled partner for customer support • Need some specialized skills that aren't readily available or attainable in-house (e.g., language skills, telemarketing skills) • Need to move extremely fast • Requirements are rapidly changing • Expect significant growth, peaks or variability in volumes, or highly unpredictable volumes • Want temporary solution until needs are further defined or in-house capability can be built • Prefer cost models that have operating expenses rather than capital investment • Don't have enough human resources to serve customer contact volumes or implement new capabilities • Need 24x7 support but don't currently provide (or want to provide) 24x7 in call center

Option	Characteristics of a Good Fit
ASP	• Have people to service contacts but are not able to or not interested in procuring and managing new technology • Need to move fast • Need to introduce new media and applications, and want state-of-the-art tools for customer support • Technology staff has little time available for additional projects • Prefer cost models that have operating expenses rather than capital investment • Believe technology will continue to evolve rapidly and want to leverage new capabilities quickly as they become available

Following are a few conclusions we've come to from our work with organizations:

• Established, larger centers tend to keep technology in-house. Many are migrating from a "build" mentality to a "buy" mentality. You can find in-house sourcing in almost any industry.

• Outsourcing is used for new centers (often called "green field" centers), smaller centers and companies which have determined that call centers are not a source of competitive advantage for them. It is also used by larger, more established centers to augment their in-house operations. Outsourcers handle specialized functions (e.g., media, sales or collections) or help with peaks. Many high-tech companies use outsourcing. Utilities sometimes use outsourcers to help with outage peaks, while retailers might use them during peak seasons (e.g., around the holidays) or when conducting a focused advertising campaign.

• ASPs were initially embraced by smaller centers and start-ups, but are now being considered by established centers that have too much to do and not enough time and resources to do it. Many use ASPs to add specialized, advanced functions like CRM and multimedia. The ASP model has great potential, but some companies shy away from it because of the financial instability many of the vendors have experienced.

Helpful Hints

Regardless of which sourcing option you pursue, or which technology you're implementing, here are some keys to help you succeed:

- Take time to define your needs and find the best solution to meet them.
- Ensure all elements are in place – people, processes and technology.
- Take a careful approach to implementation, ensuring adequate time to test and pilot before going into production.
- Carefully manage the relationship with your supplier (i.e., vendor, outsourcer or ASP) so they'll help you achieve customer contact success.
- Monitor, modify and adjust. Business needs continuously evolve and so will your contact center. So get started, but watch, listen, learn and continuously improve.

Points to Remember

- Taking time to define a contact center technology strategy can help you avoid suboptimization of your technology investments and your call center operations.

- Call center technology implementation risks can be minimized with proper testing, training and piloting. It is important to define whether the project is automating or transforming your environment.

- The vendor world is changing. Consider a supplier's past, present and future to assess their potential fit with your needs.

- Sourcing options include in-house (buy or build), outsource or application service providers.

Actions to Take

- It all boils down to taking the time and allocating the resources to get it right. When planning, take the time to build a strategy. When designing, involve the right resources. When selecting a vendor, do your homework. And when deciding which approach is best, match the options to your organization's culture and needs.

Chapter 11:

Perspectives on the Future

Key Points Discussed in this Chapter:

Good Indicators of the Future

The Changes and Challenges

A Few Predictions

What It All Means to You

We created this book as a practical guide to help you deal with today's real issues as you plan for and implement call center technologies. However, it's hard to plan for today without insight into the future. So here are a few things you need to consider about the future of call center technologies and how they will impact the decisions you make today.

Good Indicators of the Future

Some things never change, right? But we're dealing with technology, which is supposed to move at Internet speed, right? But does it really? Are the realities of the technology world, in general, and the Internet-powered world, specifically, also true of the contact center world? Let's take a look backward so that we can look forward:

• The "dumb" switch/smart CTI combination (or Hybrid switch/server or server-based routing/reporting engine) and "erector-set" telephony have been discussed for years. But today's reality is not what has been hyped. Proprietary architectures have constrained it and continue to do so. But it is still an attractive concept.

• CRM has the potential to transform businesses. How-ever, many who've tried have failed or so industry statistics tell us. Yet many still want to implement it or, at least, put in place new front ends and contact management tools. And others who've implemented it want to fix it to get the value out of it that they had intended. Overall, today's expectations are more realistic than they were a couple years ago.

• Web-enabled call centers (text-chat, Web calls, collaboration) have been the rage for three or four years. However, penetration rates are still relatively low (benchmarking studies reveal that, while penetration is low, it's growing fast). Web-enabling the center is on many companies' "wish" lists.

• The multimedia queue is the highest goal for many contact centers. Companies buy technology with that plan in mind, but few have implemented it – yet.

• Voice and data are converging. IT influence is growing (and, correspondingly, telecom influence is waning), which impacts switch architectures, application infrastructure architectures and network infrastructure architectures. These changes will prove valuable to the contact center, both in services that can be delivered, and the cost to implement and maintain them.

Note: VoIP is on the radar. Some companies are dabbling with the technology, but few are implementing it for customer contact. But when the quality of service guarantees are met and it becomes routine to talk through a PC while on a Web site, we all want to be there and we all need to be there.

These realities set the stage for the future – at least, the near-term future. Many businesses want to implement CTI-enabled CRM, seamlessly link to the Web and reap the benefits of VoIP for cost-savings. And they need to do these things in the context of a true business strategy.

The Changes and Challenges Are Real

As companies plan for the future of their call center technology environment, there are real challenges they must face. Technology does evolve rapidly. Call center change doesn't happen as fast as PC changes (which seem to get cheaper and more powerful by the minute) – but it does change. New product releases with new features hit the market almost daily. There are continuous upgrades and architectural evolutions. They're particularly influenced by IP and the shift to server-based systems (issues we discussed in Chapter 2).

The trustworthy PBX or ACD used to have a five- to 10-year depreciation cycle, with new releases coming in 18- to 24-month intervals. The newer hardware architectural elements (standard hardware servers and data-networking equipment) that are replacing traditional voice switches depreciate in three- to five-year cycles. New software releases (for operating systems, databases and application software) hit the market every 12 months (or less) with the potential for significant integration, customization or configuration efforts, or even total replacements.

As one result of these technology changes, some companies now suffer from "analysis paralysis." They spend so much time studying trends, wondering what's next and trying to adapt, they have trouble moving foward. Yet, companies can't afford to wait if they want to be competitive.

We also see companies struggle with priorities. Limited budgets and long wish lists are a bad match. As a result, the wrong initiatives sometimes make it to the top of the list, or partial solutions are purchased, or integration or training is short-changed. However, when business needs are the driver in the context of a complete call center strategy, priorities become clear. Business cases should be built within that context.

A Few Predictions

Considerations about the future should factor into your decision-making process and influence your requirements and planning today. With that in mind, we'll stick our necks out a little (but not too far) with five predictions:

1. System Decomposition

A key trend in call center technology is decomposition, which is breaking the system down into its fundamental hardware and software components. IP-architected solutions, Communications Servers and Voice XML are current examples (and they were developed from the data world's influence on telephony). Decomposition creates choice of hardware platforms, operating systems, software applications, databases and network infrastructure. New vendors or solutions emerge to provide the various elements, while existing vendors break their proprietary systems down into a variety of more open elements that interoperate. The expanded choic-

© 1995 Ted Goff

"Welcome! You are about to experience the very latest in impersonal customer service technology!"

es and competition drive down costs.

While it's not going to develop into a perfect world, there will be further decomposition of call center technology. Call center technology will move closer to a "mix-and-match" or "plug-and-play" world. Some vendors will offer one element, while others will offer many. Suites or best-of-breed solutions can be leveraged, but with greater interoperability than we've seen in the past.

2. IP Network Infrastructure

Some type of packetized voice, probably VoIP running on data networks, is here to stay. While VoIP has its challenges (which we described in Chapter 2), the quality issues are currently being addressed. The market is moving beyond the early-adopter stage, and is projected to grow quickly and significantly. It will take time, due to the large installed base of TDM-based voice switches with long depreciation cycles. But switches will evolve in place (the traditional voice-switch vendors are already offering options to add IP to existing switches or migrate to IP-based switches). When new systems are purchased, IP will become the platform of choice.

IP will be further promoted in contact centers because of its "killer application" – to enable voice calls from the Web site over the Internet. The ability to collaborate with customers in real-time with a quality voice connection will transform contact centers.

3. Server-Resident Applications Infrastructure

Applications infrastructure migration is a reality, and there are advantages to the more open platforms. The more traditional switch vendors are backing this trend (remember the Hybrid we discussed in Chapter 2?), albeit with a "somewhat proprietary, somewhat open" approach. It's proprietary because it uses its own link between switch and server, but it's also more open because of standard hardware platforms, operating systems, databases and APIs. The move to IP will help to push the applications shift along, as more options for the switching platform and IVR are introduced that don't have a legacy of internal, proprietary applications. Server-resident applications fit well with decomposition, IP and multimedia.

4. Unified Multimedia Routing and Reporting Engine

The vision of a single routing-and-reporting engine that is aware of and in control of every contact regardless of media is a beautiful one. We think it will become the norm as "call centers" complete their evolution to "contact centers" and the organizational, process and technology boundaries dividing phone calls from emails from text-chats come tumbling down. However, we don't expect the walls to fall quickly since voice calls continue to be the predominant media in most centers. This trend closely relates to system decomposition and server-based applications infrastructure – it bodes well for a unified routing-and-reporting application (one of the core elements in the decomposed environment running on a server).

A key benefit of this vision is a common system management and administration environment. A single interface or set of tools to control skills, define routing paths (or business rules) and develop or access reports will make it much easier to manage the call center technology environment. The benefits of the common application will ripple out to other technologies that integrate with the routing-and-reporting functions – quality monitoring, workforce management and other support tools will only need to talk to one system.

It's not clear which system will emerge as the "winner" to play the role of this powerful multimedia engine. Today, CTI solutions are closest to meeting this requirement, with some of the major platforms providing an integrated multimedia solution (again, somewhat constrained by the limited openness of switch links). But if CRM (or its next generation of technology applications) is the place where data is captured about every interaction with the customer, could it and should it be the engine? Or will it be some sort of converged CTI/CRM solution? Or will the Hybrid solution offered by the switch vendors evolve into the best type of multimedia engine? New VoIP platforms and Communications Servers are built from the ground up with the blended media engine concept. Stay tuned for the outcome of this interesting race.

5. Web Architecture and Technology

Our final prediction concerns the role of Web-based architecture and corresponding integration, development and interface environments. Web technologies and architecture have proven their value and the tools continue to evolve. Various markup languages, such as HTML, XML and VoiceXML, are key tools in the evolution of call center technologies, applications and integration. Clearly, the role of TCP/IP, browsers and middleware tools will expand.

The prevalence of Web tools and relatively large programmer communities will further catalyze changes in the call center technology market. The data world's influence continues to grow stronger, displacing proprietary systems of the past. This Web architecture is ideal for supporting self-service and assisted service, as customers use the Web for voice-enabled Web applications and then collaborate with agents when needed. All "users" will access the corporate knowledge base through the same core architecture – the browser, Internet/intranet and the associated applications and databases.

The Contact Center Technology Vision

Figure 11-1 shows the vision of the future for "plug-and-play," IP-based, applications-server driven, multimedia contact center technology. The differences between this vision and today's environment are:

• **The voice switch becomes a gateway.** The voice-switching matrix has little intelligence – it only does as it's told by external, server-based, application logic. It connects endpoints (IP and TDM-based) and converts PSTN circuit-based communication to packet-based (LAN and WAN) communication.

• **Vendor choice exists for each element.** Standards-based architectures and data communications mechanisms – along with middleware – enable interoperability. Therefore, how you buy call center technology elements and, potentially, from whom you buy, change.

• **All media are created equal.** The traditional voice call dominates the call center today (and may for a long time) and, as a result, the technology is voice-centric. In this new model, different media contacts are all managed equally. Each arrives on its media server, and the routing engine becomes aware of its presence and its needs. The routing engine applies business rules to route each contact to the properly skilled agent. That might mean a voice call is top priority because of its real-time nature – or maybe not. It depends!

• **The contact center becomes more tightly linked to enterprise fulfillment.** Media-independent, contact center-initiated customer requests trigger a series of downstream activities and processes like credit approval, financing options, inventory, supply logistics, manufacturing, shipping and billing. The original request flows through the organization with complete visibility. The contact center is wired into the enterprise operating system.

• **Integration is easier.** Because they are based on standards, the system elements can more readily communicate or interoperate. The value (and investment) is in the applications and business rules, not in making the diverse systems talk to each other.

• **Contact center development, management and maintenance shifts to IT and to those who know the Web and standard Web tools.** Ideally, there is a tight relationship between the IT representatives who apply these tools into the call center and the call center operation.

Figure 11-1: Contact Center Technology Vision

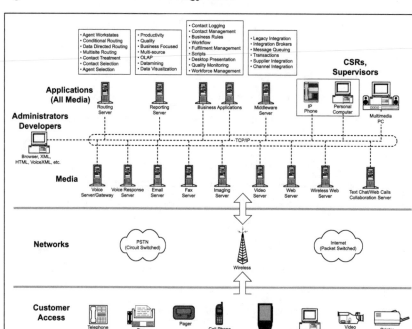

The result of these differences is that the new world incurs lower total cost of ownership – the cost to implement, integrate, manage and maintain. It's easier to find resources to work with the elements (developers, administrators, technicians), and there is more flexibility as you become less constrained by proprietary tools. But shorter product lifecycles introduce more change, more often. For this vision to become a reality, there are many requirements:

- Full migration to IP and/or more openness on TDM-based systems.
- Robust application suites on the controlling servers providing the capabilities call centers are accustomed to in their PBXs for voice. Capabilities are extended to other media, as appropriate.
- True interoperability based on standards so decomposition really allows choice.
- Integration with business applications systems.
- Minimal functional overlap between elements.
- Reliability that can be counted on for the mission-critical applications of the call center (i.e., "five-nines" or better).
- More scalable solutions so that contact centers can grow without platform or pricing discontinuities, and the same application can be cost-effectively deployed in large, small and even remote-agent environments.

What It All Means to You

How should these predictions influence what you do today? We've interwoven key principles and mantras throughout this book. We hope you remember them. They are:

1. You *need* a strategy to give contact center technology context. Business strategy, customer-contact-strategy and technology strategy must align.
2. Technology is an enabler, not a driver (see the previous principle). Start with business drivers, and focus on the users (customers and agents) first.
3. You need to make decisions and tradeoffs. Planning and prioritizing in the context of a strategy will focus your resources on the most valuable elements for your business first.
4. Technology succeeds when the people and process elements are taken care of

first (organizational change, reengineering, process redesign, cultural change, etc.). Transformation (not just automation) is often in order.

These principles will remain true – the crystal ball is crystal clear on that.

As you develop your strategy, business requirements and technical requirements, consider the changes ahead, especially in terms of infrastructure. Define what you need to put in place today, but also your vision for tomorrow. Understand the directions required for the vendors and products you are considering. For major initiatives, you will need nondisclosure briefings. Take the time to visit vendor labs, talk to developers and get product manager commitments when large purchases and core infrastructure decisions are at stake. Understand how the technology you buy today will either promote or detract from your vision of tomorrow.

And finally, monitor market developments and trends. Some of these technologies are ripe for breakthroughs. By staying informed, you'll be ready to adapt when the time is right. Keep in mind, not everyone has to be an early adopter, but most call centers that play a strategic role in the organization will want to take advantage of the benefits inherent in these trends. Bridge your strategy, operations and call center technology – today and into the future – to achieve your business goals.

Points to Remember

• Many of today's trends will influence tomorrow's call center technology. IP, server-based applications and Web architecture and tools will have a major influence on the evolution of contact center infrastructure.

• Multimedia contact center growth will lead to better ways of routing, managing and reporting on the variety of contact types. Multimedia centers will leverage the newer technology tools and platforms.

• The benefits of the technology changes include lower cost of ownership and ease of application development and management. But it will take time and many areas must align for the vision to be achieved.

Actions to Take

• Consider future directions for technology, in general, and the vendors you are considering, specifically. Monitoring trends and developments will help you to make good decisions today.

Appendix

Acronyms
Glossary
Bibliography
Index
Figures and Tables

Acronyms

ACD	Automatic Call Distributor/Distribution
ACW	After-Call Work
AHT	Average Handling Time
ANI	Automatic Number Identification
API	Applications Programming Interface
ASA	Average Speed of Answer
ASP	Active Server Pages
ASP	Application Service Provider
ASR	Automatic Speech Recognition
ATB	All Trunks Busy
ATM	Asynchronous Transfer Mode
BIC	Best In Class
BRI	Basic Rate Interface
CED	Caller Entered Digits
CGI	Common Gateway Interface
CIO	Chief Information Officer
CIS	Customer Information System (also Customer Interaction Software)
CLEC	Competitive Local Exchange Carrier
CLI	Calling Line Identification (used outside North America)
CLID	Calling Line Identification
CO	Central Office
COM	Component Object Model
CoS	Class of Service
CORBA	Common Object Request Broker Architecture
CPE	Customer Premises Equipment
CPU	Central Processing Unit
CRM	Customer Relationship Management
CSR	Customer Service Representative
CSTA	Computer Supported Telecommunications Applications
CTI	Computer Telephony Integration

DAT	Digital Audio Tape
DCOM	Distributed Component Object Model
DDE	Dynamic Data Exchange
DID	Direct Inward Dialing
DNIS	Dialed Number Identification Service
DSL	Digital Subscriber Line
DTMF	Dual-Tone Multi-Frequency
EAI	Enterprise Application Integration
ECMA	European Computer Manufacturer's Association
ERMS	Email Response Management System
ERP	Enterprise Resource Planning
EWT	Expected Wait Time
FIFO	First In, First Out
FTE	Full-Time Equivalent
GUI	Graphical User Interface
HTML	Hyper-Text Markup Language
HTTP	Hyper-Text Transport Protocol
ICR	Intelligent Character Recognition
IEEE	Institute of Electrical and Electronics Engineers
IETF	Internet Engineering Task Force
II	Information Indicator
IM	Instant Messaging
IP	Internet Protocol
IS	Information Systems
ISDN	Integrated Services Digital Network
ISO	International Stardards Organization
ISP	Internet Service Provider
IT	Information Technology
ITU	International Telecommunication Union
IVR	Interactive Voice Response
IWR	Interactive Web Response

IXC	Interexchange Carrier
J2EE	Java 2 Enterprise Edition
JTAPI	Java Telephony Application Programming Interface
KB	Knowledge Base
KPI	Key Performance Indicator
LAN	Local Area Network
LEC	Local Exchange Carrier
LED	Light Emitting Diode
LOA	Least Occupied Agent
MCU	Multipoint Control Unit
MGCP	Media Gateway Control Protocol
MIA	Most Idle Agent
MIS	Management Information System
MPLS	Multiprotocol Label Switching
NFAS	Non-Facility Associated Signaling
NIC	Network Interface Card
NOC	Network Operations Center
NSP	Network Service Provider
OA&M	Operations, Administration and Maintenance
OCR	Optical Character Recognition
ODBC	Open Database Connectivity
OLAP	Online Analytical Processing
OLE	Object Linking and Embedding
OLTP	Online Transaction Processing
OMG	Object Management Group
ORB	Object Request Broker
OSI	Open System Interconnection
PABX	Private Automatic Branch Exchange
PBX	Private Branch Exchange
PCM	Pulse-Code Modulation
PDA	Personal Digital Assistant

POP3	Post Office Protocol 3
PRI	Primary Rate Interface
PSTN	Public-Switched Telephone Network
PTT	Postal Telephone & Telegraph
QM	Quality Monitoring
QoS	Quality of Service
RBOC	Regional Bell Operating Company
RFC	Request For Comment
RFI	Request for Information
RFP	Request for Proposal
RFQ	Request for Quote
ROI	Return on Investment
RPC	Remote Procedure Call
RSF	Rostered Staff Factor
RSVP	Resource Reservation Protocol
RTP	Real-Time Transport Protocol
SALT	Speech Application Language Tags
SCP	Signal Control Point
SFA	Sales Force Automation
SGML	Standard Generalized Markup Language
SIP	Session Initiation Protocol
SLA	Service Level Agreement
SMTP	Simple Mail Transfer Protocol
SNA	Systems Network Architecture
SNMP	Simplified Network Management Protocol
SOHO	Small Office Home Office
SQL	Structured Query Language
SS7	Signaling System 7
STP	Signal Transfer Point
TAPI	Telephony Applications Programming Interface
TCO	Total Cost of Ownership

TCP/IP	Transmission Control Protocol/Internet Protocol
TDM	Time-Division Multiplexing
TLA	Three-Letter Acronym
TSAPI	Telephony Services Application Programming Interface
TSR	Telephone Service Representative
TTS	Text-to-Speech
UDP	User Datagram Protocol
URL	Uniform Resource Locator
UUI	User-to-User Information
VLAN	Virtual Local Area Network
VoIP	Voice Over Internet Protocol
VPN	Virtual Private Network
VRU	Voice Response Unit
VXML	Voice eXtensible Markup Language
WAN	Wide Area Network
WAP	Wireless Application Protocol
WFMS	Workforce Management System
WWW	World Wide Web
XML	eXtensible Markup Language

Glossary

**Glossary definitions are copyrighted
to ICMI, Inc. and Vanguard Communications Corporation**

Abandoned Call: Also called a Lost Call. The caller hangs up before reaching an agent.

Active Server Page (ASP): Microsoft-branded, dynamically created Web page that uses ActiveX scripting.

Active X: Branded software component technologies developed by Microsoft. Although these technologies can be used in any application, they are frequently associated with Internet capabilities.

Active X Controls: Microsoft-branded software components that allow a user to interact with an application. Examples include entering data, making selections or displaying information. Most commonly associated with Web-based applications in the form of downloadable applications similar to Java "applets." Active X Controls are software language-independent. Used frequently to "Webify" existing client/server applications.

Activity Codes: See Wrapup Codes.

Adherence to Schedule: How well agents follow designated work schedules. It includes the time spent handling calls and waiting for calls (availability), as well as when they were available to take calls (also called Compliance or Adherence).

After-Call Work (ACW): Work state when the agent is unavailable for calls to complete work associated with calls. Also called Wrap-Up and Post-Call Processing (PCP). It can include entering data, filling out forms, and faxing, emailing and outbound calling needed to complete the transaction. The agent is unavailable to receive another inbound call while in this mode.

Agent: The person who handles customer contacts. May also be referred to as customer service representative (CSR), telephone sales or service representative (TSR), etc.

Agent Features: Features on the switch specific to the needs of a call center agent. Typically include login/logout, changes to work states (available, not available/not ready, after-call work/wrap-up), transaction codes, supervisor assistance request, audio trouble indication, call trace indicator (for malicious calls) and queue status.

Agent Group: A collection of agents who share a common work activity. Also called Split, Gate, Queue or Skill Group. Examples include service, billing, sales, shipping and technical support.

Agent Selection: Function of ACD software to select the best agent to handle a call when there is no queue.

Agent Status: See Work State.

All Trunks Busy (ATB): When all trunks are busy in a specified trunk group. Switch reports indicate how often all trunks were busy, and how much total time all trunks were busy.

Analog: Telephone transmission technique with a continuous, low-voltage signal. Spoken words are in an analog format.

Analytics: A general term for advanced reporting and data analysis. In call centers, a set of products or methods that typically interact with CRM systems and multi-source data warehouses to collect, analyze and report on particular customer trends or buying patterns.

Announcement: A recorded verbal message played to callers.

Answer Supervision: The signal sent by the voice switch to the local or long-distance carrier to accept a call. When answer supervision starts, billing for either the caller or the call center will begin, if long-distance charges apply.

Application Service Provider (ASP): An outsourcing business that hosts software applications at its own facilities. Customers "rent" the applications, usually for a monthly fee. Applications are usually accessed via an IP network.

Applications Programming Interface (API): A defined set of programming commands that specify a set of actions that can be initiated by a program or application. It allows an application developer access to the capabilities of a specific system without having to understand the details of how it functions. For example, CTI vendors provide APIs so that third-party applications can perform additional call-control functions.

Architecture: The basic design of a system. Defines how the components work together. Architecture includes characteristics such as system capacity, scalability, upgradability and the ability to integrate with other systems.

Asynchronous Transfer Mode (ATM): A layer 2 WAN and LAN protocol for both real-time and non-real-time applications. ATM has built-in Quality of Service to enable converged network applications of voice, video and data. For call centers, it can be used with TCP/IP to enable VoIP.

Auto Available: Agents automatically go into an Available work mode after the call disconnects. If needed, they can manually go into After-Call Work.

Automated Attendant: A voice-processing capability that automates the operator/receptionist function. Callers use their telephone keypad to enter an extension or select a menu option that routes their calls to the correct destination. This function can reside in an onsite system (e.g., switch, voicemail or IVR) or in the network.

Automated Greeting: Agent's prerecorded greeting that plays automatically when a call arrives.

Automatic Answer: Answer mode that delivers a tone and automatically connects the call to the agent position (without ringing or need to push a button or go off-hook).

Automatic Call Distribution (ACD): A software application that routes incoming telephone calls and manages agent work states. At its most basic, the ACD usually routes calls, based on the trunk group of the call or the number the caller dialed (see DNIS) to the longest available or most idle agent in a group; it "queues" calls when there is no agent available. This capability may reside in a PBX, standalone ACD system, Communications Server, Centrex, Key System, ASP or a CTI application.

Automatic Call Distributor (ACD): A specialized voice switch or telephone system used in incoming call centers, serving only the call center. It is a programmable device that automatically answers calls, queues calls, distributes calls to agents, plays delay announcements to callers and provides real-time and historical reports on these activities.

Automatic Number Identification (ANI): A telephone network feature that passes the billing number of the line the caller is using to the call center. ANI may arrive over the D channel of an ISDN PRI circuit (out-of-band signaling), or before the first ring on a single line (in-band signaling). Long-distance companies provide ANI. Caller ID is the local phone company's version of ANI and is delivered in-band. Also called Calling Line Identification (CLI) outside North America.

Automatic Speech Recognition (ASR): Technology that allows people to interface with computers (including voice response and the Web) using spoken language. Also referred to as Advanced Speech Recognition.

Auxiliary Work State: An agent work state that makes an agent unavailable to take calls for nonphone call activities like training, lunch and breaks.

Available State: Work state for an agent signed on to the ACD software and waiting for a call to arrive.

Average Delay of Delayed Calls: The average delay of calls that are delayed (or queued). It is the total Delay for all calls divided by the number of calls that had to wait in queue.

Average Handling Time (AHT): The sum of Average Talk Time and Average Wrapup Time for a specified time period.

Average Speed of Answer (ASA): The average delay of all calls. It is total Delay divided by total number of calls.

Average Time to Abandonment: The average time that callers wait in queue before hanging up (without reaching an agent).

Back-Office Applications: Business applications that encompass functions that are "behind the scenes" to a customer such as finance, accounting, inventory control, purchasing, fulfillment, human resources and production. Often associated with Enterprise Resource Planning (ERP) systems.

Base Staff: Also called Seated Agents. The minimum number of agents required to achieve service level and response time objectives for a given period of time. Seated agent calculations assume that agents will be in their seats for the entire period of time. Therefore, schedules need to add in extra people to accommodate breaks, absenteeism and other factors that will keep agents from the phones. Contrast with Rostered Staff Factor.

Basic Rate Interface (BRI): One of the two levels of ISDN service. A BRI line provides two voice-grade channels (64 kbps), known as "bearer" channels, which can be used for voice and/or data and one data channel (16 kbps) for signaling. This configuration is commonly referred to as 2B+D. See ISDN.

Beep Tone: An audible notification that a call has arrived (also called Zip Tone). Beep tone can also refer to the audible notification that a call is being monitored.

Benchmark: Historically, a term referred to as a standardized task to test the capabilities of some business function or attribute against other companies (not limited to direct competitors). In quality terms, benchmarking is comparing products, services and processes with those of other organizations to identify new ideas and improvement opportunities.

Best-in-Class: A benchmarking term to identify organizations that outperform all others in a specified category.

Blended Agent: An agent who handles multiple contact types, such as inbound and outbound, or incoming calls and emails.

Blocked Call: A call that cannot be connected immediately because: a) No circuit is available at the time the call arrives; or b) the voice switch is programmed to block calls from entering the queue when the queue backs up beyond a defined threshold. A blocked call receives a busy signal.

Branch Office: A typically smaller regional or satellite office of a larger company. A branch office could be involved with sales and/or service for a defined geography. It may include call center activities.

Business Rules: A phrase used to refer to various software controls that manage contact routing, handling or followup. Often used interchangeably with Workflow.

Cable Modem: A device that provides high-speed Internet access over cable TV infrastructure. It is used for, but not limited to, application system access and VoIP for work-at-home (telecommuting) agents.

Call Blending: The ability to dynamically and automatically allocate call center agents to inbound or outbound calling, based on conditions in the call center and programmed parameters. This capability can be extended to nonvoice activities, as well (for example, email and text-chat). See also Multimedia Queuing, Blended Agent and Work Blending.

Call-by-Call Routing: The process of routing each call to the optimum destination according to real-time conditions. Typically used in the context of multisite routing.

Call Center: An umbrella term that generally refers to reservations centers, help desks, information lines, customer service centers, sales centers or similar names, regardless of how they are organized or what types of transactions they handle. See also Contact Center.

Call Classification: Determining and capturing the outcome of an outbound call. Can be done by an agent or a dialing system. Examples are busy, ring/no answer, answering machine, network tones and answer.

Call Load: Also referred to as Work Load. Call Load is the product of (Average Talk Time + Average After-Call Work) x call volume, for a given period.

Call Selection: Function of routing software to select the best call for an agent to handle when there has been a queue and now an agent has come available.

Call Treatment: Announcements, music, busy signals or ringing provided to a call while in queue.

Caller Entered Digits (CED): The digits that a caller enters on their telephone keypad to provide identifying information and/or call purpose. Generally entered into a voice processing system. Also referred to as Prompted Digits.

Caller ID: See Automatic Number Identification.

Calling Line Identification (CLI): See Automatic Number Identification.

Calls in Queue: A real-time statistic that refers to the number of calls waiting for a particular agent group and not yet connected to an agent.

Campaign Management: Process and system for defining and reporting on parameters for an outbound calling program. Includes when to call, number of attempts, retry rules and outcomes to track.

Carrier: A company that provides telecommunications circuits. Carriers include both local telephone companies (or Local Exchange Carriers – LECs) and long-distance providers (or Inter-Exchange Carriers – IXCs).

Case-Based Reasoning: Business application that aids in analyzing and resolving problems based on cases are recorded in the database. New cases are added to the database as additional problems are resolved or resolved in new ways. May be part of a bigger support system known as a Knowledge Base.

C-Club: Executives; those whose titles are things like CEO, CIO, CFO. Also referred to as CxO.

CD-ROM: Compact Disc Read-Only Memory. These discs hold as much as 660 megabytes of data, and the digital information is optically stored and read by a laser.

Central Office (CO): A telephone company switching center, or the type of telephone switch used in a telephone company switching center. Provides connections to local endpoints, routes calls locally and connects calls with an Inter-Exchange Carrier (IXC).

Centrex: A central office telephone switch service that serves a specific area. Similar to a PBX, except that it is owned by the local telephone company and is used by multiple business and/or residential customers. For call centers, it is an alternative to buying, maintaining and administering your own voice switch.

Chief Information Officer (CIO): A typical title for the highest-ranking executive responsible for an organization's information systems.

Circuit: A transmission path between two points in a network.

Circuit-Switching: A method of transferring information across a network by establishing a temporary, dedicated, end-to-end path ("circuit") for the duration of a communication. This is the technology traditionally used to transmit voice (e.g., over the PSTN).

Class of Service (CoS): A method of tagging data packets for special handling, usually at a higher priority. For call centers, this technique is used to enable VoIP.

Client: Usually refers to the client in a client/server environment. The client is a computer or computer application that has access to services (data, applications) over a network from a server application. See Thin Client and Thick Client.

Client/Server Architecture: A networked computing approach in which one computer application (client) issues a request to another computer application (server). The server application processes the request and delivers the requested information back to the client application. A computer can be a client in one application process, and a server in another process. Call center client/server applications include, but are not limited to, CTI, IVR and CRM.

Co-Browsing: A collaboration approach where the agent and customer can both see the same Web page and either can control the navigation.

Common Gateway Interface (CGI): A program running on a Web server that lets you do dynamic things with a Web page, such as collect data, access data and create unique pages.

Common Object Request Broker Architecture (CORBA): A programming standard and framework from the Object Management Group (OMG) that utilizes object-oriented programming to enable software programs to interoperate. It is programming language independent, and utilizes a software device called an Object Request Broker (ORB) to pass messages between programs.

Communications Server: An alternative to the PBX that manages and routes voice, fax, Web and email communications within a single server, and provides a wide set of applications. Typically based on a Windows server platform. Communica-tions Servers are generally seen in small to medium (fewer than 100 agents) contact centers that can benefit from an integrated solution that otherwise would be cost-prohibitive as separate point solutions (e.g., PBX, voicemail, IVR, ACD, CTI, quality monitoring).

Component Object Model (COM): A Microsoft term describing the base model used for building components in an object-oriented programming language.

Computer Telephony Integration (CTI): The functional integration of various computer and telephone system elements to enable voice and data networks to work together and share information. CTI enables a number of useful call center applications, including screen pops, intelligent routing, multimedia, cradle-to-grave reporting and voice/data transfer.

Conditional Routing: Intelligently routing calls to the right group(s), position or treatment (e.g., announcements, music, options) based on current call center conditions, defined time/day parameters, information on the call or caller type, or other parameters. Implemented through routing tables and decision trees.

Contact Center: A group of agents who not only take phone calls, but handle additional forms of contact such as email, text-chat, Web calls, mail, fax and other interactions with customers. See Call Center.

Contact Management: Business application that creates a record of and tracks each contact made with the customer. Also provides contact history information. Creates a database that enables informed communications with customers, database marketing and proactive communications. Includes functions such as contact history database and triggers for follow-up contacts. One function of a CRM system.

Cookie: A small file in a Web browser that uniquely identifies a user to a Web server to provide personalized content. It is used as an enabling technology in eCRM and Web integration applications.

Coordinated Voice/Data Conference: A CTI application that provides the ability to conference a data screen along with a voice call, enabling both parties on the conference to view information about the caller.

Coordinated Voice/Data Consultation: A CTI application similar to Coordinated Voice/Data Conference, except that the caller is put on hold while the originally called party consults with a colleague.

Coordinated Voice/Data Delivery ("Screen Pop"): A CTI application that delivers an incoming voice call to an agent at the same time as a data screen about the calling party.

Coordinated Voice/Data Transfer: A CTI application similar to Coordinated Voice/Data Conference, except that the voice call and the data are transferred to a colleague. Often used when transferring a call from an IVR to an agent position with a screen pop.

Cost Center: An accounting term that refers to a department or function in the organization that is expected to incur costs only (doesn't generate profit).

Cost of Delay: The 800 service expense incurred to queue callers.

Cost Per Call: Total costs (fixed and variable) divided by total calls for a given period of time.

Cradle-to-Grave Reporting: Call center reporting term that includes all call center touch points (human and systems) from the time a caller dials an 800 number to the time of disconnect. It can include, but is not limited to, voice-switch routing, IVR, multisite flows, all agent activity and business application activity. The key enabler for cradle-to-grave reporting is typically CTI.

Customer Information System (CIS): A database application or series of linked database applications that provides information about the customer and their relationship with the business. Also referred to as Customer Interaction Software. See CRM.

Customer Relationship Management (CRM): The strategy and process of holistically managing a customer's relationship with a company through marketing, sales and service. It takes into account their history as a customer, the depth and breadth of their business with the company, as well as other factors. CRM generally uses a sophisticated applications and database system that includes elements of Data Mining, Contact Management, and Enterprise Resource Planning allowing agents to know and anticipate customer behavior better.

Customer Service Representative (CSR): See Agent.

CxO: A person with a "C-level" position, e.g., Chief Financial Officer (CFO), Chief Infomation Officer (CIO), Chief Executive Officer (CEO), etc.

Data-Directed Routing: Routing approach that looks into a database for information about the customer, current status or other factors to use in the routing decision. Generally CTI-enabled.

Data Mining: The use of sophisticated analysis tools to identify patterns within one or more databases (usually data from a Data Warehouse). Data-mining tools can proactively discover relationships between variables without being expressly programmed. Data Mining helps companies learn more about their customers and leverage that information to provide customized service and expand relationships.

Data Switch: A LAN or WAN networking device that connects a series of computers via high-speed transmission paths. Each computer has its own bandwidth to the switch.

Data Warehousing: A large database that stores data generated by an organization's multiple business systems. Data can be extracted using report generators, sophisticated decision support systems or other analytical tools. See Data Mining.

Datamart: A subset of a data warehouse, typically with data that is of interest to a particular department of an organization.

Desktop Statistics: Real-time and/or historical call center activity accessed from a desktop PC. This function enables a supervisor to view call center activity or agents to view their own activity.

Dialed Number: The number that the caller dialed to initiate the call.

Dialed Number Identification Service (DNIS): An enhanced network service offering – generally associated with 800 service – where a unique set of identifying digits is passed to the voice switch and act as a code to identify the call type (purpose) and intended destination. Companies often use DNIS to route different types of calls (e.g., sales vs. service) to different agent groups. See Direct Inward Dialing.

Digital: The use of a binary code (1s and 0s) to represent information.

Digital Subscriber Line (DSL): An integrated, digital, high-speed (>384kbps) Internet access and voice service for small offices and residential users. For call centers, it is an enabling technology for work-at-home (telecommuting) agents.

Direct Inward Dialing (DID): A network service offering – generally associated with local service – where a unique set of identifying digits is passed to the voice switch. By mapping each set of digits to an internal extension, the switch can provide direct dialing to a particular extension, bypassing the attendant. See Dialed Number Identification Service.

Directed Dialog: Speech recognition approach that recognizes what is being said based on guided or structured interactions. The caller is given examples of phrases to use. Also referred to as Structured Language.

Dual-Tone Multi-Frequency (DTMF): A signaling system that sends pairs of audio frequencies to represent digits on a telephone keypad. It is often used interchangeably with the term Touchtone (an AT&T trademark).

Dumb Terminal: A phrase used to describe the user device (terminal) in a computing environment where all of the processing occurs on a central computer or mainframe. No computing intelligence resides on the terminal.

Dynamic Data Exchange (DDE): A Microsoft function allowing information from one application to be transferred to another via the Windows operating system. Also referred to as "copying and pasting" or "cut and paste," it involves the temporary storage of information in the Windows Clipboard.

Electronic Documentation: Information for an application, product or process that would normally be in paper format, but is converted into digital format for display on a desktop computer.

Enterprise Resource Planning (ERP): A large-scale business application or set of applications that encompass some or all aspects of "back-office" functions (e.g., human resources, finance, manufacturing). There is an evolution within the ERP industry to either provide add-on modules or integrate with third-party applications for "front-office" functions such as sales, marketing and service. Applications that combine these "front-office" functions are generally referred to as Customer Relationship Management applications. See CRM.

Erlang: One hour of telephone traffic. For example, if circuits carry 120 minutes of traffic in an hour, that's two Erlangs.

Erlang B: A formula developed by A.K. Erlang, widely used to determine the number of trunks required to handle a known calling load during a one-hour period. The formula assumes that if callers get busy signals, they go away forever, never to retry. Since some callers retry, Erlang B can underestimate trunks required. However, Erlang B is generally accurate in situations with few busy signals.

Erlang C: A formula developed by A.K. Erlang, widely used to calculate service level and queue (delay) times based on three things: the number of agents, the number of callers (call volume), and the average amount of time it takes to serve each call (handle time). It can also predict the resources required to keep waiting times within targeted limits. Erlang C assumes no lost calls or busy signals, so it has a tendency to overestimate staff required in call centers.

Ethernet: A standard networking technology for putting information on a Local Area Network. The IEEE standards body defines it, and it is the most popular LAN technology today. It is implemented with Network Interface Cards and Ethernet switches and hubs, and it is tightly tied to TCP/IP.

Expected Wait Time (EWT): A formula that uses real-time and/or historical queue data to approximate how long a caller will have to wait for an agent. Depending on the wait time, callers may hear a message and be offered options of staying on hold, hanging up, leaving a call-back request or transferring to an IVR.

Expert System: Business application that aids the user in analyzing and resolving problems based on logic trees and known solutions to identified problems. (Also known as a Knowledge Based System.) Includes functions such as problem analysis and problem resolution.

eXtensible Markup Language (XML): A language derived from the Standard Generalized Markup Language (SGML), primarily used to pass information between Web pages, applications or systems. A standard for passing data that provides the definition of the type and format of the data, as well as the data, in information passed between systems and applications. Enables very open interchanges between systems. See also Voice XML.

Extranet: Networks typically connected via the Internet, providing for direct and secure business-to-business access between a company and its vendors or other partners.

Extraprise: Refers to a business entity that includes a company, its vendors or other partners.

Facsimile (FAX): Technology that scans, encodes and transmits a document over a telecommunications circuit and reproduces it at the receiving end.

Fax-on-Demand: A system that enables callers to request documents to be delivered to specified fax numbers. May be a function of a voice-response system.

Five-Nines: Level of reliability often quoted for traditional voice switches. Means system is working 99.999 percent of the time (all but a few minutes per year).

Forecasting: In a call center, the process of predicting call (and other types of contact) volumes and workload based on history, growth or other parameters. Forecasts are used to staff and trunk appropriately to meet desired service level, accessibility and response time goals.

Frame Relay: A Wide Area Network data transmission service for connecting multiple Local Area Networks. Enabled by routers, this service is obtained from local and long-distance phone companies, as well as Internet Service Providers.

Front Office: Business applications that deal with customer interactions, such as customer service, help desk, sales or customer relationship management.

Fulfillment: The process of fulfilling a request for literature or other information (e.g., product information, user guides, billing policies, forms, etc.). This can be a manual or automated process and the information sent via mail, fax or email. Fulfillment can also refer to fulfilling an order and sending product(s).

Full-Time Equivalent (FTE): A term used in call center scheduling and budgeting to indicate the number of staff required. Derived by the number of scheduled hours divided by the hours in a full work week. The hours of several part-time agents may add up to one FTE. FTE can also be used to indicate the number of staff on a payroll or allocated headcount in a budget.

Gate: See Agent Group.

Gateway: A server dedicated to providing access to a network. Also, software and hardware that interprets and translates different protocols from different networks or devices. For example, a VoIP gateway translates between TDM and IP.

Grade of Service: The probability that a call will not be connected to a system because all trunks are busy. Grade of service is often expressed in the form "p.01," meaning 1 percent of calls will be blocked.

Graphical User Interface (GUI): An interface that uses icons, menus and a mouse to manage interaction with the system. Windows and browsers are GUIs.

H.248: An ITU standard, also known as Megaco, for defining the components of a voice-switching system. It is also referred to as the "softswitch" standard. It disaggregates a monolithic voice switch into gateways, software controllers and protocols.

H.323: An ITU standard for putting real-time information onto an unreliable packet network. This standard is used for most VoIP applications today.

Handled Calls: The number of calls received and handled by agents or peripheral equipment. Handled calls does not include calls that abandon or receive busy signals.

Handle Time: The time an agent spends in Talk Time and After-Call Work handling a transaction.

Help Desk Software: Applications that deal with customer interactions, usually of a technical nature (e.g., computer support). The application not only captures and manages contact information but also tracks and manages a problem from initial request to resolution. Often has links to an expert system for the purpose of problem analysis and resolution, and workflow for escalation and follow-up.

Historical Reports: Reports that track call center and agent performance over a period of time, such as day, week or month.

Home Agent: See Telecommuting and Remote Agent.

Hunt Group: A basic routing method for linear or circular distribution of calls to a group of agents.

Hybrid: A voice-switch application infrastructure approach from PBX vendors that uses an external server attached to the PBX to provide the call center application software capabilities (routing, work state management, etc.).

Hyper-Text Markup Language (HTML): A language derived from the Standard Generalized Markup Language (SGML), primarily used to create Web pages.

Hyper-Text Transport Protocol (HTTP): A protocol in the Web environment that links addresses entered into a browser URL line with a Web server and presents the appropriate HTML pages.

Imaging: A technology to scan printed documents such as mail into electronic documents for processing, storage and/or routing.

In-Band Signaling: Passing information about a call in the same channel as the voice information. For example, Caller ID into a home uses in-band signaling, sending the information between ringing cycles.

Incoming Call Center Management: The art of having the right number of skilled people and supporting resources in place, at the right times, to handle an accurately forecasted workload, at service level and with quality.

Information Indicator Digits: Information sent in an ISDN D channel setup message that provides additional information about the call source, such as payphone, cell phone, calling card, prisons and hotels. This information can be used in call centers for advanced routing applications.

Instant Messaging: A form of text-chat used primary for noncommercial communications between two or more Internet users. Several incompatible addressing and protocols issues have limited its use for business-to-business or business-to-consumer applications.

Integrated Reporting: The ability to track a call from its inception to culmination and tie business information and results together with call data (a.k.a. "cradle-to-grave" reporting). Each point the call touches (e.g., IVRs, announcements, CSRs) and the business results of those transactions (sales, complaints, contact record) are tracked on a single database record and/or via a common tracking identifier. This enables more accurate tracking of caller treatment and contact results.

Integrated Services Digital Network (ISDN): A set of international standards for telephone transmission. ISDN provides an end-to-end digital network, out-of-band signaling and greater bandwidth than older telephone services. The two standard levels of ISDN are Basic Rate Interface (BRI) and Primary Rate Interface (PRI). ISDN is often used in call centers to deliver signaling and caller information (such as ANI, DNIS, prompted digits, UUI, information indicator digits), as well as for faster call setup and teardown. See Basic Rate Interface and Primary Rate Interface.

Intelligent Character Recognition (ICR): Technology that reads handwritten text and determines what it says. Can be used with an imaging system to determine information about mail or fax items for routing and handling.

Inter-Exchange Carrier (IXC): A long-distance telephone company (e.g., AT&T, Worldcom, Sprint).

Interactive Voice Response (IVR): Systems that enable callers to use their telephone keypad (or spoken commands if speech recognition is used) to access a company's computer system for the purpose of retrieving or updating information, conducting a business transaction or routing.

Interactive Web Response (IWR): Systems that enable customers to use the Internet to access a company's Web site for the purpose of retrieving or updating information or conducting a business transaction.

Internet: A worldwide, expanding network of linked computers, founded by the U.S. government and several universities in 1969, originally called the Arpanet and based on the TCP/IP protocol. Made available for commercial public use in 1992.

Internet Protocol (IP): A data communications protocol for addressing endpoints. Part of the TCP/IP protocol suite. IP helps control communications activity on the Internet, and an IP address is assigned to every computer on the Internet.

Internet Service Provider (ISP): A company that provides Internet access to customers either through a modem or direct connection.

Intranet: A company's private data network that is accessed using browser technology and TCP/IP.

IP Phone: An end-user device that enables users to place voice calls through a data network (LAN, WAN or the Internet) using the Internet Protocol. The device can be an IP-enabled telephone or a PC with soundcard and software. Either device encodes analog voice into data packets.

IP Telephony: Technology that enables voice telephone calls to be carried over a data network (a private intranet or the public Internet) using protocols from the TCP/IP suite. Voice is transmitted in data packets. Also referred to as Internet Telephony.

Java: An object-oriented programming language developed by Sun Microsystems. It is designed for creating and executing operating system independent applications.

Java Applet: Small Java-based applications that can be downloaded and run within browsers on virtually any operating system without modification, making them ideal for use over the Internet.

Java Telephony Application Programming Interface (JTAPI): An object-oriented application programming interface for Java-based computer-telephony applications. Allows Java applications to initiate, control and disconnect telephone calls.

Knowledge-Based Systems: See Expert Systems.

Knowledge Management: A method of organizing a company's internal and external processes, product and service documentation, expert systems or case-based reasoning information, and information about customers, prospects, competitors, partners, etc.

Law of Diminishing Returns: In call centers, the declining marginal improvements in service level that can be attributed to each additional agent as successive agents are added.

Least-Occupied Agent: A method of distributing calls to the agent who has the most idle time (lowest occupancy) for a given period of time.

Legacy Systems: Existing information systems or databases that house core business information, such as customer records. May be based on older technologies (e.g., mainframes, mini-computers) but are still used for day-to-day operations.

Linux: An open source Unix operating system. Some call center applications, such as Communications Servers, are being run on Linux.

Load Balancing: Balancing traffic between two or more call center destinations.

Local Area Network (LAN): The connection of multiple computers within a building or campus to share information, applications and peripherals.

Local Exchange Carrier (LEC): Telephone companies responsible for providing local connections and services.

Logged On: A state in which agents have signed on to a system (made their presence known), but may or may not be ready to receive calls. Contrast with Logged Off, when they are no longer active in the system database.

Loggers or Logging Systems: Tools that automatically record and archive calls in a call center. Can be used to record every call, record on demand or conduct event-based recording. Used by companies such as insurance, financial services and utilities that must keep detailed records of transactions for verification or legal purposes.

Logical Agent: An agent defined in ACD software by the login, not their physical position or phone number. Enables an agent to log in at any position and receive call types appropriate to their skills.

Mainframe: A computer system that is a large, monolithic system. Generally has its own operating system, and databases and applications resident on the same system.

Management Information System (MIS): For call centers, a system that facilitates the capture and reporting of activity within the telephony or computing infrastructure.

Manual Answer: Answer mode where an agent position must push a button or go off-hook to connect the caller.

Manual Available: An ACD software setting where the voice-switch automatically puts an agent into After-Call Work after call disconnect. When agents complete any After-Call work, they put themselves back into Available mode.

Megaco: A pending IETF VoIP standard that is the equivalent of the ITU's H.248. The joint IETF/ITU standard is sometimes referred to as Megaco/H.248.

Middleware: A generic term for software that mediates between different types of hardware and software on a network so that they can function together. Typically uses open interfaces and Applications Programming Interfaces (APIs) to access and move information. In call centers, middleware is typically used in CRM and CTI application integration. Also refers to Windows or Web tools for passing information (e.g., COM/DCOM, CGI).

Modem: A contraction of the terms Modulator/Demodulator. A Modem converts analog signals to digital, and vice versa, for data communications.

Monitoring: Also called Position Monitoring or Service Observing. The process of listening to agents' telephone calls for the purpose of maintaining quality. Monitoring can be live or recorded, silent or with a warning tone, and remote or side-by-side.

Most-Idle Agent: A method of distributing calls to the agent who has been sitting idle the longest. Also known as the Longest-Available Agent.

Multimedia: Combining multiple forms of media in the communication of information. Generically used in call centers to mean nontelephone communications (email, fax, text-chat, etc).

Multimedia Queuing: Handling customer contacts through different channels (inbound calls, outbound calls, voice messages, email, Web calls, text-chat, fax, video, etc.) in a common queue. Allows customers to choose the method of contact and ensures all contacts are handled according to business rules in a timely way. Requires advanced technology to integrate, route and report on all media channels.

N-Tier Architecture: A systems architecture term that means that there can be any number of applications and databases integrated together for a business purpose.

Natural Language: Technology used in speech or text recognition that recognizes what is being said or requested through free-form communication (no structure or required words or phrases).

Network Control Center: Also called Traffic Control Center. In a networked call center environment, the centralized command and control center where people and equipment monitor real-time conditions across sites, change routing routines and thresholds, and coordinate events to positively impact call center performance.

Network Management System: A management and diagnostic tool for managing a network of devices, usually via the protocol SNMP. This allows network managers to have visibility into devices like PCs, servers, data switches, routers, IP phones and voice switches for remotely diagnosing and troubleshooting problems.

Network Reports: Reports that provide historical or real-time information on network call activity. For example, network reports can indicate how many network busies were delivered, trunk utilization, call volumes, total traffic (volume x holding times), calling numbers, etc., for each trunk group or DNIS number.

Network Routing: The ability to make routing decisions in the network before selecting a location to route the call. Network routing can be based on such factors as the time of day, day of week, percentage of calls to be handled at each site, area code of the calling party, DNIS or information gathered from databases via CTI.

Non-Facility Associated Signaling (NFAS): A method of aggregating the signaling for multiple ISDN T1s or E1s onto a single D channel, thereby reducing expenses.

Object Linking and Embedding (OLE): The ability of Windows to embed an object in another object, and link the two so that when information is updated in one it is updated in the other. For example, an Excel spreadsheet can be embedded in a Word document, and the embedded document will be updated if the original Excel document is changed. OLE is part of Microsoft Active X.

Occupancy: Also referred to as agent utilization. The percentage of time agents handle calls out of staffed time. For a half-hour, the calculation is: (call volume x average handling time in seconds) / (number of agents x 1800 seconds). See Adherence to Schedule.

Off-the-Shelf: Hardware or software programs that are commercially available and ready for use "as is."

Offered Calls: All of the attempts callers make to reach the call center. There are three possibilities for offered calls: 1) They can get busy signals; 2) they can be answered by the system, but hang up before reaching an agent; and 3) they can be answered by an agent Offered call reports in ACDs usually refer only to the calls that the system receives.

Online Analytical Processing (OLAP): A category of software reporting technologies that provide dynamic, multidimensional access to consolidated data for the purpose of extrapolating trends. Commonly used with Data Warehouses.

Online Transaction Processing (OLTP): A category of business applications where multiple users access and update business records in real-time. OLTP is highly scalable, fast, secure and fault tolerant. In a call center, order-entry and account-inquiry applications are usually of this type.

Open Database Connectivity (ODBC): A standard method of accessing databases on a variety of platforms. Defined by the SQL (Structured Query Language) Access Group.

Optical Character Recognition (OCR): Technology that reads printed text and determines what it says. Can be used with an imaging system to determine information about mail or fax items for routing and handling.

Out-of-Band Signaling: Passing information about a contact (e.g., ANI or DNIS) in a channel separate from the one that carries the voice conversation. For example, ISDN services carry voice conversations in a B (bearer) channel, and ancillary information about these contacts in a D (data) channel.

Outsourcing: Contracting some or all call center services and/or technology to an outside company. The company is generally referred to as an Outsourcer or Service Bureau.

Overflow: Calls that flow from one group or site to another. More specifically, intraflow happens when calls flow between agent groups and interflow is when calls flow out of the ACD to another site.

Packet-Switching: A method of transferring information across a network by passing it in small pieces ("packets") of information. Typically used to transmit data (e.g., over the Internet). Now being applied to voice, as well. See Voice over IP.

Page Pushing: A Web collaboration technique in which the agent can send a page to the customer desktop.

PBX/ACD: A PBX that is equipped with ACD functionality.

Percent Allocation: A carrier-based call-routing strategy used in multisite call center environments. Calls are allocated across sites based on user-defined percentages.

Percent Utilization: See Occupancy.

Pooling Principle: The Pooling Principle states: Any movement in the direction of consolidation of resources will result in improved traffic-carrying efficiency. Conversely, any movement away from consolidation of resources will result in reduced traffic-carrying efficiency.

Post-Call Processing: See After-Call Work.

Post Office Protocol 3 (POP3): A standard for retrieving email used by most email systems.

Predictive Dialing: A system that automatically places outbound calls, classifies calls and delivers answered calls to agents. Call classification detects busy signals, answering machines, ring/no answer, etc., and the dialing software tracks and acts on the outcome based on the defined campaign. See Campaign Management.

Preview Dialing: An application that instructs the switch to outdial a specific phone number under control of an agent or a timer. The agent previews a screen containing information about the person to be called, monitors the call for connection (or other classification), and updates the database accordingly. Used for callbacks or other contacts where the agent needs to review information before placing the call.

Primary Rate Interface (PRI): One of two levels of ISDN service. In North America, PRI typically provides 23 bearer channels for voice or data and one channel for signaling information (commonly expressed as 23B+D). In Europe, PRI typically provides 30 bearer lines (30B+D). See Basic Rate Interface and Integrated Services Digital Network.

Private Automatic Branch Exchange (PABX): See Private Branch Exchange.

Private Branch Exchange (PBX): A telephone system located at a user's premise that handles incoming and outgoing calls and provides many features for call-routing and management. By adding ACD software, a PBX can provide call center functionality. A PBX serves both the call center and administrative users. Also called Private Automatic Branch Exchange (PABX).

Private Network: A network made up of circuits for the exclusive use of an organization or group of affiliated organizations. Can be regional, national or international in scope. Common in large organizations.

Profit Center: An accounting term that refers to a department or function in the organization that is expected to generate a profit. See Cost Center.

Progressive Dialing: Similar to Predictive Dialing, but ensures no call is launched unless an agent is available.

Public Switched Telephone Network (PSTN): The circuit-switched network that interconnects our homes and offices.

Quality-Monitoring Tools: Tools used to assess agent contact-handling skills, allowing specific or random selection of positions, trunks, queues or other entities to monitor. Monitoring can be real-time or recorded and may include data as well as voice. Quality-monitoring tools include scoring, reporting and trending capabilities. Quality-monitoring tools now monitor email and Web contacts, as well.

Quality of Service (QoS): A data-networking management method to provide different packets different priorities when there is congestion. For call centers, QoS is critical for VoIP applications. Packets are tagged for QoS with a Class of Service header.

Queue: Holds callers until an agent becomes available. Queue can also refer to a line or list of items in a system waiting to be processed (e.g., email messages).

Queue Time: See Delay.

Random Availability: The normal variation in the availability of agents in a call center, due to variations in talk and wrapup time.

Random Call Arrival: The normal variation in the arrival of incoming calls at a call center.

Readerboards: Also called Display Boards, Wall Displays or Wallboards. A visual display, usually mounted on the wall or ceiling, that provides real-time and historical information on queue conditions, agent status and call center performance. It can also display user-entered messages. This function can also be provided by software on a workstation.

Real-Time Adherence Software: Software in a Workforce Management System that tracks how closely agents conform to their schedules. See Adherence to Schedule.

Real-Time Data: Information on the current condition in a call center. Some "real-time" information is real-time in the strictest sense (e.g., calls in queue and current longest wait). Some real-time statistics require some history (e.g., the last X calls or Y minutes) in order to make a calculation (e.g., Service Level and Average Speed of Answer).

Real-Time Management: Making adjustments to staffing and thresholds in the systems and network in response to current queue conditions.

Reengineering: A term popularized by management consultant Michael Hammer that refers to radically redesigning processes to improve efficiency and service.

Remote Agents: Fully integrated call center agents residing at home or other remote locations. Requires both telephony and data connectivity from a main site to the agent's location, and the same features and functions available to agents onsite.

Remote Office: A group of agents or a single agent working at a site separate from the main call center, but using the same technology infrastructure (voice switch, applications and other elements). The agent(s) could be located in a branch office or another center.

Response Time: The time it takes the call center to respond to transactions that do not have to be handled in real-time when they arrive (e.g., correspondence or email). See Service Level.

Rostered Staff Factor (RSF): Alternatively called an Overlay, Shrink Factor or Shrinkage. RSF is a numerical factor that leads to the minimum staff needed on schedule over and above base staff required to achieve your service level and response time objectives. It is calculated after base staffing is determined and before schedules are organized, and accounts for things like breaks, absenteeism and ongoing training.

Router: A data-networking device that connects LANs through a WAN. It contains sophisticated algorithms for calculating the best paths between two end devices.

Sales Force Automation (SFA): A class of business applications designed to automate the marketing and sales process. The term usually refers to any technology-enabled sales tools and often includes Contact Management and Customer Relationship Management. See CRM.

Satellite Office: A call center location that operates using a cabinet or carrier of a switch from a main location. Used to extend one switch to another site to operate virtually without purchasing a second switch. See Remote Office.

Schedule Compliance: See Adherence to Schedule.

Scheduling: Allocating call center agents and other resources in a way that will meet service level and other goals for specific days and times. Scheduling is generally based on historical call center activity, projected volumes and associated staff needs, agent skills, performance and availability, and knowledge of planned events.

Scheduling Exception: When an agent is involved in an activity outside of the normal, planned schedule.

Screen Monitoring: A system capability that enables a supervisor or manager to remotely monitor the activity on agents' computer screens. Can be viewed in real-time or recorded.

Screen Pop: A CTI capability where callers' records are automatically retrieved (based on ANI or identifiers gathered through prompting) and delivered to agents along with the calls. See Coordinated Voice/Data Delivery.

Screen Refresh Rate: The rate at which real-time information is updated on a display.

Scripting: An application that provides agent guides for call-handling (for example, product descriptions, information to gather, promotional offers, upsell scripts). Scripts can accommodate various situations and individuals (for example, different levels of experience, full scripts vs. reminder lists, generic or customized). Sometimes referred to as "dialog manager."

Server: A computer that shares its resources with other computers on a network. For example, file servers share disk storage with other computers. Database servers respond to requests from other computers on the network (clients) with specific data records. Application servers respond to requests from clients for processing or presentation of data.

Service Bureau: See Outsourcing.

Service Level: Also called Telephone Service Factor or TSF. The percentage of incoming calls that are answered within a specified threshold: "X percent of calls answered in Y seconds." See Response Time.

Service Level Agreement: Performance objectives reached by consensus between the user and the provider of a service, or between an outsourcer and an organization. A service level agreement specifies a variety of performance standards, such as response time when there is an outage or service level for call answering.

Service Observing: An ACD software feature that enables a supervisor position to listen to calls. See Monitoring.

Session Initiation Protocol (SIP): A pending IETF standard for VoIP, utilizing Internet-based development tools. SIP holds the promise of being less complex than H.323.

Shrinkage Factor: See Rostered Staff Factor.

Signaling System 7 (SS7): A method of signaling within the PSTN that uses a separate packet-switched data network ("common channel signaling") to communicate information about calls. In a multisite virtual call center environment that is CTI-enabled and conducting pre-arrival routing, SS7 can be used to pass signaling information requesting the call route, and then route the call based on CTI instructions.

Silent Monitoring: See Monitoring.

Simple Mail Transfer Protocol (SMTP): A standard for sending email used by most email systems. Used for transmission of email over the Internet or private TCP/IP networks.

Simplified Network Management Protocol (SNMP): A protocol from the TCP/IP suite that enables network devices to be remotely monitored and managed by a Network Management System.

Simulation Tools: Tools used to replicate contact activity to test process changes, new technologies, staffing and traffic scenarios prior to actually making the change. Simulation tools show performance, costs or other outcomes for the various scenarios defined.

Skill Group: See Agent Group.

Skills-Based Routing: A specific form of intelligent routing that matches the compentencies of each agent with information about the call to route it to an appropriate agent. When an agent logs in, the database associates a defined skill set with that position and the application routes call types that match the skills to that position. An agent can have multiple skills, preferred skills and unique combinations of skills.

Softphone: The ability to access telephony functions through the desktop computer interface of a PC instead of a telephone. For a call center agent, softphone can include login/logout to both the voice and data systems via a single action on the PC, point-and-click changing of work states (available, unavailable/not ready), visibility into availability and statistics, outbound calling, and entry of transaction codes via the PC. Softphone is a CTI-enabled function.

Speaker Verification: A method of verifying the identity of a caller by comparing his voice to a previously stored voiceprint. Also referred to as Voice Authentication or Voice Recognition.

Speech Recognition: See Automatic Speech Recognition (ASR).

Split: See Agent Group.

Standalone ACD: A specialized voice switch with software specifically designed to perform ACD routing and other call center functions. Standalone ACDs typically exclude many PBX capabilities such as least-cost routing, camp-on or other functions targeted toward general business use, and may co-reside with a PBX in many office environments.

Structured Query Language (SQL): A standard language for requesting data from relational databases.

Supervisor: The person who has frontline responsibility for a group of agents. Generally, supervisors are equipped with special telephones and computers that enable them to monitor agent activities.

Switch: A device that connects other devices for communication. The term can refer to a Data Switch or a Voice Switch. (In this book, when switch is used, it refers to a voice switch.)

T1 Circuit: A high-speed digital circuit used for voice, data or video, with a bandwidth of 1.544 megabits per second. T1 circuits offer the equivalent of 24 analog voice lines. The European equivalent is known as E1 and it offers the equivalent of 31 analog voice lines.

Talk Time: The time an agent spends with a caller during a transaction. Includes everything from "hello" to "goodbye."

Telecommuting: See Remote Agent.

Telephony Application Programming Interface (TAPI): API developed by Microsoft and Intel to enable computer-telephony functions on Windows-based systems. It is one of the de facto standards by virtue of Microsoft's large installed base.

Telephony Services Application Programming Interface (TSAPI): A CTI API developed by Novell and AT&T/Lucent/Avaya.

Text-Chat: Allows agents and customers to have a "conversation" over the Internet by typing on their computers. Generally enabled through a "click-to-chat" button on a Web site, and then a separate window opens for chatting (via a Java Applet or Active X control). Also called Chat or Web Chat.

Text-to-Speech: Enables a voice processing system to speak the words in a text field using synthesized – not recorded – speech. Sometimes used for large, dynamic database applications where it is impractical to record all speech phrases, such as addresses or product names. Also used to "read" email or other text-based information over the telephone.

Thick Client: A workstation in a client/server environment that performs much or most of the application processing. It requires programs and data to be installed on it and requires significant computing resources (CPU and memory) at the desktop. The client is "thick" in that it has much of the smarts of the overall application running on it. Contrast with the Thin Client.

Thin Client: A workstation in a client/server environment that performs little or no application processing (applications run primarily on the server). Often used to describe browser-based desktops. The primary function of a thin client is to manage presentation. Contrast with the Thick Client.

Three-Tier Architecture: An information system architecture where processing functionality is split into three discrete functions: 1) Presentation (desktop PC), 2) Application (business rules), and 3) Data (database system). By keeping the functionality cleanly separated, three-tier architectures are scalable and flexible.

Tie line: A private circuit that connects two or more voice systems.

Time Division Multiplexing (TDM): Multiple conversations are placed on a common transmission circuit. Common in voice-switching technology.

Toll-Free Service: Enables callers to reach a call center out of the local calling area without incurring calling charges. In North America, 800/888/877/866 service is toll-free. In some countries, there are also other variations of toll-free service. For example, with 0345 or 0645 services in the United Kingdom, callers are charged local rates and the call center pays for the long-distance charges.

Total Cost of Ownership (TCO): Estimated lifetime expenses of a technology including acquisition, implementation, maintenance, management and upgrades. TCO should include costs for hardware, software, and internal and external resources.

Touchtone: See Dual-Tone Multi-Frequency.

Transmission Control Protocol/Internet Protocol (TCP/IP): A standard set of protocols that govern the exchange of data between computing systems. TCP/IP was originally designed by the U.S. Department of Defense to link dissimilar computers across many kinds of networks. It has become the de facto standard for commercial equipment and applications. TCP/IP specifies how information that travels over the Internet should be divided and reassembled. In call centers, TCP/IP is the underlying protocol of VoIP; it is also widely used in IVR, CTI and CRM systems.

Trunk: Also called a Line, Exchange Line or Circuit. A communications link connecting two switching systems. The two systems can be company-owned voice switches or a company-owned voice switch and a central office.

Trunk Group: A collection of voice circuits usually used for a common purpose. In call centers, usually there are separate trunk groups for 800 services, local service and long-distance calling. A trunk group can handle multiple DNIS numbers or be dedicated to a number.

Trunk Load: The telecommunications traffic that trunks carry, measured in Erlang units. In call centers, it includes both Delay and Talk Time.

Trunk Utilization: Percentage of time that a trunk (or group of trunks) is in use.

Two-Tier Architecture: A computing systems arrangement where functionality is split between two computing devices. At the client layer (usually a PC), presentation (GUI) and application level (business rules) reside. In the server, the application and data (database) reside. Application functionality can be split between the client and the server, or reside all in the client or all in the server. Compare with Three-Tier, N-Tier and Client/Server.

Un-PBX: A term sometimes used for Communications Server.

Unavailable Work State: An agent work state used to identify a mode not associated with handling telephone calls.

Uniform Call Distributor (UCD): See Hunt Group.

Uniform Resource Locator: The alphanumeric address for a Web page that is translated to an all numeric IP address.

Universal Agent: Refers to: a) An agent who can handle all types of incoming calls; b) an agent who can handle both inbound and outbound calls; or c) an agent who can handle multimedia calls (for example, fax, email, video and text-chat).

User-to-User Information (UUI): A method of passing information between communications systems via an ISDN D channel. Information passed can be prompted digits, call identifiers or custom application information. UUI is more widely used in multisite call center networking applications.

Virtual Call Center: Multiple networked call centers that operate as a single logical system even though they are physically separated and geographically dispersed. This permits economies of scale in call-handling, as well as supporting disaster recovery, call overflow and extended hours coverage. Ability and degree of networking varies with system type, similarity of systems and approach to integration. It is enabled to varying degrees using network features, voice-switch features or CTI.

Virtual Private Network (VPN): A method for using a public network (like the Internet) for a company's private business purposes. To address security, information is encrypted at the sending site and then decrypted at the receiving site.

Visible Queue: When callers enter a queue, they are given announcement feedback on queue length or queue position. The source of the announcement can be the voice switch or an IVR system.

Voice Over Internet Protocol (VoIP): Transmitting voice conversations as packets of data from one communications device (voice switch, PC or IP phone) to another over a TCP/IP network.

Voice Processing: An umbrella term that refers to any combination of voice technologies, including Voicemail, Automated Attendant, Audiotex, Interactive Voice Response and Faxback.

Voice Response Unit (VRU): See Interactive Voice Response (IVR). Note: VRU is sometimes used to refer to the piece of equipment, while IVR is used to refer to the capability.

Voice Switch: The PBX, ACD, Communications Server, Centrex, key system or other switching system for voice communications.

VoiceXML (VXML): An emerging standard for developing voice-processing (IVR) applications with Internet and Web-based tools. The promise of VXML is that millions of Web developers will be able to develop voice applications.

Wallboards: See Readerboards.

Web Call: A voice call initiated by a customer from a company's Web site. Web calls can be accomplished in two ways: the caller can speak by VoIP over the Internet or be immediately called back over the PSTN. Regardless of calling method, the caller and agent speak while collaborating on a Web-based application.

Web Integration: Incorporating Web contact into the call center by providing access to an agent over the Internet. Provides the customer with additional support, information and guidance during a self-service transaction. Can be enabled through text-chat or a Web call. Email is sometimes included offered as part of this integration. Often includes "co-browsing" or "pushing" Web pages to the customer.

Whisper Transfer: An IVR integration technique where the IVR temporarily connects to the agent and speaks the account number or other information before connecting the caller to the agent. Allows the agent to access information without the customer having to repeat information already entered into the IVR. Sometimes called "poor man's CTI."

Wide-Area Network (WAN): The connection of multiple geographically dispersed computers or LANs, normally using digital circuits. The device that connects LAN to a WAN is usually a router.

Work Blending: The ability to dynamically and automatically allocate call center agents to any media, based on conditions in the call center and programmed parameters. See also Multimedia Queuing, Blended Agent and Call Blending.

Work State: Status indication of a call center agent's availability or activity. Used to control when an agent can receive a call and to track their activity in reports. Part of ACD software.

Workflow: A business application that enables work tasks to be executed consistently and thoroughly, driven by business rules. The movement of each task can be tracked throughout the duration of the process providing both current status and historical activity. Workflow management can be used to track contact-handling at specific stages or for the life of a contact. Workflow is an element of CRM solutions. The term workflow can be used to describe routing, handling or following up on a contact.

Workforce Management System (WFMS): A software system that, depending on available modules, forecasts call load, calculates staff requirements, organizes work schedules and tracks performance compared to projections. Enables the manager to project work volume and corresponding resource needs based on historical information and other parameters, such as growth.

Workload: Often used interchangeably with Call Load. Workload can also refer to noncall activities.

World Wide Web (WWW): The capability that enables users to access information on the Internet in a graphical format.

Wrap-up Codes: Codes agents enter into the voice switch to identify the type of call handled. The call center MIS can then generate reports on call types, by handling time, time of day, etc. Generally entered at the completion of each contact.

Wrap-Up: See After-Call Work.

XML: See EXtensible Markup Language.

Zip Tone: See Beep Tone.

Bibliography

2001 Call Center Best Practices Report: Management and Operations Edition. ProSci Research. 2001

2001 Call Center Best Practices Report: Special Technology Edition. ProSci Research. 2001

Call Center Management on Fast Forward: Succeeding in Today's Dynamic Inbound Environment. Brad Cleveland and Julia Mayben. 8th edition. Call Center Press. 2001

Call Center Planning & Design Toolkit. ProSci Research. 2002

Competitive Advantage: Creating and Sustaining Superior Performance. Michael E. Porter. Simon and Schuster Trade. 1998

Competitive Strategy: Techniques for Analyzing Industries and Competitors. Michael E. Porter. Simon and Schuster Trade. 1998

The Discipline of Market Leaders: Choose Your Customers, Narrow Your Focus, Dominate Your Market. Michael Treacy and Fred Wiersema. Perseus Publishing. 1996

In the Age of the Smart Machine: The Future of Work and Power. Shoshana Zuboff. The Perseus Books Group. 1989

On Competition. Michael E Porter. Harvard Business School Publishing. 1998

The Prosci Reengineering Series. ProSci Research. 2002

The Loyalty Effect: The Hidden Force Behind Growth, Profits, and Lasting Value. Frederick F. Reichheld. Harvard Business School Publishing. 2001

Standards

H.323. ITU

H.248. ITU

802 standards. IEEE

RFC 2705. IETF

RFC 3015. IETF

VoiceXML 2.0 specification. VoiceXML Forum

Index

Figures

Tables

About the Authors

Lori Bocklund has 15 years' experience in the call center industry, nine of them as a consultant with Vanguard. The majority of her time is spent on consulting projects, but she also teaches, speaks and writes articles on call center technology, strategy and operations. Lori is a proud graduate of South Dakota State University (go Jackrabbits!) and George Washington University with B.S. and M.S. degrees in Electrical Engineering. Lori lives in Vienna, Virginia, where she can be found running, bicycling with her husband, Mike, and walking in the woods with Harley, her big yellow Lab.

Dave Bengtson has more than 13 years' experience in the call center and telecommunications industries, including a variety of consulting, sales and sales support, and product management positions. He is a call center algorithm patent holder and a frequent speaker at call center conferences and industry events. Dave holds a B.A. from Boston University and an M.B.A. from Pennsylvania State University. He resides in Denver with his wife, Sheila. When not consulting, he can be found surveying the world from a bicycle seat, killing plants in Sheila's garden, searching for the perfect microbrew and messing up the kitchen.

Lori is a Certified Associate of Incoming Calls Management Institute (ICMI) and course developer and seminar leader for "Understanding and Applying Today's Call Center Technologies."

Contact the authors at demystify@vanguard.net.

About Vanguard Communications Corporation

Vanguard Communications is a leading independent consulting firm with more than 20 years of experience in customer contact. Vanguard combines an in-depth understanding of traditional call center technologies, processes and operations with emerging e-commerce and Web-based interactions. Vanguard's core consulting services include strategic planning, contact center operational audits, call flow and workflow design, technology assessments, requirements definition and project management.

Vanguard expands and revitalizes its clients' visions of customer contact, and helps align business, call center and technology strategies. Vanguard's approach to technology projects is to evaluate the business needs first, and then link those needs to new ways of doing business. As a result, solutions are technology-enabled, not technology-driven.

Vanguard is based in Morris Plains, N.J., with offices throughout the United States, and locations in Europe and Asia-Pacific. As an independent company, Vanguard does not partner with, distribute for, or represent any vendor of products or services.

For more information, and for articles, white papers and resource links, visit www.vanguard.net.

⚠VANGUARD

Vanguard Communications Corporation
100 American Road
Morris Plains, New Jersey 07950
973-605-8000 • 800-872-6678
demystify@vanguard.net • www.vanguard.net

About the Publisher

Incoming Calls Management Institute (ICMI), based in Annapolis, Maryland, offers the most comprehensive educational resources available for call center (contact center, interaction center, help desk) management professionals. ICMI's focus is helping individuals and organizations understand the dynamics of today's customer contact environment in order to improve performance and achieve superior business results. From the world's first seminar on incoming call center management, to the first conference on call center/Internet integration and subsequent research on multichannel integration, ICMI is a recognized global leader. ICMI is independent and is not associated with, owned or subsidized by any industry supplier; ICMI's only source of funding is from those who use its services.

ICMI's services include:

- Public and onsite (private) seminars
- Web seminars and e-learning courses
- Certification review seminars and study guides
- Industry studies and research papers
- Consulting services
- Software tools for scheduling and analysis
- Books (including the industry's best-selling book, *Call Center Management on Fast Forward*)
- QueueTips, the popular (and free) monthly e-newsletter
- *Call Center Management Review*, the authoritative monthly journal for call center leaders

For more information and to join a network of call center leaders, see www.incoming.com

Incoming Calls Management Institute
Post Office Box 6177
Annapolis, Maryland 21401
410-267-0700 • 800-672-6177
icmi@incoming.com • www.incoming.com

QTY.	ITEM	PRICE
	Call Center Technology Demystified: *The No-Nonsense Guide to Bridging Customer Contact Technology, Operations and Strategy* 375 pages, paperback, more than 100 figures and tables $39.95 each* *Multiple Publication Sales Discount	
	Call Center Management On Fast Forward Book – 281 pages, paperback, more than 100 charts and graphs – $34.95 each* *Multiple Publication Sales Discount	
	Call Center Management On Fast Forward Book on Tape – Six cassette tapes with charts and graphics booklet – $49.95 each	
	Call Center Recruiting and New Hire Training: The Best of *Call Center Management Review* – $16.95 each* *Multiple Publication Sales Discount	
	Call Center Forecasting and Scheduling: The Best of *Call Center Management Review* – $16.95 each* *Multiple Publication Sales Discount	
	Call Center Humor: The Best of *Call Center Management Review* Volume 3 – $9.95 each* *Multiple Publication Sales Discount	
	Industry Studies Monitoring Study Final Report II *(published 2002)* – $99.00* Multichannel Call Center Study *(published 2001)* – $99.00* Agent Staffing and Retention Study *(published 2000)* – $79.00*	
	Call Center Sample Monitoring Forms – $49.95 each*	
	Call Center Sample Customer Satisfaction Forms Book – $49.95 each*	
	CIAC Certification Study Guides Module 1: People Management – $199.00*** Module 2: Operations Management – $199.00*** Module 3: Customer Relationship Management – $199.00*** Module 4: Leadership and Business Management – $199.00***	
	QueueView – Software Tools For Incoming Call Center Managers $49.00 CD ROM*	
	Easy Start™ Call Center Scheduler Software – $299.00 CD-ROM*	
	Easy Start™ Call Center Calculator Software – $49.00* CD-ROM	
	Call Center Management Review – monthly 20 page journal $337 (1 year subscription)	
	Shipping & Handling @ $5.00 per US shipment plus $1.00 per book/tape set and $.50 per software order. Additional charges apply to shipments outside the US.	
	Tax (5% MD and 7% GST Canada)	
	Total in U.S. Dollars	

Shipping & Handling @ $5.00 per US shipment, plus .50¢ per* item, $1.00 per** item and $2.00 per*** item. Additional charges apply to shipments outside the US.

❏ Yes, please send me a free issue of *Call Center Management Review* and information
on other publications and seminars.

Please ship my order and/or information to:

Name _____

Title _____

Industry _____

Company _____

Address _____

City _____ State _____ Postal Code _____

Telephone ( ) _____

Fax ( ) _____

Email _____

Method of Payment (Check one)

❏ Check enclosed (Make payable to ICMI Inc.; U.S. Dollars only)

❏ Charge to: ❏ American Express ❏ MasterCard ❏ Visa

Account No. _____

Expiration Date _____

Name on Card _____

Fax order to: 410-267-0962

call us at: 800-672-6177
410-267-0700

order online at: www.incoming.com

or mail order to: ICMI Inc.

P.O. Box 6177, Annapolis, MD 21401